Praise for *Witchful*

"*Witchful Thinking* is here to inform and
witch take you on a magical tour throu   ... can
make your life sparkle. With methods b....u on her own experiences, Howe invites in other practitioners to offer expert advice, too.
Turn up the music and make some magic."

—Dr. Kate Laity, author of *White Rabbit*

"Zoë Howe is the wise and seasoned guide I wish I had at the beginning of my magical journeys. *Witchful Thinking* feels like sitting at
the table with Zoë, enjoying a cup of tea, as she warmly shares practical, accessible, and powerful methods for creating a mindful and
enchanted life. Written with more than a bit of wit and genuinely
solid life advice, this book is a sweet gift from a truly witchy heart."

—Amy Hale, PhD, anthropologist, folklorist,
and author of *Ithell Colquhoun*

"Encouraging us to forge our own way guided by intuition, imagination, heritage, and preferences, this is both personal magical primer
and an enchanting, self-blossoming guide. There are spells, tips, and
simple positive practices ... We are led to consider our own extra-
mundane connections and become aligned with them, to benefit
ourselves and the wider community, letting magic flow into the real
world of here and now."

—Caroline Wise, international presenter on the goddess, folklore,
and Mythic London and coeditor of *The Secret Lore of London*

"The author presents us with a plethora of information and guidance drawn from our wonderful eclectic journey that is witchcraft, with a little history and personal experience thrown into the mix for good measure. A practical and useful guide for those wishing to embark on working and living a magical life in today's modern age."

—Rachel Patterson, witch and author of *Curative Magic* and the Kitchen Witchcraft series

"Packed full of smart, practical tips and techniques for living your best, most empowered life, *Witchful Thinking* is the equivalent of a powerful magical tool kit. The author's kind, warm tone makes this book very accessible; reading it is like speaking with a fun friend... Whether you are a novice or an adept, let *Witchful Thinking* lead you toward a more magical life."

—Judika Illes, author of the *Encyclopedia of 5,000 Spells*

"Zoë Howe has created an engaging new work of witchery for the modern era, studding it with gems from her personal magical experiences, British folklore, and her family's own traditions. Zoë's warm personality comes through the page as she welcomes everyone to join her on the journey of the Wise Woman... We agree with Zoë: let's all bring more 'witchful thinking' into our lives!"

—Sue Terry & Erzebet Barthold, directors of the Magickal Women Conference

WITCHFUL THINKING

About the Author

Zoë Howe is an internationally published author, artist, broadcaster, sometime musician, and "rock 'n' roll witch" based in East Anglia, UK. Her popular radio show *The Rock 'n' Roll Witch* broadcasts on the award-winning Soho Radio, blending music and magic and featuring guests including Judika Illes, Byron Ballard, Rachel Patterson, astrologer Shelley Von Strunckel, and others. Known for her work in support of radical and marginalised women, Zoë has had thirteen books published, including bestselling biographies of punk queen Poly Styrene—a collaboration with the singer's daughter Celeste Bell—and rock's witchy woman, Stevie Nicks. Zoë was also screenwriter on the award-winning documentary *Poly Styrene: I Am A Cliché*. She has appeared on UK TV and radio outlets, including the BBC and Sky Arts, and her work has been acclaimed by publications including *The Guardian*, *The Independent*, *Teen Vogue*, *Rolling Stone*, and elsewhere. She is currently the Royal Literary Fund Writing Fellow at Newnham College, University of Cambridge.

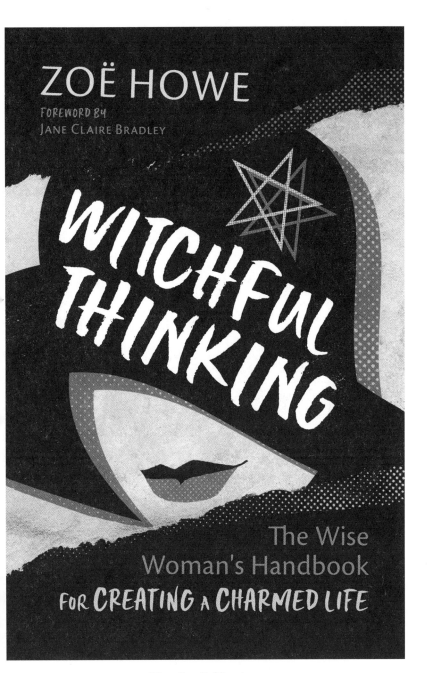

ZOË HOWE

FOREWORD BY
JANE CLAIRE BRADLEY

WITCHFUL THINKING

The Wise
Woman's Handbook
FOR CREATING A CHARMED LIFE

Llewellyn Publications
Woodbury, Minnesota

FIRST EDITION
First Printing, 2022

Book design by Valerie A. King
Cover design by Shira Atakpu
Interior Illustrations by the Llewellyn Art Department

Llewellyn Publications is a registered trademark of Llewellyn Worldwide Ltd.

Library of Congress Cataloging-in-Publication Data (Pending)
ISBN: 978-0-7387-6843-4

Llewellyn Worldwide Ltd. does not participate in, endorse, or have any authority or responsibility concerning private business transactions between our authors and the public.

All mail addressed to the author is forwarded but the publisher cannot, unless specifically instructed by the author, give out an address or phone number.

Any internet references contained in this work are current at publication time, but the publisher cannot guarantee that a specific location will continue to be maintained. Please refer to the publisher's website for links to authors' websites and other sources.

Llewellyn Publications
A Division of Llewellyn Worldwide Ltd.
2143 Wooddale Drive
Woodbury, MN 55125-2989
www.llewellyn.com

Printed in the United States of America

Other Books by Zoë Howe

Typical Girls? The Story of the Slits
(London, Omnibus Press, 2009)

How's Your Dad? Living in the Shadow of a Rock Star Parent
(London, Omnibus Press, 2010)

Florence + The Machine: An Almighty Sound
(London, Omnibus Press, 2012)

Wilko Johnson: Looking Back at Me
(Coauthored with Wilko Johnson. London, Cadiz Music, 2012)

British Beat Explosion: Rock 'n' Roll Island
(Anthology edited by JC Wheatley. London, Aurora Metro, 2013)

Barbed Wire Kisses: The Jesus and Mary Chain Story
(Edinburgh, Birlinn Books/New York, St Martin's Press, 2014)

Stevie Nicks: Visions, Dreams & Rumours
(London, Omnibus Press, 2015)

Lee Brilleaux: Rock 'n' Roll Gentleman
(Edinburgh, Birlinn Books, 2015)

Shine On, Marquee Moon (London, Troubador, 2016)

Dayglo: The Poly Styrene Story
(Coauthored with Celeste Bell. London, Omnibus Press, 2019)

50 Women of the Blues (Coauthored with Jennifer Noble,
Cheryl Robson. London, Aurora Metro, 2020)

For my family.
For Marion Weinstein, my North star.
For Meggs, and all who suffered for the freedoms we enjoy today.
And for Bibi, and the new generation of wise women.

CONTENTS

Disclaimer ... xiii

Acknowledgments ... xv

Foreword by Jane Claire Bradley ... xvii

Introduction ... 1

PART 1 EVERY WITCH WAY ... 11

Introducing the Wise Woman Archetype ... 12

   Witch & Wisdom: Author and Activist Syd Moore ... 19

Speaking of Witch ... 21

Which Witch Are You? ... 26

Golden Rules ... 32

Quiet Revolution: Magic by Stealth ... 34

   Witch & Wisdom: Claire Powell, a Modern-Day Wise Woman ... 36

   Magical Musing: Unicorn Energy versus Toxic Masculinity ... 37

PART 2 AS ABOVE, SO BELOW ... 39

Aligning with the Divine ... 40

Elementary, My Dear Witchy: Earth, Air, Fire, Water, and Spirit ... 44

   Witch Tip: It's as Quick as a Thought ... 52

Pentagram Power ... 53

Creating a Sacred Space ... 56
    Witch Tip: The Microcosm and the Macrocosm ... 60
    Witch & Wisdom: Candle Magic with Madame Pamita ... 61

Lunar Lore: Working with the Cycles of the Moon ... 62
    Witch Tip: Using Your "Flow" ... 67

Retromania: When Planets Go Backwards ... 76

The Wise Woman's Calendar: The Wheel of the Year ... 78
    Witch Tip: Making Eggshell Powder ... 82
    Witch Tip: A Cheerful Apple Charm ... 88

Everyday Planetary Magic ... 92

Weather Magic ... 96
    Witch Tip: Storm Water and Lunar Drops ... 97

Working with Crystals ... 99
    Witch Tip: Nature Gifts ... 110

Scent from Heaven: The Fragrant Magic of Essential Oils ... 112

Perfumes Per Se ... 118

Let the Florida Flow ... 120
    Witch Tip: A Simple Sealing Ritual ... 122

Plant Magic ... 123

Plant and Flower Remedies ... 128
    Witch Tip: Say "Aloe" to Fresh, Healthy Skin and Hair ... 132

Witchful Drinking ... 137
    Witch Tip: Dress for Success ... 141

Pots of Protection ... 145

Smoke Cleansing with Herbs ... 151

Soul Signs, Messages, and Gifts ... 153
    Magical Musing: Respecting the Soul in Everything ... 156

PART 3 AS WITHIN, SO WITHOUT ... 157

Sympathetic Magic ... 158

Energy Centres or Chakras ... 160
Exercise: Colour Me Calm ... 164

Prioritising Protection ... 166
Exercise: The Auric Egg ... 171

Feeling "Other" ... 174

Magic Words and Affirmations ... 176

Placebo Power ... 180
Witch Tip: The Ultimate Love Potion ... 181

"Why Aren't My Spells Working?" ... 182

Energetic Perception: Spirit Lights and Orbs ... 185

Pyramid Power ... 187

Distant Healing ... 189

Meditation for Personal and Universal Healing ... 194
Witch Tip: "What Does This Mean?" ... 195

Divination Techniques ... 197
*Witch & Wisdom: Meeting Freya Ingva, Diviner
and Tea-Leaf Reader ... 204*

Our Intuitive Bodies ... 205
Witch Tip: Notice What You Notice ... 206

Setting Intentions: Use It or Lose It ... 207
Witch Tip: Make That Move ... 212

Working with Sigils ... 213
Witch & Wisdom: Art Witch Laura Keeble ... 215
Magical Musing: A Note on Spare Time and Awareness ... 217

PART 4 EQUAL DARK, EQUAL LIGHT ... 219

Don't Be Afraid of the Dark ... 220

Good Vibrations: Changing State with a Song ... 223

Navigating and Interpreting Life's Jolts ... 225

The True Beauty of Authenticity ... 227

The Power of Deciding ... 229
    Witch Tip: Choices, Choices ... 232

False Modesty and Imposter Syndrome ... 233
    Witch & Wisdom: Dream Expert Linda Yael Schiller ... 236

Doing What Comes Naturally ... 238

The Trick of Treats ... 240

"Please Adjust Your Set": Creating New Channels ... 242
    Witch Tip: Lighten Up and Laugh ... 243

Engaged, Expressive, Extraordinary You ... 244
    Witch & Wisdom: UK Artist and Therapist Jane Woollatt ... 248

The Best Is Yet to Come? ... 250
    Witch Tip: Stop Saving It for Special ... 251

Want Change? Change Your Channels ... 252
    Magical Musing: The Transformative Magic of
    Standing Up Straight ... 255

Conclusion: Embracing the Wise Woman Within ... 257

Recommended Reading ... 259

Bibliography ... 267

Endnotes ... 273

Disclaimer

This book is designed to provide information and inspiration. It is sold with the understanding that the publisher is not engaged to render any type of psychological, legal, or any other kind of professional advice. The content is the sole expression and opinion of its author, and not necessarily that of the publisher. Neither the publisher nor the author shall be liable for any physical, psychological, emotional, financial, or commercial damages, including, but not limited to, special, incidental, consequential, or other damages.

ACKNOWLEDGMENTS

The biggest bouquet of thanks and love goes to my family, who continue to fill each day with love and magic; to my husband, Dylan, and cat, Marzipan; and also to Kizzy Thomson, for believing in this project. It's a big step out of the broom closet, and it wouldn't have seen the light of day without your encouragement. Thanks to my brilliant and patient editor, Heather Greene, for taking on this project and inviting me into the incredible Llewellyn family. It is an honour.

I was keen to invite other voices to be part of *Witchful Thinking* and create a merry band of wise women, so a heartfelt thank-you to those who took the time to contribute their perspectives, encouragement, and guidance, namely Jane Bradley, Claire Powell, Laura Keeble, Jane Woollatt, Madame Pamita, Linda Yael Schiller, Susan Chritton, Freya Ingva, Michelle Bappoo, Syd Moore, and Caroline Wise. Love and thanks to friends who took an interest, and to those who went before who shared their lessons and experiences for the benefit of the greater whole. To Red Feather, B and Alwyn, Judika Illes, Amy Hale, Rachel Patterson, Kate Laity, and Sue Terry and Erzebet Barthold at the wonderful Magickal Women Conference.

Love across the Great Divide to Marion Weinstein for being my North Star for at least the past twenty-five years, and to all of those, known and unknown, who have played a part in this project seeing the light of day.

FOREWORD

What does it mean to be a witch? People far wiser than me have filled entire libraries with their attempts to answer that question, and if I'm honest, I've never yet read one that captures it completely. If anything, it's the opposite: the more I read and explore the concepts and practices of witchcraft, magic, and assorted adjacent esoterica, the more I've come to recognise how much is revealed by our fascination for questions like these. We hunger for definitions. We want a map we can use to orientate ourselves in this strange territory. And there's wisdom in that, for sure. If you're venturing forth into unknown-to-you lands, it makes sense to want guidance and directions. You want to know where the edges are, the jagged rocks and the dark sections marked with warnings of "Here Be Monsters."

So, granted, some of our curiosity is practical, but there's more to it than that. If all we needed was a magical how-to manual, there wouldn't be such an endless array of books, films, music, art, and everything else devoted to exploring the countless multifaceted elements of the witch: the witch as archetype, the witch as an identity, the witch as an ever-shifting creature with an infinite list of stories, passions, perspectives, and skills. A figure with so much history, mythos, and lore. There's a tangible appetite for works exploring all these topics and more. It's an appetite that has existed for a long, long time, and—with the state of the world being what it is right now—one I can completely understand. We already know there are monsters here. What we want is understanding. Empowerment. Armour. A connection to a global heritage and community of witches, all using what the iconic Granny Weatherwax from Terry Pratchett's Discworld series would call "headology" to create real, tangible shifts. And a way of finding and celebrating beauty, joy, pride, trust, and magic even when times seem tough and dark.

So, that question about what it means to be a witch: maybe some of the spell it continues to cast on generation after generation comes from there actually being no one answer. More, that there are millions of answers, at least one for each witch, and probably more, depending on the day, the hour, the position of the moon, and the mood the witch is in. Combined, all of these answers come together to create a glorious, messy, multihued patchwork quilt that may in places be torn, stained, half-formed, or unraveling, but no less beautiful for it. A source of comfort and warmth.

More than anything, I think that's what Zoë has created with *Witchful Thinking*: a warm and gorgeous guide that can function as map, armour, and comfort blanket while exploring these concepts and areas and developing your own definition of what witchful thinking means to you. And lest we forget, creating our own language for the magic we make—as Zoë does with the concept and exploration of *Witchful Thinking*—is in itself a powerful act. This, I think, is what makes this book so special: the sense of empowerment and agency Zoë gives you, the reader, while still collecting an extensive array of wisdom and experience to make sure you're well-supplied for your journey.

There's a balance that books like this have to strike, between being accessible and being irresponsible. But in this book, Zoë encourages creativity, experimentation, playfulness, and personal discovery while never forgetting the importance of ethics and responsibility. Whether you're a "baby witch" or a longtime practitioner, there will be something for you in these pages, and it warms me to see these experiences and insights being shared with such a powerful focus on intersectionality and inclusion. Books like this build on a tradition that goes back centuries, and over that time language, context, and so much else has changed. So each book has a role in reflecting where things are *now*, in this continual reflection, celebration, and evolution of what's gone before. Which makes it more important than ever that contemporary texts like this one have a commitment to justice, diversity, equality, and inclusion.

That's something I've always loved about Zoë's work: from contributing to the Slits claiming their rightful place in rock 'n' roll history with her debut *Typical Girls?*, to her work with luminaries from the worlds of music, art, and more, there's a constant theme of compassion, curiosity, and commitment to telling stories that might not otherwise be shared, along with that punk grit of courage, tenacity, and creativity to get it done, often against significant odds. Whether it's in her journalism, fiction, art, or radio work, Zoë's integrity and ethics are always evident, and—in a subject area in which those things can sometimes seem invisible or altogether absent—they give *Witchful Thinking* a grounding and context that will support its readers in exploring and developing their own witchy ethics and approach.

In some ways, *Witchful Thinking* might seem a departure from Zoë's previous writing. But if you delve deeper into her brilliant back catalogue, I'd say the clues have always been there that this is a woman who brings her irreverent rock 'n' roll stardust and magic to everything she does, while always having the guts, know-how, and commitment to back it up. As with everything Zoë does, there's both style and substance in *Witchful Thinking*, and that in itself feels like an important celebration of what magic can do and be. And there's a generosity to how much Zoë's shared of her own heritage, knowledge, and experience in this book: while witchcraft and magic might have had a headline-hitting resurgence in recent times, it feels relevant to acknowledge how risky and vulnerable this wisdom-sharing has been and still can be. So treasure this book for its contents but also as a talisman for the possibility of being out of the broom closet and publicly open about one's witchy skills and approach to life. While *Witchful Thinking* builds on Zoë's previous work, it nevertheless represents a claiming of power and identity that I'm sure will resonate with its readers and imbue its contents with even more potency.

As a mental health practitioner, I have seen recent times reinforce the role and responsibility we all have in developing a fluency and skill set for managing our own resilience, mental health, and well-being. This isn't to victim-blame anyone struggling: external challenges and sources of oppression still exist, of course, and it's our collective responsibility to recognise and challenge these wherever we can and support each other in this process with as much empathy and understanding as possible. But what I've seen over and over in my therapeutic work is that a sense of self-empowerment and ownership over our respective mental health can be a key aspect of resilience, well-being, and recovery. Feeling powerless contributes to stress, grief, anxiety, and even trauma. Taking steps to identify our needs and move towards them—even if that movement takes time and happens in millimeters—can be an important act of self-care, self-compassion, and self-discovery. Although I didn't have a term for it until reading Zoë's book, that's what my own version of witchful thinking has given me: Rituals. Power. A framework for understanding the interconnectedness of the world and a recognition of my place in it. In the form of covens both formal and fluid, magic has given me collaborators and comrades, instruction, accountability, and confidence. Magic has brought people across my path who have gone on to become close friends and family. It's given me independence, yet also community. And all of those play an essential part in my day-to-day well-being.

I'm aware some of this might be controversial to some. That some of my peers in the mental health and therapeutic fields would say these areas are worlds apart. That if you could illustrate their relation to each other, they'd be at opposite ends of a miles-long strip. But I'm not a believer in binaries. Not when it comes to gender, sexuality, or morality. And not with this. So what if that miles-long stretch of paper or ribbon is actually a Möbius strip? Give it a twist, glue the ends together, and what you've got is overlap between areas that once seemed diametrically opposed. And *that*—that crossover, liminal place where all these things come together—is a place I find infinitely fascinating, exciting, and full of possibility. To me, that's the place *Witchful Thinking* will take you. I hope it brings the magic you need.

~*Jane Claire Bradley*

INTRODUCTION

*W*elcome, witches and wise women of every walk of life. It is my sincere hope that this book will be a life-affirming companion for you, weaving warmth, wit, and enchantment into your days, all while keeping you earthed in reality—well, the reality of your choosing, anyway.

The techniques and secrets inside this spiritual tool kit are largely notes from my own personal practice, shared from the heart: they work for me and can work for you. Take what you need, and expect that to change over time. Treat this book like a jewellery box: some items you'll feel more drawn to than others, depending on the day, your mood, and what's happening in your life. But whether you dip in or read it from cover to cover, you'll soon be injecting mysticism into everything from brewing your tea to beating the patriarchy—if you aren't already. Like everything, it all begins with a thought and a word.

The lighthearted but dynamic act of "witchful thinking" initiates a shift in mindset by utilising our natural cycles and inbuilt magic powers: essentially, our words and awareness. Moment by moment, we'll be connecting with the natural divinity that surrounds us and gives us structure, well-being, and even amusement. If you haven't noticed that the Universe has a kooky sense of humour, you might need to tweak your perspective. Witchful thinking will help. But it will also serve as a reminder that, whether you are a magical practitioner or not, we all have far greater control over how life goes than we are often led to believe.

Wise Woman Ways

The concept of witchful thinking is underpinned with the archetype of the wise woman, or "cunning woman." She'll encourage you to refine your awareness, get tough, get kind, get creative, live more freely, and age more joyfully. Yes, you read that right. It can be done, especially if you learn what to notice and what to ignore. It has been a pleasure to invite other voices to be part of the witchful conversation, so expect to meet some real-life wise women in the "Witch & Wisdom" sections throughout the pages that follow.

The more open you are to the magic within and around you—and not just when you want to cast spells, read the tarot, or meditate—the more it reveals itself, washing up ever more relevant treasures onto the shores of your precious life. And your life is precious, even if it doesn't feel like it is right now. We are rarely as powerless as we assume, but we sometimes need a friendly hand to guide us along the way. More often than not, that hand has to be our own. When we connect with nature and our higher self, this makes more sense.

While *Witchful Thinking* is aimed at all ages, this is the book I wish I'd had by my side as a teenager: a manual, sprinkled with humour and a little stardust, that would help me process what I was feeling and discovering, taking me all the way to cronehood. This world can be tough on sensitives and outsiders, and, no matter how much support we have around us growing up, sometimes it's hard to ask the right questions—or even know what those questions are. While I'm not claiming *Witchful Thinking* contains all the answers, it does include thoughts, workings, and reminders that have been an anchor for me, and I hope they will be for you as well, should you need them.

What to Expect

The playful but potent practice of witchful thinking is as individual as it is effective. It can see you tuning in to the quiet energy of a forest, stirring enchantment into your coffee, and using the electricity of a storm to charge your intentions. Prepare for life to get richer, a little curious, and certainly more fun. We should *always* make time for fun: it is magnetic to the good stuff. Never underestimate the power of a party.

Together we will explore symbolism, divination, our dreams, the power of our words, charms for health and beauty, herb lore, connection with Spirit, planetary correspondences, and the language of flowers, scent, and colour. We'll work consciously towards wisdom, acknowledging that this gift of the years and our experiences is not guaranteed, but earned. We'll learn how better to interpret the messages we are being shown *all the time*, if only we pay attention.

While you will be introduced to, or reacquainted with, many of the cornerstones of witching life, this book is essentially about magical *thought*. Magical thinking must always precede magical doing. You can have all the tools in the world, but it's when you've mastered the mindset that things really happen.

This is not a book of spells per se; plenty already exist. Indeed, you'll come across a list of my favourite magical books in Recommended Reading. I treasure my ever-expanding occult library and love that we can freely share such information now. Books are essential friends on our respective journeys. No matter how instinctive we are, clear guidance from those who have walked the path before us is precious, all the more so when we consider that at one time this knowledge would have been hidden, outlawed, or burned by our persecutors—or ourselves, for safety's sake.

It doesn't matter if you're just starting your magical journey, you've been on it for a while, or you're simply interested in enlivening your life with greater spiritual connection: this book will see you thinking magically as a matter of course. It's like learning a new language: you don't simply expect to speak it perfectly at the very moment you need it. We should be *thinking* in that language as much as possible if we want the best results.

Remembering Ancient Truths

In the witching life, the onus is on personal responsibility. Many of us look to a Divine Power, while others identify as atheist witches, but we are all united in that we do what we can for ourselves and others rather than handing over our power and looking only to external forces for help. We are all co-creators. Magic is our true nature; we were just told it wasn't by people who wanted to keep us under their thumbs. This is changing as more people embrace the idea of living consciously and tuning in with what Mother Earth is telling us—and she's talking loud these days. Ultimately, these modes of thought and ways of being are hardly "New Age"; they're centuries old and trusted throughout time and space. I'd say they've aged pretty well.

My hope is that you will retreat to this book as if it were a cosy, candlelit grotto: a fire in the grate, incense wafting about you, and a draught of something restorative at your side. This is a place to rest and revive—a place some may find curious or strange at times, but there is a reason for everything I have chosen to share.

My own path is largely rooted in the Celtic tradition with some nondenominational spiritualism woven in, so that's the predominant flavour of this book. But all are warmly welcomed here—and by that I mean *everyone*, of all cultures, all ages, and every gender. The wise woman archetype is a universal ally, as she always was. You will find reflections that pertain specifically to the issues women commonly face, because I am writing from my own experience. However, there is never any intention to exclude or deny the experiences or existence of others.

As with any such work, there will be parts you relate to more than others. So take what you need, and know that every word is delivered from the heart with a sincere wish for your happiness as a fellow human being.

My Witchy Beginnings

Once, it was considered perfectly reasonable to practice a little folk magic to nudge things in the right direction. It was normal to read the future in the fire, to tell our secrets to the river, to venerate the trees and the stones—at least it was before the "heresy" of magical living became demonised and thus had to be concealed in order to survive. It is unsurprising that so many in the West know more about Eastern spirituality, at least superficially, than the traditions embedded in our own DNA. Still, our instincts will take us where we need to be if we listen.

On a personal level, I was gravitating towards herb lore before I could write. When I was a toddler, I made flower and herb infusions and solemnly presented my mother, laid up with a migraine, with a neat arrangement of feverfew leaves from the garden. No one had told me that this herb was good for headaches. I had "brought the knowledge with me," as my mum put it, perhaps learned in a previous incarnation or guided by an unseen influence. Children are, as we are often told, closer to Source and have fewer layers to impede their connection. Nowadays, I won't use an unfamiliar herb unless I've Googled it fifteen times before popping it into my teapot, naturally.

I wrote secret letters to spirits, and when I was older, I was drawn to cartomancy: using playing cards as an oracle, a Gypsy witch technique historically favoured by the Roma community. Of course, traditional witchery across the board would see practitioners using whatever they had in or around their home. No expensive decks or mass-produced runes here—rather, your grandfather's old playing cards, or the bones and peelings in the kitchen, tossed onto a surface and "read" according to the shapes they'd fall into. This was also a more discreet way to follow the witching path. No visitor would question the broomstick, the deck of cards, the chicken bones, or the candles: these were staples in every home across the land.

Hereditary Witches

At the time of this writing, many practitioners are self-identifying as hereditary witches, which seems to imply, intentionally or not, a sense of hierarchy, justification, even "added value." But you don't have to be a hereditary or "natural-born" witch to work with energy for magical transformation, although if you are strongly drawn to this work, you may be one anyway without realising it. After all, few of us really know that much about the private lives of our family lines throughout the generations.

For a long time, it was not deemed sensible to use the word *witch* openly if you valued your life, or at least your reputation. It was, and to an extent remains, an emotive term that risked ostracism, ridicule, and suspicion. Old fears last lifetimes, and one can see why some still refer to this work as "the Nameless Arte." However, in the interests of giving you a sense of my own family tree, I can tell you it is full of psychics, healers, and people with an intuitive knowledge of plant lore. There are artists, poets, and musicians—all magical practitioners in their own way. Indeed, these professions actually would have been considered "magical" in ancient times.

My mother directed a company of mummers of which I was a part, although I was too young to remember very much. Mumming is an anarchic and very old theatrical tradition, and there are many bands of mummers around still, performing their colourful plays for the community on Twelfth Night, mingling Pagan and early Christian traditions. My mother also always had interesting occult-themed books in the house, and my sister and I were brought up with a strong sense of Spirit, as well as the power of nature and our own creativity. The modes of thought and natural lore that subtly wove their way in and around every day would instantly chime with those who identify as modern witches today.

The Magic of a Determined Thought

Magical thought worked effectively for me as a child because I never believed it wouldn't. I didn't give it the name "magic"—the word was charged with far-fetched fairy-tale connotations—but I never doubted I could influence things with energy and focus, although I have had to remind myself of this as I've aged. For example, I "decided" menstruation would be easy for me (it was), and I also "decided" my height. Being unusually tall as a prepubescent child, I felt self-conscious and so chose, with great determination, to cease growing. For better or worse, my body responded, and I indeed have remained the same height since I was eleven years old, despite having a tall father, a medium-height mother, and a sister who is a good head and shoulders taller than me. I kind of wish I hadn't done that now, but either way it illustrates the point that our thoughts and will are potent. I also recall reviving dead cellphones with focused intention and "fixing" my dad's electric car window when it stopped working. The window was energy, and my mind power is energy, so I found that when we're all tuned up, we can influence things with alarming ease, especially if we are stressed or excited. I know I'm not the only one who can do this, and I also know most people don't think to try. But witchful thinking means living with one foot in the world of the "seen" and the other foot in the world of the "unseen," all the time.

Teenage Seeker

My mum became dubious about any dabbling when I was in my teens, and understandably so. We are like radio receivers at that age, wide open to whatever's coming through and not experienced enough to know what to do with it. But I was a seeker and keen to delve deeper. I had a few whimsical spell books, I'd always gravitate to the spiritual section of libraries, and I reverently treated myself to a deck of Egyptian oracle cards at the historic Atlantis Bookshop in London, separating the Isis card and keeping it with me like a talisman.

But it was when I left home in my late teens that this whatever-you-want-to-call-it sprang fully into life, probably because I needed all the help I could get. Spirit definitely stepped in from time to time, and I realised I was developing clairaudience—literally "clear hearing," the ability to perceive sound and speech intuitively. Like many growing up in a pre-internet world, I kept it all to myself, although those who knew, knew. Some can spot a witch straight away, and I've found that witches are rather good at inadvertently finding each other, which is always fun.

I strayed from the path for a few years, although I always kept my magical books, crystals, and journals close as I moved from one place to the next. The candle guttered during my mid-twenties as I tried to fit in to a world of Muggles, Machiavellians, madness, and mundanity, but I found my way in the end.

Old Ways for the New Wave

For me, spirituality is personal, not prescriptive: it can and should evolve with us, and our needs, over time. Witching is an autonomous, innately creative practice. Yes, we draw on Old Ways, but when you consider that much of our history was destroyed, well, we must take the embers of what we can find and nurture them as best we can, adding our own flavour and even updating where appropriate. There's nothing to say that some of the newer spells and magical ideas weren't unknowingly channeled from those who went before—witch elders guiding the new guard from across the veil.

I encourage you to be guided by your intuition, imagination, heritage, and preferences, as well as the existing material you are called to research. In fact, if you need to be told what to do, think, and say at every step, this might not be the path for you. Witchcraft is a way of independence and sovereignty; it is the way of the freethinker, the artist, the radical, and the rebel. No wonder it scared the pants off the patriarchy.

WITCHCRAFT IS A WAY OF INDEPENDENCE AND SOVEREIGNTY; IT IS THE WAY OF THE FREETHINKER, THE ARTIST, THE RADICAL, AND THE REBEL.

PART I

EVERY WITCH WAY

Meeting the Wise Woman and Deciding
"Which Witch" You Wish to Be

INTRODUCING the WISE WOMAN ARCHETYPE

If you find people from all walks of life are magnetised to you and can't resist telling you their problems, chances are your inner wise one is shining through. Embrace it—but learn to shield your energy too. We'll talk more about how to protect yourself later on. First, it's time to mount our broomsticks and fly back in time to meet some very special ancestors who are waiting to hold up a mirror, and a sounding board, to our own practices across time and space.

Traditionally, the wise woman or man of the village would be the port of call for everything from health advice to the banishment of curses (or just warts), from tea and sympathy to the safe delivery of a baby. The wise one of the community was often one of the only people in the village able to read. They understood not just human nature, but Mother Nature, and they were generally surrounded by creatures of all kinds—from cats to dogs, bats to frogs, and even spiders, who often found a safe space within or close to the home of the practitioner. These furry, hairy, or scaly brothers and sisters would be referred to as animal "familiars," and they were and continue to be considered sensitive, protective presences during magical work.

Village healers, charmers, astrologers, and what we would now refer to as mediums were said to be mostly practicing "low magic," or magic with a practical use in the material world, rather than "high magic," which refers to ceremonial or ritual magic typically more concerned with celestial matters. Most contemporary followers of this path, such as myself, employ a blend of both. Every culture has its own version, but we draw from the same well in that we all acknowledge the fundamental importance of the elements (fire, water, earth, air, and spirit, or ether), the heavens, the natural world, and the power of focused thought, developed through meditation.

Cunning Folk and "Blessing Witches"

The British term *cunning folk* was often used to describe these usually solitary workers. Cunning folk worked with herbalism, natural lore, astrological knowledge, and folk magic—literally "people magic"—on behalf of the community. While the Industrial Revolution saw pagan magic or country magic dwindle as rural folk sought work in towns and cities, keepers of the old flames remained and still exist to this day. The term *hedge witch*, coined by the contemporary witch Rae Beth,[1] is often used to describe this kind of "natural magic" worker now.

Some referred to the cunning folk of the past as *white witches*, because they generally worked positive or at least protective magic. Historically, however, most would have been unlikely to refer to themselves as white witches for fear of persecution. The hysteria sporadically whipped up by reports of "Devil worship" and the subsequent witch hunts, from the mediaeval and Early Modern periods onwards, meant that many adepts risked being stitched up even by those they had tried to help. White or "blessing" witches could be called upon to heal a child only for the child to sicken and die after a brief improvement; this might then be blamed on the witch having cursed the child with further illness in order to extort more pennies for another healing cure. Hindsight indicates that in all likelihood, the child would have had a disease too complex or advanced to be cured in this way, and the temporary reprieve the witch offered had just delayed the tragic inevitable. But blame was sought, and witches—and those who just looked or acted like they *should* be "witches," to use the term in the pejorative sense—were scapegoated.

While there will no doubt have been some magical workers who were not exactly pure at heart, in most cases, the village witch or wise one worked to assist the community, to bless those coming in and out of the world, to heal, to guide, and to bring harmony. This was often done in secret and with no expectation for any credit: the work was enough. This is, of course, at odds with the image of the witch during the years of persecution. It bears recognising that many who were executed in those days were not witches, and many actual witches would not have been executed. When I was little, I believed that true witches would surely have been able to protect and conceal themselves during these dark times. Now that I'm older, I am certain many did exactly that.

Dark Ages and "Devilry"

We have to consider the spiritual and socioeconomic climate of Merrie England and her neighbours during the Dark Ages and beyond to better understand why negative witchcraft—and specifically "Devil worship"—was such a concern. As the Church swept in and pushed the old nature religions out, there was a crossover period in which the old gods were demonised and turned into a symbol of all that was dark, impure, "earthy," and wrong. The idea was that if something was not of Christ—heavenly, pure, and perfect—it was dark by default. It was literally the "anti-Christ." As a result, some who continued to hold the old gods and nature deities dear were now believed to be venerating "the Devil," to use the manipulative vernacular of the Church. In reality, they were doing nothing differently at all.

However, we also have to recognise that there was a feudal system that kept many in abject poverty. Church and government were one and the same, so if you rebelled against the government, you were denying the Church in turn. This, according to the research of author and witch Marion Weinstein, led to an underground minority, disempowered and in some cases crazed by destitution, that was seeking a different authority to turn to.[2] Once they had recognised how the Church was trampling their values and practices, this minority felt sufficiently motivated not only to reject but to actively desecrate all that was Christian.

But more prevalent than any real threat from "anti-Christians" and supposed Devil worshippers was the archaic fear of the Devil and his cults. The establishment stoked and propagated this terror, as it was a useful tool for social control. But, as Weinstein observed, "Satan is a thought-form. As a thought-form derives power from human thought, so its power may dissipate when people no longer give it power. For people who do not believe in Satan, 'he' simply does not exist."[3]

This is not to say that darkness doesn't exist—it does, in the form of negative energy and negative emotion. Give it a pointy red tail if you like, but it's ultimately the same thing, and it can be as intense as hate or as apparently innocuous as apathy or resignation. These are all energies that can potentially create chaos, destruction, and sabotage, keeping us down and pushing us off course. But with our conscious thought, a healthy perspective, and reasonable discipline, we easily keep "the Devil" away.

Old Ways in (Early) Modern Days

Most cunning folk in the British Isles, at least from the Early Modern period onwards, were followers of the Christian faith rather than any of the Pagan or ancient Goddess-centred religions. This is simply because they were now living in an established patriarchal society: any residual connection to the Great Mother or Divine Feminine would have been transferred to the Virgin Mary or other female saints,[4] who fulfilled the enduring ancient need to acknowledge both the Divine Feminine and the Sacred Masculine. The Church was very much the norm by this point. Some people may have been more casual churchgoers than others, but this was the cultural structure in which they would have been brought up.

There were reports of subversive outliers who openly rejected the Christian faith and apparently claimed not to know the Lord's Prayer if asked. This was supposedly one way of being able to spot a witch,[5] although evidently it was not a very reliable one. Imagine randomly stopping an old lady and commanding her to recite the Lord's Prayer: it's likely that the shock of being accosted in this way—possibly with prosecution, torture, and execution hanging on her response—would cause her to hesitate or go blank.

There was more of a lingering crossover between the two paths of Christianity and country mysticism than some may realise. It was common for magical practitioners across Europe to work Christian references into spellcraft, and there was an acceptance amongst witches and cunning folk that holy water and the sign of the cross would protect against evil. Some would use the Lord's Prayer as a kind of shield, as it had become a charged tool of protection after centuries of being used and turned to for this reason. Amusingly, during the early 1600s, a preacher in the county of Essex wryly commented that the standard of Christian worship locally was so poor that "only witches and sorcerers use the Lord's Prayer."[6]

Apotropaic marks

As ambiguous as their image could be, many cunning men and women managed to remain safe, as they were regarded as useful members of society and were often called upon to cast counter-charms against suspected works of malevolent witchcraft. They worked to protect, break curses, and send negative energy back to the sender. Apotropoaic marks and symbols are evidence of counter-magic and can be found everywhere from the lintels of old houses to the pews in a church. Other items of folk magic, such as animal skeletons, shoes, hair, and so on, are still being found in the walls of crumbling old dwellings.

Superstitious Minds

Their qualities of empathy and intuitive wisdom and their knowledge of astro weather, folk medicine, and herb lore meant that cunning folk were always in demand, not least to heal those who had fallen ill. This was rather to the chagrin of orthodox physicians fearful of losing paid work. As a result, many working in this way were subject to propaganda that, in order to seed mistrust, trivialised their work as superstitious, primitive nonsense, at best.

Admittedly, the lines between folk magic and superstition can sometimes seem to blur, but one important distinction is this: Magic is empowering, placing the power in the hands of the practitioner. Superstition is disempowering, as it places our power outside of ourselves.

Some superstitions admittedly have sensible origins. For example, walking under a ladder could cause walkers to have something dropped on them accidentally from above. Likewise, the belief that opening an umbrella indoors is unlucky would have made more sense during the Victorian era, when every surface was cluttered with fragile ornaments. But most superstitions have lost any discernible meaning, developing lives of their own as a result of having been taken literally by generations of unquestioning people. If we see a single magpie and subsequently decide we're going to have a bad day, we probably will—because that's what we're expecting. We will be looking out for things that relate to that "omen" and will eventually justify it.

Like many, I grew up with old superstitions and think they can be fun if not taken too seriously. It's best not to allow one's fate to rest on the behaviour of a single bird, for example. Although if that bird's behaviour is unusual, pay attention: symbolism is the language of magic.

MAGIC IS EMPOWERING, PLACING THE POWER IN THE HANDS OF THE PRACTITIONER. SUPERSTITION IS DISEMPOWERING, AS IT PLACES OUR POWER OUTSIDE OF OURSELVES.

WITCH & WISDOM
Author and Activist Syd Moore

Syd Moore has written novels about witchcraft and the witch hunts, including The Drowning Pool, Witch Hunt, Strange Magic, *and the rest of the* Essex Witch Museum Mysteries. *Her work changes people's perceptions of witches, the motivations behind the witch trials, and indeed women overall. I asked about some of the common misconceptions about the witch hunts and how they affect our perceptions of powerful women to this day, and here is her answer:*

Syd Moore: Many people think the witches of the English hunts were actually practicing witchcraft, [but] most were scapegoats blamed for unrelated tragedies: famines, storms, illness, crop failures, stillbirths, miscarriage, et cetera. When people couldn't understand why these things happened, they often blamed the grumpy old woman who lived down the road, especially if she often came begging for food and cursed them if they refused.

Although they could have been spiritual and certainly had a greater awareness of the natural world than our post-industrial society, most of the accused would have identified as Christians. They didn't really know of other paths, and the term *witch* wasn't something that was used to self-identify but a label (think "lasso") thrown at women—and men—who did not display conventional behaviours.

Women who stray outside the norms of socially approved behaviour are often perceived as threats, something to be feared and contained. Power has for so long been the privilege of men that women who wield it are often seen as perversions of femininity, as the witches once were. And God help any powerful woman who is attractive: often they are referred to as "charming," "bewitching," and with many allusions to "glamour," thought to be a magical spell [that gave you] the ability to make yourself more attractive, richer, or finer than you were.

[This kind of language implies] that these women couldn't be what they were: they had used magic or had "done" something witchlike to get where they were, something unnatural. The "witch," and all the preconceptions that go with the word, is never far under the surface of the way we talk about women.

SPEAKING OF WITCH

For me, *witch* is a compliment: it signifies wisdom and mirth, divine connection, and empowerment. After years of being misinterpreted as "scary woman with green skin," the term has burst into full bloom and is now largely seen as a positive, at least in the West. In fact, the word *witch* now seems to represent everything from "independent creative spirit" to "rebellious feminist warrior," from "wise, powerful person with a foot in both worlds" to "person who wears black nail polish and posts mysterious selfies on Instagram."

It *is* positive—and very healing—to see people enjoying the word after centuries of fear and secrecy, but to tag yourself a "witch" just because you dig the aesthetic and think it makes you sound intriguing is like proclaiming yourself Hindu because you do yoga and think you look cute when you wear a stick-on bindi. Obviously, you're not going to do that—and I think the Old Ways, and those who have quietly lived them throughout time and space, deserve the same respect.

The above behaviour might seem innocuous, but to some it can feel like appropriation, such as when people adopt elements of practices from cultures that are not their own, with little comprehension of the sanctity of those practices. To me, and others, what we refer to as witchcraft is a life choice, present since childhood in many cases, and most likely before that. A daily commitment—and sacred.

While I rejoice in how open we can be in our conversation, I wonder what our ancestors would make of the fact that the way of the witch—a lifestyle many died for, whether they subscribed to it or not—is now "in fashion" and treated casually by so many. Still, I love the spirit with which a lot of magical information is being shared, and a global community of sensitives, adepts, and healers growing and communicating with each other can only be a good thing. We teach, learn from, and embolden each other when we share our practices, and we also draw unconsciously on the work of those who went before.

The pendulum swings to the opposite extreme before finding its balance, and certainly it's better that the witching life is now accepted and appreciated than viewed erroneously as all-out evil. Yes, there will always be practitioners who choose not to work for the greater good, but let us consider this: as my mother told me, those who are gifted—say, with psychic awareness, natural ability, or healing hands—risk losing those gifts if they exploit them. Mirroring our cunning ancestors, a humble appreciation and the question "How can I develop my abilities to serve others and the planet?" should always be in our minds.

Reclaiming the Witch

As the word *witch* is reclaimed, the perception of it changes—and that, to me, is magic in action. It heals the past, working backwards in time to reach out to those who lived in a very different era, one that was hostile to who they naturally were.

We can't pretend the evil eye doesn't exist—this can be as simple as negative energy—nor that baneful spells were never cast. Plenty of evidence, from blasting rods to pierced animal hearts, survives and now resides in museums. But how many spells were cast in vengeance against abusers, manipulators, or simply ignorant neighbours whose idle words had caused ostracisation? "Keep away from her, she's strange": that kind of social alienation, whether subtle or blatant, would make one take a dim view of people, and perhaps as a result someone's horses might start misbehaving or the milk in the churn would sour. Petty victories would no doubt be claimed, but this didn't mean a witch was to blame *every* time the buttermilk went off or the carthorse refused to budge.

History is written by the oppressors, and so we must question everything. It was only the alleged crimes that were reported, written down, and archived, rather than the good deeds, blessings, and healings. The facts we are presented with are skewed. My own research and intuition still assures me that these people were largely acting as they would now: as a positive force and an "independent advisory body," if you like, not to mention a bridge to other realms. They were the ones with the skills and the spirituality to see a soul into, and out of, this world, after all.

Making Peace with the Outsider

Witches have always offered assistance to rebels and outsiders because we are outsiders ourselves. Life gets better when you accept that you don't fit. Look at the world: if you don't fit in with all this, I'd say, for the most part, that's a positive. You'll only cause yourself pain and confusion when you try to square-peg it, so say it if you feel it: "I don't fit with any of this—and that is fine."

Striving to fit in is futile. It's all about other people and what they think, which is none of our business. Nature says that you fit in perfectly, you are infinitely lovable, and you absolutely belong. Spirit says the same. That's all I need, although it took me a while to understand that.

Witches, Bitches, "Nasty Women": The Rise of the Divine Feminine

There have been movements of "nasty women," "dangerous women," "bad girls," and so on—I've been involved with them myself—and these terms are being used by creative, adventurous women who are breaking the glass ceiling and fulfilling their life's work. This is no different from what most men have been allowed and expected to do since forever. But here's the thing: they're just called "men." They're not "supermen" or "nasty men" (although some of them are). They're just men.

"Nasty woman" refers to Donald Trump's put-down of Hillary Clinton in 2016, and the phrase was immediately adopted by millions of women around the world.[7] To embrace the word *nasty* in the face of this is radical and liberating. To use the phrase "nasty woman"? Even more so. But if you are an introvert who is every bit as capable of self-fulfillment in your own quietly subversive way, is the fierce, hardcore, "badass" tag off-putting? Must self-empowerment be ferocious and startling and explosive for it to even count? "I want to do this and this, but I'm not 'fierce' or 'badass,' I'm just me. Is that not enough? Do I have to pretend?"

The message is potentially confusing, and we risk alienating those who can't relate to it. Too often it's the squeaky wheel that gets the grease, but we must underestimate no one's power. Being absolutely ourselves isn't really dangerous or wild or crazy. It's about being alive and free—free to be as loud *or* as quiet as we want to be, moment by moment.

To be fair, a lot of women have had to be genuinely dangerous, violent, and aggressive to ensure we got the vote, got heard, and got the respect we deserve. But the idea that more often than not a woman has to be an all-out rebel just to express herself creatively, speak her truth, and be heard—something we should be free to do every day anyway—seems retrogressive in this era. Women are creative by nature, resilient and strong, powerful and mystical. This applies to all we do, whether creating art, making a splash in the political arena, or holding up society at home by keeping a family together and ensuring that the next generation of adults will be compassionate, wise, stable, and emotionally intelligent.

The Divine Feminine is rising. The fact we are now seeing these very words emblazoned on T-shirts tells us a lot. For something to infiltrate popular culture indicates a great change. Just make sure that by fighting the monster, we don't become the monster. It's alarmingly easy to let righteous rage incinerate *everything*—for it to cloud our vision until all we see is enmity to be fought at every turn. That was certainly me for a while. It's also not unknown for some members of the sisterhood to not be so sisterly when they think no one's looking. We are so much stronger when we truly unite. Indeed, it's the only way we can really succeed.

Wise Women of Today

Wise woman knowledge evolves with time, political shifts, and changing social and cultural needs. While it can never really be lost, it needs conscious relearning, as it has been muted, drowned out, and repressed by conditioning—and I'm not talking about the kind that makes your hair look less like the business end of a broomstick.

Today, the concept of the wise woman has expanded to reflect the tropes of modern society and can mean many different things. A wise woman can be someone who wittily guides us away from self-obsession and neurosis over our looks, like the plain-speaking British actor and director Kathy Burke; someone who empowers us with body positivity, like the pop singers Beyoncé and Lizzo; someone who infects children with a love of reading—and provides the books, to boot—like Dolly Parton; someone who turns their life into a peace campaign, like Yoko Ono; or someone who casually smashes down the walls of male-dominated worlds with intellect, artistry, and spirit, like the historian Mary Beard or the rock star, poet, and "godmother of punk" Patti Smith.

These are just a few of my go-to contemporary wise women. I'm sure you can think of many of your own. They might not be casting spells in a traditional sense, but their power is clear and can leave you feeling changed—and that's magic.

WHICH WITCH ARE YOU?

Labels can be reductive, and I'm not crazy about defining things too much, not least because we all must allow ourselves the space to shift, flow, and develop over time. I just follow my heart, and I suggest you do the same.

While some people believe that all witches must be Wiccan, this is not the case. I have family members who do identify as Wiccan, and I find Wicca fascinating and inspiring in many ways. But, if I had to pin down my own practice, I would call myself a "positive" kitchen witch with roots in the Celtic tradition and nondenominational spiritualism. That description reflects my own practice, and it's where I feel most at home. However, I give myself space to grow and change, and I acknowledge that I may feel called to work with others at some point. As always, listen to your soul and what it needs, and the best way to do this is to take yourself aside every day and spend time in silence. Meditating is at the heart of many paths and practices, and with good reason. We shall explore this further later on in the book.

There are myriad paths, and it is often said that there are as many types of witch as there are witches. There are traditional witches, Wiccans, Alexandrian witches, and hedge witches. There are sea witches, Dianic witches, Druids, heathens, hoodoo practitioners, root workers, and kitchen witches, to name but a few. Witches can be any gender—and male witches don't much like the term *warlock*.

My mother is a perfect example of what some would now term a *green witch*, although she would never refer to herself that way. Gardens flourish under her touch, and she only needs to think, "I'd love it if I had foxgloves (or snapdragons, or London Pride) in my garden..." for the plant to self-seed from nowhere and burst into bloom within a matter of weeks. No hocus-pocus—just the magnetic power of a sincere wish is enough for her. She is definitely living with a foot in both worlds, so this happens more naturally than it might for most. I sometimes wonder whether one of her spirit guides is a gardener who links in with her passion for nature. Either way, my mum explains the magnificent responsiveness of her garden thus: "It knows it's loved." Nothing can grow without that.

Eclectic Witchery and Cultural Appropriation

You don't have to give yourself a label, although some favour *eclectic witch* these days. It's appropriate for some, as it avoids more specific categorisation if your practice is still quite new and you're finding your feet. To be honest, most witches do embrace a bit of eclecticism: information freely shared leads to inevitable cross-pollination, after all. It is our nature to seek and find, to connect, and to be curious. We have much to share with each other, and when we do, it's exciting to see how our own ways of observing the Craft move forward. Most of us are also living, breathing multicultural mixes, and the world's the better for it. So, with that in mind, *eclectic* seems about right overall.

However, the term can also indicate a "pick 'n' mix" approach to spiritual paths, sending us veering into the territory of appropriation. Ideally, we draw on our own ancestral heritage, researching it with commitment and love and building a secure foundation that we connect with on a soul level. But many of us are sensitives and can unwittingly tap into something profoundly relevant to us, whether from a previous incarnation or from an ancient, unknown ancestral link. We also can't rule out the possibility that our "spirit team" are nudging us towards a deity or practice that was sacred to our guides when they were on the physical plane. Spend time in meditation if you're unsure, and see what comes through in the stillness—or in your dreams.

It is vital that we do not casually or inadvertently exploit practices, symbols, and tools sacred to living traditions that are not our own. At the same time, our view can become very narrow if we never look beyond our own backyards to at least learn about and appreciate the traditions of our neighbours in the global community. When we do this with sensitivity and respect, we make the world smaller and more integrated. Often, we find out how similar our values and ideas really are.

Exploring Your Connections

My own homeland is a melting pot, and the cultural lines often blur. I am a mix of English, Irish, Scottish, French, and Scandinavian Jewish—and those are just the bloodlines I know about. Those of us with old roots in the British Isles are likely to connect naturally with pre-Christian Celtic or Pictish (Scottish) deities, but also Norse and Roman, as their traditions fed into ours by way of invasion over the centuries. The Celts themselves were originally a nomadic Indo-European people; they arrived in Ireland in 500 BC.[8] Granted, that is quite a long time ago, but still we can't be too surprised if we of Celtic stock find ourselves as drawn to Athena as we are to Brighid or if we sense an inclination towards Sumerian goddess Inanna. Magic evolves like language. Cross-fertilisation and cultural exchange help us grow and develop, widening our horizons and enriching our lives.

Think about where your connection stems from. For example, you may feel a link with the energy of Thor. Rather than reject this feeling because you don't know of any Vikings in your bloodline, follow the instinct, look into it. Find a meditation that will allow you to glimpse your past lives, or look into your family trees. Above all, honour it with respect and humility, and see where it takes you.

There are so many reasons a figure can turn up as a guide. Could it be that a certain deity embodies a quality that you need right now?

Follow the spiritual breadcrumbs with sincerity, and see where they lead you.

Whatever path we identify with, we are all made of magic: the rest is mostly semantics. Much time can be wasted categorising and arguing over the validity of different terms—time that is better spent doing the work. Staying focused on what really matters is how we create a charmed life, both for ourselves and for others.

Coven or Solitary?

You don't have to join a coven to tap into your inner wise woman, and you don't have to be initiated by another person to feel you can legitimately identify as a witch, if that's who you authentically feel yourself to be. Often, the traditional wise woman would have worked alone; she knew who she was and did as she pleased, and this holds true today. However, many witches do prefer to work with others, and as always, this is a personal choice that may or may not alter with time or your circumstances and needs. There are also traditions that require ceremonial initiation to represent a step from one way of life into another, and I certainly respect the significance of that. But it very much depends on which path you wish to pursue, so don't feel inadequate—or superior—should you choose one way over another. All that matters is the work.

Working magic in a group can be a transcendent experience: collective energy is potent. But, as with any recipe or spell, you want to be sure of the right mix of ingredients if you are going to commit. As always, listen to your instincts and do what feels right at this time. Whether you join a coven or not, there is magic in the mere act of getting together to listen to each other. Too often we don't feel heard or acknowledged, and we need support networks to blast through the sense of separation and competition that can stop us from being the sisters (and brothers) we all could be. You just need to find the right blend and to know that everyone is on the same page in terms of intention.

As for working "solitaire," you will quickly find that you are never really alone when working with Spirit, Nature, and the Divine.

You Do You

We're all learning, so don't let anyone make you feel you have to justify yourself or your developing practice. Similarly, don't let anyone make you think they know everything. If there was nothing more for them to learn, they wouldn't be here. Call a young seeker a "baby witch" if you wish, but remember, they may be continuing a journey they have been travelling for many lifetimes, while this might be your first. Unless you're acting as someone's mentor, guide, or high priest or priestess, you can never know what stage anyone else is at—nor is it your business, unless they choose to make it so.

Women in particular often live in a cycle of waiting for validation and legitimisation from others before they can feel confident in who they are and what they are doing. We become resigned to fitting the many roles others foist upon us, to the extent that we risk losing touch with our essence, and that starts early. It's no surprise that we get angry and frustrated, but these feelings get pushed down so much that when they do rise up, we can't understand them, let alone explain them to anyone else. We find ourselves resorting to passive aggression to try to get our messages across, because we've been trained to find more palatable ways to express ourselves. Everything has been skewed to making the other person more comfortable. Now, in this age of information, there is another level of validation neurosis: this sense that unless the things you do, say, and feel are plastered online for the approval of others, they essentially didn't happen. This is a strange and destructive way of being that we must challenge and preferably detach from as much as possible—and yet it's the way in which we, in the digital age, are now being trained.

It's time we got used to defining and determining who we are, where we shine, and how we want things to go. It's never too early or late, although the earlier we do this, the better. This is, for me, at the heart of witchful thinking. There's no right or wrong way to witch. Just stay true to what you feel works at this time, and proceed accordingly. Salem witch Laurie Cabot put it beautifully when she said: "If you are truly a witch, you will behave as one. You will have integrity. You will have balance [and] focus. Your personal power is important […]: that power is to bring goodness to the world, to yourself and all that surrounds you."[9]

STAYING FOCUSED ON WHAT REALLY MATTERS IS HOW WE CREATE A CHARMED LIFE, BOTH FOR OURSELVES AND FOR OTHERS.

GOLDEN RULES

Many—but certainly not all—modern practitioners of the Craft observe the following basic tenets, which you no doubt will have encountered somewhere even if you've barely set foot on your witching path:

- "Harm none," a phrase from the Wiccan Rede: "an' (meaning 'if') ye harm none, do what ye will." First publicly uttered by Wiccan high priestess Doreen Valiente, the mother of modern witchcraft, in 1964, although it is believed this rule was based on much older witchcraft tenets.[10]

- Work should be for the good of all and according to free will.

- The good old law of "what goes around comes around"— in different and unexpected ways, AKA karma. Sometimes known as the Threefold Law, indicating that that which we put out returns to us three times. At least.

Admittedly, these are all open to interpretation, but they are good principles to observe whether you are spiritual or not. But in the main, many of those in today's witching community are good at reminding each other that negative work has consequences that can reach far beyond what we had imagined, always affecting ourselves as well as our "target." It should be clear that this is also a choice that we are all free to make. The important thing is that we proceed with informed judgement.

White magic is supposed to be "good," black "bad," and gray a mix of both, but in today's world, talk of white being good and black being bad sounds dangerously rooted in racist ideology. Additionally, magical work tends to be nuanced and complex, so using binary terms is not always helpful or accurate. Still, inspired by the late New York witch Marion Weinstein, I generally enjoy using the terms *positive magic* and *negative magic* instead, and identify as a positive witch.[11] Magic is energy, and energy is neither good nor bad, but neutral. It's what we do with it that counts.

All humans work with energy, albeit not always in conscious ways. We need to get conscious about it. Magic is music; magic is nature, art, poetry, song, and dance; it is science and it is *a* science. At the risk of repeating myself, magic is about transformation and energy, the stuff we're all made of.

Turn your attention on like a spotlight and shine it on what you love, what excites you, what you want more of—it will expand and grow under the focus of your gaze. That's how we change our world for the better.

MAGIC IS ENERGY, AND ENERGY
IS NEITHER GOOD NOR BAD, BUT NEUTRAL.
IT'S WHAT WE DO WITH IT THAT COUNTS.

QUIET REVOLUTION: MAGIC BY STEALTH

Witches have always beavered away behind the scenes to help their communities, generally by stealth. At odds with the performative, virtue-signalling culture of the digital era, magical workers and healers of the past would rarely talk openly about their work, not only because of the trouble it could lead to, but also because going public dilutes the results.

Humility is also vital. We are working with elemental forces and Spirit, acting as a channel for divine light to come to Earth and go where it is needed. This is deep work, and we must question and inspect our intentions. Ask yourself if you are coming from a pure place with this or if you are doing it mainly so you can post about it on social media. Stealth normally makes one think of sneaky behaviour, but how about when you just want to silently do some good with no agenda? It's hard for humans to do a nice thing without wanting credit for it, but when we work as witches—often in silence—we know the grip of ego is at least a *little* looser.

This kind of work is more effective when it is not talked about. When you discuss it with others, you risk your plans or results being inadvertently polluted or knocked off course by people's attitudes, doubts, or negativity. "To know, to dare, to will, to keep silent" is a law many magical folk live by. *Occult* means "hidden," but sweet Venus, how open things are now. Even twenty years ago I would cover my witchy books in silver paper so I could read them on public transport without arousing curiosity, and I'd bury them deep in drawers so nosy landladies wouldn't see them as they snooped about. Let us not forget the value—necessity, indeed—of silence and mystery.

What can you do by stealth to help others? Here are some ideas:

+ Leave tokens, notes, or positive messages around in public spaces for people to find.

+ Donate to a charity.

+ Deliver a pack of healthy pet food to a struggling animal shelter.

+ Start a community garden.

+ Post a hamper of goodies to someone who would appreciate it.

+ Send a cheerful message to someone who is unwell or feeling blue.

The last two don't have to be anonymous (we don't want to freak anybody out), but, similarly, you don't have to "go public" about your act of kindness.

Another idea would be to tap into old-style cunning ways by assisting the journey of souls passing from this world to the next. One way to do this would be to spend time in private meditation and ask the appropriate angels or deities—the goddess Hecate, who lights the way, for example—to guide souls safely and easily to the light. You may also write a heartfelt prayer to those who have passed or are about to, and light a candle at twilight or just before dawn: these liminal, "thin" times are considered psychic portals. Imagine yourself grounded, with roots travelling from the soles of your feet into the earth, and picture yourself suffused with protective divine light. Now speak the words, aloud or in your head, while linking in with any other people who are doing the same on both sides of the veil. You can bet those already in Spirit will be chiming in to amplify this lightwork too. This is a simple but profound act of compassion, and it makes a difference.

WITCH & WISDOM

Claire Powell, a Modern-Day Wise Woman

I asked my friend Claire Powell, Celtic medicine woman, Druid, and practicing witch, how we can better access our inner wise woman. Her answer was characteristically rich and overflowing with healing energy:

Claire Powell: A good place to start is with a definition of wisdom. I can only speak of what it is to me, in this moment, as I understand it right now. Wisdom is "knowledge perfected," understanding gained, information experienced, evaluated, understood, and then interrelated and brewed in the cauldron of Cerridwen to become consciously focused purpose and potential. It is alive, self-aware, and its purpose is the experience, knowledge, and love of itself.

How do we access the wise woman within? Live. Be willing to embrace life fully, consciously—to engage. Trigger experience. Without experience, you can never know wisdom. Be willing to be aware of the life that flows to and through you, of your impact upon it and its impact upon you.

Seek out your own understanding of your experiences; they are your gifts and unique to you. Know that in each hurt is a hidden blessing, a healing, and a magic that is absolutely yours if you care to seek it out, understand it, heal it, love it whole, and give it purpose. Each experience has a right to fulfil itself; how it is fulfilled is the work of the wise woman.

Magical Musing
Unicorn Energy versus Toxic Masculinity

At this time of increased female empowerment, it's hard to ignore the fact that unicorns are everywhere. They arrive in the form of toys, tattoo designs, and colouring books. People are even referring to themselves as unicorns. I think this is significant: the Divine Feminine is rising and unicorns are intrinsically connected with women. Legend has it that no man could capture a unicorn: male hunters would be savaged, and only a maiden could draw this creature near.

The language of magic is symbolism, so rather than discount mythical creatures as made up for fairy tales, consider what this persistent idea might be trying to tell us. After all, most fairy tales themselves speak to us in thinly veiled symbols and riddles, often communicating deep truths connected to menarche and the female life cycle: maiden, mother, crone.

As well as being linked with feminine power, the unicorn, with its phallic horn, is also associated with bisexuality and polyamory. Some sense the magic of the unicorn drawing close as we prepare for a shift in consciousness that will usher in a more accepting world of inclusivity and sensitivity. The symbolic energy of these light beings supports us as we rise, with savage consequences to any toxic masculinity that rears its ugly head.

At this point in history, female power is becoming more respected, and attitudes are changing in connection to people of colour and the LGBTQIA community. Much-needed conversations are being held. Many of us are also returning to ancient nonbinary ideas that we all contain masculine and feminine aspects and indeed that the Divine is gender-fluid, manifesting in different guises.

I see all of these phenomena as connected.

PART 2

AS ABOVE, SO BELOW

Working with Nature and Celestial Cycles

ALIGNING WITH THE DIVINE

When it comes to the Divine, there are multiple terms we can use: Universal Energy, the powers that be, God or Goddess, the Creative Source, Divine Intelligence, the Infinite. There will be many more names to add to this list besides, but the thing to note is that they are essentially the same. We work with what we feel is right for us. We have a choice.

My parents sent me to a Church of England primary (elementary) school during the mid-1980s, because it was the nearest decent school to where I lived. C of E, as it is known, is not generally assumed to be *too* hardline these days, at least not in comparison to some branches of the Church. However, I never felt comfortable with the religious aspect of school life—and I tried, I really did. I read the Bible, I sang the hymns, I listened in horror to my fire-and-brimstone teacher, who warned me of all the things that would send me to hell, and I played an angel in the Nativity play every year. While I still love angels, the Christian way overall did not feel authentic to me.

I didn't like the imagery, often tragic and gory, nor the elements of emotional blackmail. I also didn't appreciate the fact that this path didn't seem very female-friendly, unless you were a virginal matriarch, which didn't make sense. No one really explained that the teachings in the Bible are mostly symbolic—and, in some cases, actually quite useful, sexism aside. I'm not trying to disrespect anyone; this is just my experience and what I took from it.

The idea that I could feel my way to something that suited me better was thrilling and a great comfort. We are products of our circumstances and environments, but that doesn't mean you can't step outside of them and ask your soul where it wants to go, where it finds its solace, and what it wants to worship, if anything. It may surprise you.

I hadn't grown up using the term *Great Mother*, but some years ago, while worrying about something, I decided to meditate and I heard a distinct voice calmly say, "The Great Mother is taking care of it." I occasionally experience clairaudience, and while it is easy to assume we have imagined things at times, all I can say is, there's a difference. Ever since then, in my meditations, I send appreciation to the Great Mother or ask for her protection and guidance. I interpret the Great Mother as the all-powerful loving energy of Mother Earth and the Divine Feminine. Some may interpret this symbolic figure as the Virgin Mary. To me, the essence is the same. Much of what we believe is either a choice, an agreement based on what resonates with us, or just part of our upbringing. But the above experience came unbidden, and I felt privileged to have that glimpse into something so loving and authentic.

All Is One

The way of the wise woman is a way of self-government, and we adapt in ways to suit our own characters while maintaining respect for the natural world and the Divine. We take responsibility for our actions, and we always have one eye on potential consequences. Some of us are monotheistic, some work with Spirit and elementals, some are atheists, and others are polytheistic, worshipping several or many deities. Like many, I turn to different deities depending on my situation: from abundant Brighid to the Morrigan, protector of witches, and from Isis, the mother of all magic, to Bastet, the Egyptian cat goddess. (I invoke her aid when someone's feline has gone missing; she always answers sincere petitions in return for an offering, usually catnip and treats.) Personally, I recognise the various deities as different aspects of one Divine Power. I never could fully relate to the concept of a specific goddess or god being in charge of the whole thing; for me, they are all representations of a greater divine whole and the energy that flows within and all around us. While it took me years to know how to articulate this, the growing conversation concerning gender has helped me nail down my discomfort, in that I don't really relate to the gendering of the ultimate Source or Divine Power. This Intelligence, however you wish to refer to it, is bigger than gender, which seems a very Earth concept.

Humans like to externalise and anthropomorphise that which we don't quite understand. I feel that we've created imagery of gendered, humanised beings because we can more easily try to communicate or project onto them if they look a bit like us—multiple limbs and cat heads notwithstanding. All the same, I believe the Divine Feminine and Sacred Masculine are qualities that are real, and we translate them or imagine them as we see fit. They are also part of us, within us and without. By placing them "out there," we risk losing sight of the divinity within, and of the fact that it is all the same energy.

Magical Collaborators

We are never alone, even when working solitaire. You may be consciously working with the Universe, a deity, or your guides and angels—whatever chimes with you is perfect at this time. Different people connect with different things spiritually, and while some guides and light beings may stay with us for life and beyond, others come and go depending on our needs and where we are in our respective journeys.

Brew a cup of mugwort tea in the evening and see what, or who, comes through the veil in your dreams. Pay attention to what comes up, and always say thank you to those helpers, known and unknown, who have got your back. You will draw them closer this way too.

On the other hand, if you feel the energy is getting overwhelming, you are allowed to call time. As always, your word is your wand, to quote the metaphysical writer Florence Scovel Shinn.[12] Politely but firmly state that you'd like some space if need be, or invite your spiritual guardians and guides to draw close if you prefer. You are always in charge.

YOU MAY BE CONSCIOUSLY WORKING
WITH THE UNIVERSE, A DEITY,
OR YOUR GUIDES AND ANGELS,
WHATEVER CHIMES WITH YOU
IS PERFECT AT THIS TIME.

ELEMENTARY, MY DEAR WITCHY: EARTH, AIR, FIRE, WATER, AND SPIRIT

Knowledge of the elements—earth, air, fire, water, and spirit—and their areas of influence is crucial to witchful thinking. We draw upon them in all we do. We encompass all of these, all the time, whether we are conscious of it or not. Students of herb lore will be aware of the ancient concept that we contain the elements in our bodies by way of humours—physical qualities of hot, cold, dry, and moist—and we work on balancing them in order to maintain good health.

The elements are such a fundamental part of everyone's lives—witch or nay—that we may take them for granted. With this in mind, let's take a moment to connect with them and the qualities over which they preside.

The symbol for spirit (sometimes drawn as a sacred spiral or wheel)

Spirit

Also known as *ether* or *quintessence*, which literally translates as "the fifth element" in Latin, spirit is associated with the Divine, the Universe, and the archangel Metatron, believed to be the highest of the archangels. In its perfection, it does not have earthly correspondences like the other elements listed, as it is not physical.

When we think of spirit, we think of pure energy, of our connection with the Divine, of the infinite love and wisdom of the Universe.

We also think of our higher selves and of our soul's path throughout time and space, travelling through different lives, different selves, even different realms or galaxies. In terms of colour, spirit is associated with white or golden light, and it is with the light of spirit that we are cloaked when we call upon divine protection.

The symbol for earth

Earth

The Great Mother: life starts, ends, and starts again with earth. This element represents strength and security, stability and structure, deep roots and strong foundations. Earth rules our health, both mental and physical, and presides over deep learning—that which is ancient but still evolving. Earth is associated with the north, with dark goddesses like Hecate and the Morrigan, with the archangels Uriel and Sandalphon, with hardworking elementals such as dwarves, trolls, and brownies (often thought of as house elves), and with the signs of Capricorn, Taurus, and Virgo—strong, reliable, tough, and, well, *earthy*. Plants, earthenware, and crystals connect us with this element (although do your research to ensure your crystals have been ethically sourced).

Consciously connecting with earth keeps us grounded when we are amid life's chaos, when we are coming back from a deep meditation, or when we've spent a long time in the virtual world. If you feel you need grounding, imagine roots coming down from the soles of your feet, pushing into the soil, and going further still through layers of mud, clay, rock, and crystal. Send any energy you no longer wish to hold on to down into those roots to be received by the earth and utilised in positive ways. Then see your roots drawing up golden light from the centre of the earth. This is a good exercise for when you feel in need of a bit of stability, or just every morning and evening to keep yourself in balance.

The symbol for air

Air

Air rules communication, divine connection and inspiration, clarity, wisdom and the intellect, cleansing, purity, thought, and movement. If you want to get a message across, air will clear the way. Mercury the messenger, also known as Hermes, rules this element, as does the archangel Raphael. Air is associated with the east, with air spirits known as sylphs, and with the zodiac signs Aquarius, Gemini, and Libra, all signs known for being lighthearted, witty, communicative, and charming—and for sometimes blowing hot and cold.

We honour the element of air when we burn incense and watch the smoke rise, listen to wind chimes, appreciate a breezy day, or simply go outside and consciously take in a few lungfuls of the good stuff. Whisper your intentions into the wind when you want it to blow something out of your life. Alternatively, take a breath in for a count of five, hold it, and then exhale forcefully for six—a great way to change state and cleanse the lungs. It's a top tip from my Gemini mum for everything from releasing pain to centring energy. It's also a good way to prepare for meditation.

The symbol for fire

Fire

Fire is light and heat, purification and transformation, the positivity of sunshine, the warmth of a summer's day, the alchemy of the forge, and the spark of inspiration. With fire, we blaze through negativity and light the way to a brighter world. Associated with the south and the sun; with solar deities such as Ra, Sulis, Sol, and Sunna; with the archangel Michael; with the elemental salamanders; and with the signs of Aries, Leo, and Sagittarius, it can destroy as swiftly as it can heal us, and care must be taken when working with this element.

We use fire magic more than we realise, from the candle on a birthday cake to the lighting of a bonfire to create warmth and light as temperatures drop. With fire, we transform and transmute. Literally, we can witness a profound change of state: from a lump of dough to a loaf of bread, or from an ex-lover's jumper to a pile of ashes. When we gaze at a fire, we often see images and symbols in the flickering light. Write a wish on a leaf, cast it safely into the flames with a handful of herbs or fruit peel, and inhale the scent as you watch your leaf change. Now prepare for life to do the same. For the good of all, so mote it be.

The symbol for water

Water

Water brings flow, harmony, healing, grace, love, illusions, and deceptive strength. We turn to the west to honour water, which is associated with the moon and the tides, with Neptune and the lunar goddesses Diana, Selene, and Hecate, with the archangel Gabriel, and with undines, the watery elementals. Water presides over Pisces, Cancer, and Scorpio—sensitive and imaginative signs. Psychic work is associated with this element, which conducts energy with ease. I often see faces in steam, for example, when the veil thins between the worlds during the darker months of the year.

Water rules emotions, but it also encourages us to flow flexibly around obstacles. But things are rarely as they seem when we see them underwater, and if we resist life's flow, we can get knocked down by powerful waves and end up far from where our souls should really be. Water is also easy to program with words and intentions, something we will look at in depth later on. It's vital to bear this in mind, because we ourselves consist of a great deal of water: if water can effortlessly be manipulated, so can we. Use this power for good.

An Elemental Spell to Refresh Your Soul

Here is a simple charm encompassing all five elements that will leave you feeling revived. The meditative act of simply doing this spell will connect you with the element of spirit and the Divine. All you will need is:

> A glass or cup (to represent both earth and fire, as both elements were used in the forming of it)
>
> Filtered or spring water to fill your receptacle
>
> Your breath (to represent the element of air)

Place your cup of water in front of you. Think about how you would like to feel. Let's say you want to invite a greater sense of harmony into your life. Choose a colour that you associate with that quality. Personally, that would make me think of pink, but substitute if a different colour speaks to you.

Close your eyes and deepen your breathing, connecting in your mind with the element of spirit, or the Divine, and ask for a little assistance, explaining simply in your mind what you wish to do.

Begin to see a heavenly shade of pink in your mind's eye. Spend a few moments on this, imagining it flooding your vision. If visualising is difficult for you, bring to mind objects of the same hue, such as a piece of rose quartz, coconut ice, marshmallows, cotton candy, or a glass of rosé.

When you are ready, open your eyes and gaze at the water, imagining it turning a perfect pink. Stare at it for five minutes while breathing as deeply as is comfortable, charging it with colour and the feeling you associate with it. Imagine every inhalation draws in that celestial pink from the heavens, and every exhalation focuses the energy right into the water in front of you.

Once you feel the water is sufficiently infused, speak your intention—e.g., "I now invite love and harmony into my life"—and drink. Imagine with every sip that you are absorbing divine love and harmony. Drain your cup, or share with a thirsty plant. Do this as often as is needed.

Release Rituals

Sometimes you have a list of things you would love to see the back of but feel too overwhelmed to know where to start. Fortunately, there are plenty of quick, decisive ways to tangibly dissolve and release that which no longer serves, all utilising the elements. You can use them at any time, although full moons and dark moons are especially favourable times for release.

Keep forgiveness and peace in your heart if you can, and even gratitude: everything that happens to us brings a lesson, and nothing turns up uninvited, as hard as that may be to believe. Read on for some of my favourite elemental tips and tricks for clearing the decks.

Gone to blazes: This is a classic technique loved by many—including those who do not otherwise consciously practice magic. Write a list of everything you want to release and then burn it safely and release it to the Divine, asking it to transmute the energy into something new. If you don't have an open fire, a fireproof container will do: I use a steel saucepan. Keep the paper folded small and use metal sugar tongs to hold it safely while you light it. You can then work with the element of air to blow the ashes out of your life. Just make sure they blow in the right direction, not into your neighbour's clean washing or, worse, into your face.

Flushed with success: If you can't use fire for safety reasons, invoke the power of water. Take a ballpoint pen and write down that which no longer serves on a piece of toilet paper and flush it away. Alternatively, write a list in water-soluble ink, drop the list into a jar of water—the ink will dissolve into nothingness swiftly—and then pour that water down the drain. You could even use a cocktail stick or toothpick to carve a symbol or word that represents that which you wish to say goodbye to onto an ice cube, cast it outside, and let it melt out of view, watering the grass as it does so.

Blow it all away: If you connect more with the element of air, use a lit joss stick (or other incense stick), write a word or symbol in the air with the smoke, and then blow it away, shooing it out of the open window. It's satisfying to see the smoke dissipate into nothingness. Alternatively, you could shout your list of unwanted things into a strong wind and let the power of nature blast it far away from you. Open up your windows and cleanse your home with incense smoke, imagining your troubles dissolving into thin air as the fragrant fumes guide them out of your environs.

Dead and buried: I love to turn to the solid, tangible element of earth when it comes to banishing. Try carving a word or image that represents the thing you wish to release onto a fruit or vegetable, and then bury it in the ground. You could even use a leaf, and if you used a particularly large leaf, you could write down more fully the list of things that you want to release. Once you have committed your chosen biodegradable item to the earth, it will break down, nourishing the earth and the insects as it does so, and your problem will disintegrate with it. I love the sense of permanence, purification, and change of state that working like this brings.

Avoiding the Void

If you do try any of these practices, I suggest following a practice like this with writing a new list to fill the void with things you do want or that you feel grateful for. Always follow a negative with a positive. Otherwise, not only have you used significant energy and thought writing down things that made you unhappy, but in the act of banishment, you have created a space that needs filling—and nature abhors a vacuum. Make sure you're filling that vacuum with positive intention, and seal the rite with love and thanks.

You can cast wishes into the Universe in similar ways to the above. I might eschew the toilet-flushing ritual for anything you want to attract, but a wish written with love and then transformed by fire (for example, heading up to the heavens by way of smoke) is a classic way to "put it out there," as is a wish blown into the air, pressed into the earth to "grow," or cast into running water (not a pond, as ponds don't lead anywhere).

✳ WITCH TIP ✳
IT'S AS QUICK AS A THOUGHT

Wishing might sound wishy-washy, but it isn't if you supercharge those wishes so they don't just trickle out dreamily and then evaporate.

If I am wishing but I know I have doubts in my mind, I swiftly follow up with these words: "And it's as quick as a thought." That way, I can convince my mind to at least open up to the idea that I don't need to strive or stress. The intention is out there, it's been stated, it's in the physical world already, and the result is on its way—express delivery, thank you very much. Try it and see if it makes a difference to how you feel.

Be easygoing and trust the process. Treat it like anything else you depend upon. When you switch on a light, you don't concentrate to give it a better chance of working: you know it will work. You don't have to understand how. The more you get out of hoping and trying and coaxing and get into knowing and trusting and relaxing, the more things work out. It's the same with receiving guidance. The voice of Infinite Intelligence does not come with a choir of angels and a giant hand tapping you on the shoulder. It's more likely to manifest as a simple, quiet thought of, "I feel like doing this now." Follow those feelings.

PENTAGRAM POWER

To expand on the subject of the elements, it is time to introduce the pentagram. Rarely has a spiritual symbol been so misunderstood, so I'd like to take this opportunity to define it in terms of what it means to me, and to many witches and Neopagans around the world.

The pentagram

The five points of the pentagram represent the four elements, with spirit at the top; it also portrays the human form. The physical talisman depicting this shape is referred to as a pentacle, and the star is often but not always encased within a circle, which denotes eternity and also protection. It can be drawn with one sweep of the hand, without having to lift the pen from the paper. While ultimately symbols will always mean what we decide them to mean, to the witch the pentagram is not "evil"—quite the opposite. I agree with Salem witch Laurie Cabot's soulful take on the symbol's significance: "Each time I see a pentacle I am reminded of the encircling power of the All that surrounds and protects us, assuring us that each human being is at the center of divine life."[13]

The sixteenth-century occultist Heinrich Cornelius Agrippa openly propagated the positive use of this symbol;[14] however, the mainstream demonisation of magic has ensured that other interpretations still hold sway. Sadly, an element of suspicion can often arise when a symbol is associated with largely secretive traditions.

But just because a practice is kept under the radar, it does not mean evil is being carried out. Remaining occult—hidden—can be vital, protecting the work and the worker from outside forces, unwanted attention, distractions, or downright persecution.

Many witches and Pagans wear a pentacle for the same reason a Christian would wear a cross, although many still wear their pentacle under their clothes, imprinted as we are by centuries of discretion. But the symbol has been used within Christianity itself, denoting the five senses or the five wounds of Jesus Christ when he was crucified. Still, it is not taken seriously as a religious symbol, and we see pentagrams etched on schoolbags, printed on miniskirts, and dangling from ears of teenagers keen to shock. We also find pentagrams emblazoned on heavy-metal T-shirts, often inverted. If you invert any sacred symbol, you start to get into different meanings and connotations. The idea of an inverted pentagram makes me instinctively uncomfortable, but the truth is, it does not always signal negative intent. For example, the symbol can be used in both its upright and inverted forms by followers of the Kabbalah, a discipline of Jewish mysticism.

The ill-informed casually malign the pentagram without bothering to understand it, and they mock it at Hallowe'en, linking it with "black magic," but ultimately, the pentagram is a protective symbol. We don't just wear it as a shield: we draw it in the air to seal a spell, to bless a circle, or to protect our doorways or our cars or our pets. Every time I finish a meditation, I open my eyes and close down by drawing a pentagram of light in the air in front of me.

We often find the pentagram in nature: in the form of starflowers, for example, and famously inside apples, revealed when cut horizontally. I even spotted a naturally occurring pentagram on my Mount of Jupiter. (If you aren't a palmistry enthusiast, this is situated underneath the index finger.) It's always a thrill to spot a five-pointed star in the wild. It also gives the witch a little chuckle when we suddenly start seeing five-pointed stars everywhere during the Christmas season.

It is up to us to gently educate others about the true nature of this spiritual symbol. If in doubt, just remember it symbolises earth, air, fire, water, and spirit—everything we are made of.

WE OFTEN FIND THE PENTAGRAM IN NATURE: IN THE FORM OF STAR-FLOWERS, FOR EXAMPLE, AND FAMOUSLY INSIDE APPLES, REVEALED WHEN CUT HORIZONTALLY.

CREATING A SACRED SPACE

If you're anything like me, you'll doubtless see your entire home as a sacred space. Candles, incense, and crystals will abound, and specific colours will dominate, depending on the purpose of each room. Most importantly, vibration and feel will be important to you: those of our ilk generally keep our homes blessed, cleansed, and filled with things that make us feel good, so that as soon as we step over the threshold, we feel safe and closer to that which we hold sacred.

Still, it is a good idea to have one particular space where you can quietly do your spiritual work, meditate, weave magic, and write down ideas for spells and workings: a space devoted to these activities where Spirit can habitually come closer. We can do this by creating an altar.

Making an Altar

An altar can be simple and functional or ornate and majestic. It can be small and discreet or take over the whole spare room. Most altars feature the basics: candles, incense, perhaps a bell, and something that represents the Divine. But it's entirely personal, and in my opinion there's no right or wrong.

Don't feel discouraged if you're short on space: a kitchen table, the top of a cupboard, or even a shelf can work. It's not the end of the world if you have to clear your magical ephemera away after your work is complete. Kitchen witches across time will have worked this way, not least for the purpose of discretion. You can always keep your magical items in a special box, taking them out to set up when and where it is most suitable. All the same, it is lovely to have a permanent space set up if you can.

You can buy altar kits, but my own altar space has evolved organically over time. At the time of this writing, my basic items include an oil burner, a pentagram candle holder, beeswax candles, my oracle deck, and a bell. I use the bell to clear energy and to signify a beginning and an end to the work. I also have crystals, incense, and figurines of the deities I feel closest to depending on the working that's about to unfold.

Preparing the Space

Some people use altar cloths, and you can find ones with pentacles, Celtic crosses, or other spiritual designs on them. I use coloured silk or satin scarves collected from thrift stores over the years. I'll use a vibrant red scarf if I'm casting a spell for strength or if I want to connect with the qualities of Mars. Pink is perfect for love spells, black for protection, white for spiritual connection—you get the idea.

I clean the surface with a ceremonial wash: either Florida water or an elixir of my own making, with filtered water, gemstones, and essential oils (more on these later) to lift the vibration. I then cleanse the area, and all of the items within it, with incense smoke. Frankincense is a good go-to incense for general magical workings, as it is reverent, protective, and grounding.

Like many, I don't have a great deal of room and do have a slight need for discretion, so my altar is a shifting space that also doubles as a dressing table. Almost all of the items can masquerade as ornaments if need be.

Casting a Circle

A magic circle is the ultimate sacred space, and they are marvellous things to work within. They keep good energy in and unwanted energy out, amplify our intentions, and hone our focus. They also represent eternity, renewal, death, and rebirth. Created and cast with power and intent, they provide a space between the worlds within which we work our magic and link with Spirit.

I don't always cast a circle if I'm just casting a quick charm, although I do precede any work, simple or complex, with a moment of quiet, a visualisation of light, and a request for protection and divine assistance. However, when you are about to embark on a ritual, a more complex spell, or even a deep meditation for which you really want to boost your sense of security, a magic circle of protection and focus is a must.

Here is a method for casting a circle that you can adapt as you see fit. The basics you will need are:

> Incense of your choice
>
> A bell (optional)
>
> Markers for the four directions, such as candles, stones, or crystals
>
> A wand (or your index finger will work nicely)

Cleanse the space with sound using the ringing of a bell. You can clap your hands if you prefer. Then mark the circle by walking around the area clockwise with incense and a prayer, bringing down the light and requesting the Divine and your team in Spirit to bless the space and assist the work.

Place a representative marker in each of the four directions. This is to honour the guardian spirits of the north (earth), east (air), south (fire), and west (water). With each placement, bid the guardians "hail and welcome" with a short prayer tailored to their areas of expertise (see previous chapter on the elements).

Another popular option is to place a dish of salt or soil (or a stone or crystal) in the north to represent earth, incense in the east for air, a dedicated candle in the south for fire, and a cup of water in the west. I have an antique fortune-telling cup, appropriately bought in a seaside town, that I sometimes use for this last purpose.

Once you have acknowledged the four directions, raise your hands or your wand and honour Spirit itself, asking to be divinely guided, protected, and assisted, requesting a blessing on your magical work and asking that it be for the good of all. Now draw with your hand or wand an imagined circle three times around the space, visualise it blazing bright, and declare the circle cast. You are now ready to make some magic.

You can be as creative as you like when it comes to casting your circle. You can encircle yourself with candlelight if you have the space and are sure you can be safe doing so. Alternatively, you could surround yourself with your favourite crystals, with images of your loved ones in Spirit, or with herbs, flowers, powdered eggshell, or salt. It may suit you to do things exactly the same way each time, or you may want to customise the proceedings according to the time of year, the phase of the moon, or other elements.

You can, of course, create your circle without physical items, and this may be necessary if you are away from home. You can cast the circle with your imagination, walking thrice around with incense (if you have it), a wand, or just your finger and the power of visualisation. Just know and trust it is there. If you forget something on the other side of it once the circle is cast, don't just walk straight through it: cut an etheric door for yourself to walk through with your wand, athame (ceremonial knife), or finger—and remember to seal it back up.

Drawing Up the Circle

When your work is complete, respectfully draw the circle up in whatever way you wish. I walk the circle thrice widdershins (anticlockwise) and bid each of the four directions an appreciative "hail and farewell." This is important: I've known people who hadn't closed down their circle properly and were subsequently beset by issues pertaining to the element that had not been acknowledged—think burst pipes, pan fires, and even sinking foundations.

Thank and respectfully dismiss the four directions with care and love, and thank the Divine, your guardians and guides, and all light beings, known and unknown, for their assistance and protection. State that the ritual is now complete, and *voilà*: the circle is open, the work is done. Have something to eat or drink and play some music to earth you as you tidy up.

✳ WITCH TIP ✳
THE MICROCOSM AND
THE MACROCOSM

Whether we are making magic or just thinking thoughts, we are always working with both the microcosm and the macrocosm. Keep in mind that when you are casting spells for yourself, the effects of your work are creating ripples in the wider world too, whether you are aware of them or not.

Go one step further: when you are working magic, saying a prayer, or making a wish for something personal, make sure you also add a wish for the planet and its inhabitants, sending out loving energy for the Divine or the Universe to direct where it is most needed. We are all one anyway.

WITCH & WISDOM

Candle Magic with Madame Pamita

Madame Pamita is a tarot reader, root worker, teacher, and author. She also runs the Parlour of Wonders, an online emporium of magical resources and spiritual supplies. Candles are often a key element of many people's sacred space: they create a high-vibrational atmosphere and, of course, they look beautiful. But the simplicity of working with candles is part of what makes them such effective magical tools. Madame Pamita, who writes extensively on this subject in The Book of Candle Magic,[15] *shares some excellent tips on how to use candles in our work:*

Madame Pamita: Candles are the modern-day version of fire magic. Ancient people harnessed the element of fire, and it was transformational. With the control of fire, humans could live in colder climates, cook food, and connect to the spirit world. Using fire is a sacred magical act and connects us to our ancestors going back to prehistoric times. Asking the spirit of fire to assist us in our visions, dreams, and manifestations is inviting in powerful elemental spirit help.

Candle magic helps the spellcaster to be focused. You can't light a match and get distracted—you'll end up with burnt fingers. Strictly on a practical level, if you have a hard time focusing on things like visualisations or intentions, a candle spell will help you to be present in the moment, mindful and centred. Candles also act as support to our spell intention. When we bring in elements to the candle spell such as colour, shapes, essential oil blends, and herbs, we are inviting allies that help give energy to our wishes. The more you craft and align your candle spell to your intention, the more you support your outcome.

LUNAR LORE: WORKING WITH THE CYCLES OF THE MOON

It was long considered perfectly sensible to live and work guided by the stars, lunar phases, and the landscape. Those who work the land have always done this, cultivating an innate sensitivity to the messages being delivered by the weather, the planets, and the behaviour of birds. Look at *The Old Farmer's Almanac*, for instance: it's as practical as can be. It can teach you how to garden by the moon and when the best time is to plant your crops, harvest, weed, and much more—even when to cut your hair to speed or slow growth.

Many witches refer to full moon and new moon observances as *esbats*. These fortnightly lunar events are times of psychic potency, times that lend themselves to feasts, celebrations, meditations, and magical work. Many witches worship the moon as a triple goddess—Diana, Selene, and Hecate—representing the traditional three female phases of maiden, mother, and crone.

There are thirteen moon cycles in a year, which means there should really be thirteen months in a year, but the Roman calendar put paid to that. As a result, we have one month with two full moons—the extra moon being referred to as a *blue moon*—and we must factor in a leap year every four years.

The full moons throughout the year have distinct personalities according to the season: we have the Birch Moon, the Flower Moon, the Snow Moon, the Worm Moon, and so on. Research them if you're called to, because there are intriguing stories behind the different moons that can give us a greater understanding of the turns of the year and a stronger bond with nature.

Full Moons

The full moon is a time of power, completion, conclusion, and high energy. Everything amplifies and reaches a peak, from our intentions to the effects of drink and drugs. It's no coincidence that hospital emergency rooms are busiest during a full moon—as are maternity wards.

Those of us who work with crystals often like to charge them in the moonlight. I also do this with silver jewellery, silver being a lunar-goddess metal. You can charge yourself up with a spot of moonbathing, weave some spells, manifest your dreams, or just light a candle. You can, of course, simply pause and reflect. Like the moon, we ourselves are cyclical, shifting and changing all the time, so don't worry if you feel like doing different things—or nothing at all—from month to month.

Other popular full moon practices include writing a list of what you wish to release, conclude, or forgive and uttering a few words of acknowledgment to the Lady, to the planet, and to the Universe. Give thanks for all projects or workings that have rounded up successfully. It's good to keep a notebook to monitor what is starting and finishing in your life: it's thrilling to see how life effortlessly synchronises with these natural cycles.

New Moons

New moons are times of initiation and new beginnings; the new moon is an auspicious time for making wishes, starting new projects, creating new friendships, and stimulating increase. The moon is invisible on the actual night of "New Moon," astrologically speaking, and this is what many of us refer to as the dark moon, a time of stillness and reflection. The "Witches' New Moon" is actually a night or two afterwards, when you see that silver sliver in the sky. It is always worth making a wish if you spy it. My family turns silver coins over in their pockets while looking at the new moon: it's an old charm said to increase turnover.

Make a wish in your head, on a pebble before casting it out to sea, on a candle (preferably atop a cake—it doesn't have to be your birthday), or by tying a ribbon on a tree. If you wish to try the last suggestion, reduce your environmental impact by ensuring the ribbon or cloth is made of natural fibres rather than synthetic. Write the wish on the material—or just charge it with your intention—and then tie it loosely to a branch. Tying it tightly risks restricting the growth of the branch or trapping the legs of animals and small creatures. Once this simple ritual is complete, say thank you, as always, and let the elements, tree spirits, and moonlight do their stuff. Celtic Pagans call this a *clootie tree*, with *clootie* or *cloot* being traditional Scottish slang for "cloth." There's a famous clootie tree near Glastonbury—the planet's heart energy centre—that continues to be festooned with thousands of multicoloured wishes.

It is worth waiting that extra couple of nights after the new moon until the Witches' New Moon is visible in the sky. The aforementioned dark moon period can be an anxious time: it is the moon's still and quiet crone period before it rebirths into a fresh phase as the maiden, so not the perfect time for action. If you find yourself feeling uncomfortable during the dark of the moon, as many do, think about why. Might it correlate to your feelings about darkness, stillness, your shadow side, or even death, whether your own or that of others? The more you connect with the lunar phases this way, the more you will recognise opportunities for deeper understanding of yourself and others.

Another aspect that can affect both magic working and mood is the lunar pause in which the moon is "void of course." This occurs every couple of days, when the moon moves from one sign to the next. It's useful to know about, because, put plainly, actions undertaken during this time rarely come to anything. Sometimes the void-of-course period lasts a few minutes; other times it can last for hours, even a couple of days. During these windows, avoid planning your big launch or doing anything in which you hope to make progress. Instead, use the time to rest or plan if possible. You can find these dates and times and other useful information at Lunarium.co.uk or Moontracks.com.

Respecting Our Cycles

When we take time to consider our own personal ebb and flow along with planetary phases and the seasons of the year, we can sync with Universal Energy and get more out of every day. They don't teach us this in school, but thankfully more people are waking up to knowledge that our ancestors have understood for eons. Some days, for example, you will be better off snuggling under the covers and conserving your energy. We are trained to believe we are failing if we aren't going for it every day, hell for leather. It takes a while to nix the guilt, but we are more productive when we respect a few natural laws.

We all experience cycles whether we menstruate or not, and it can be interesting to note physical and mental shifts month by month: in doing this, we can spot potential patterns and plan accordingly. It can be especially interesting to chart how we feel from day to day according to the cycle of the moon. It's a long-held popular opinion that women are particularly affected by the moon's waxings and wanings, but we are all affected: I have male friends who feel especially overwrought when the moon is full or feel dark and nihilistic around the time of the dark moon, shortly before it waxes to the Witches' New Moon.

Each of us has a different experience, but for the most part, each lunar cycle consists of four phases and associated traits. Please note that if you do menstruate, the menstrual cycle does not always sync with the lunar cycle in the way set out below: this is merely to illustrate the range of characteristics.

New moon (preovulation): The springtime of the cycle. This is a time of renewal, energy, and even impatience to get on with life after the stillness of the dark moon or menstruation phase. This is a more resilient you, reflective of the adventurous maiden aspect of the goddess. Stay in balance and keep one eye on where you are and another on where you will be in your cycle while making plans.

Waxing moon (preovulation to ovulation): The maiden archetype shifts towards the symbol of the mother; spring burgeons and brightens into summer. Opportunities for growth are increasing, and you will find yourself feeling more positive as the moon waxes full. Focus on increase and abundance. If you want to encourage faster hair growth, now is the time to for a trim.

Full moon (ovulation): The mother phase. Fulsome, summery, and fertile—and this fertility is as much about creativity as it is about children. We often feel at our most attractive, sunny, and buoyant during this phase, and the overall feeling is that of ripeness as Nature primes for pregnancy. Things fall into place a little more (and not just your hair). A time of conception, in every sense.

Waning moon (premenstruation): Turning inward. You are likely to be more irritable, especially if you don't allow yourself a bit of quiet time, but this is also a powerful phase for cutting out anything superfluous and eloquently speaking your mind. This is a time of contradictions, but accept them and stay wise, stay kind, and don't go kamikaze. Ensure any righteous anger you feel is channeled creatively and constructively. It's when we don't allow our different phases full, healthy expression that tension rises.

Dark moon (menstruation): Retreat into your cave whenever possible. Embrace the darkness, think about what you want to release, and then imagine it flowing away. Prepare for a reflective time of deep intuition: meditation is easier than usual and can be revelatory. This is a psychic time, and it is an opportunity to learn how to treat yourself with more patience, acceptance, and care.

We're different people from phase to phase. Get to know your various selves, learn what they respond to, and find out how to treat them so well that every cycle is a breeze rather than a thundering typhoon.

✳ WITCH TIP ✳
USING YOUR "FLOW"

If you menstruate, I invite you to embrace the joy of pads. I admit it doesn't have the same ring as *The Joy of Sex*, although this does concern some of the same body parts. When your monthly flow comes around, consider using washable cloth pads instead of disposable sanitary items, especially those with plastic casings that end up on beaches or in the throats of creatures. You'll be saving money, improving your menstrual health, and helping the planet. When our period swings around, the blood wants to flow *out*, so we should support this process and allow that which wants to go, to go with ease.

You can sling cloth pads into the washing machine, but some people soak them first and then pour the water onto their plants; many conventional fertilisers contain blood anyway. I brought an old cut rose back to life this way, and it bloomed so lustily that the sepal, which normally hugs the base of the rose, opened into the shape of a five-pointed star.

If you have a garden, pour this water over your plants with a blessing. They will flourish. To make this visceral connection with the earth is special: menstrual blood contains our very essence. For generations, we have been told that menstruating is a curse, to be hidden and denied. Anything that can change this perception is extremely healing. UK writer Lisa Lister has written extensively on this subject in her game-changing book *Code Red*. More information can be found in the Recommended Reading section.

Esbats and Astrology

If you've ever heard astrologers referring to "the New Moon in Scorpio" or "a Full Moon in Aries" and wondered what that means, this section can shed some (moon) light on the subject. All new and full moons are powerful times, but if you work with specific astrological influences, your intentions will really pack a punch. There's more to astrology than sun signs: when the different heavenly bodies—specifically the Moon, in this case—travel through the constellations that make up those signs, we are all affected. These astrological events can flavour the general mood—and influence magical work and meditation in turn. Tap into this knowledge and act accordingly.

These are my hot takes on how these distinct astro personalities can affect us when they combine with new and full moons:

Aries, the ram

Aries New Moon: Aries is number one in the zodiac. Everything begins with the bold and bumptious ram, so while all new moons are excellent times for starting projects, a dynamic New Moon in Aries will give an extra injection of energy to anything you initiate.

Aries Full Moon: This energy can be intense and agitated, so watch your words and behaviour. Aries is impulsive and quick-tempered and can engage mouth before brain, so take extra care. This goes for others too: we are all affected by these influences, so bear this in mind before you react to someone's sharp tongue.

Taurus, the bull

Taurus New Moon: This New Moon brings staying power to anything you "plant," and it may boost your finances too. Taurus is a materialistic, practical, fixed sign with a fondness for luxury, classic elegance, and the finer things. You'll likely find yourself insisting upon everything from softer towels to better-quality coffee. Whatever you wish to seed at this New Moon will be substantial and built to last.

Taurus Full Moon: This Full Moon places the onus on stability, abundance, and sensuality. You may feel the urge to ramp up the old-fashioned charm. Taurus's Venusian influence introduces a heady dose of love, fun, and harmony, so eat, drink, be merry, avoid bullishness, and see what delights are in store.

Gemini, the twins

Gemini New Moon: Gemini is all about communication, intellect, wit, wisdom, and brainwork, so if you want to start a course of study, launch a broadcast career, or start a correspondence, the New Moon in this sign would be your moment. Airy and light, you'll probably not take too much to heart at this time.

Gemini Full Moon: A Full Moon in this sign blows away the cobwebs but can also find us conflicted: think of the twins, the Gemini symbol. Also, while there's nothing wrong with quicksilver thinking, you may find your attention span is low. Collect your thoughts and write a list of what you need to do. Better still, make two lists. This is a Gemini Moon, after all.

Cancer, the crab

Cancer New Moon: The Moon is very much at home in sensitive, emotional Cancer. The New Moon here will bless intentions that involve self-care, family or domestic matters, and protection of that which is vulnerable, although the Dark Moon that precedes it may feel a little anxious.

Cancer Full Moon: Hunker down and focus on consciously releasing hurts. All Full Moons are key times for forgiveness, but you may have to try harder with this one: Cancer tends to hold on to resentments with those formidable pincers. Your emotions will be coming to a head now, so find a way to express them without anyone getting hurt.

Leo, the lion

Leo New Moon: This time brings positive energy to fresh starts, infusing our intentions with sunshine and strength. This is definitely an appropriate moment to magnetise wealth and abundance. Leo is royalty, after all, and thrives in opulence.

Leo Full Moon: Charismatic Leo is a natural performer and is happiest when lavished with attention, so you may feel the desire to dress up and be seen on this most enjoyable Full Moon. You'll want to be heard too, but watch that roar. Channel righteous Leonine anger into a good cause and make a difference.

Virgo, the virgin

Virgo New Moon: Thoughtful, practical Virgo brings a more sober vibration, helping us get organised with our finances and goals. You will find it easier to pin down the specifics of what you want with Virgo on your side. You may also feel the need to declutter during the Virgo Dark Moon to prepare for a fresh start.

Virgo Full Moon: This grounded Full Moon will find us striving for perfection, but stay realistic as your projects reach completion and make sure you aren't obsessing over the unattainable. Be open to intuitive flashes and revelations: Virgo has her feet on the ground, but her psychic powers are always spot-on.

Libra, the scales

Libra New Moon: This is where Venus feels most at home. A New Moon in aesthetic Libra is the time to try a new look, go clothes shopping, and beautify your home. On a less superficial level, if you are embarking on a new partnership, romantic or not, ask this benevolent New Moon to bless your connection.

Libra Full Moon: Libra is represented by the scales, so reflect on any areas of your life that need balance. Relationships are in the spotlight: Is there a situation that could benefit from a little peace-keeping? Or one in which you have been sitting on the fence for too long? This Full Moon will reveal it. Indecisiveness is a Libran trait, so ask those moonbeams to illuminate your path with divine clarity.

Scorpio, the scorpion

Scorpio New Moon: Scorpio is passionate and single-minded, so a New Moon in this sign will have you concentrating on the essence of what you need and conjuring up the exact energies required to make it happen. This sign is associated with the occult, so expect psychic dreams and synchronicities.

Scorpio Full Moon: Scorpio is about transformation, so use this time to slough off the old once and for all. Here, we lift up the stones to reveal what is beneath: we need truth and knowledge to complete our goals as the Moon waxes to full in this uncompromising part of the zodiac. Sexual energy is high at this time, as is spiritual energy. Combine them.

Sagittarius, the centaur

Sagittarius New Moon: Enthusiastic Sag turns all the lights back on after the dark depths of Scorpio. This New Moon shines blessings upon any plans to hit the road: Sagittarius loves travel, forward movement, and adventures, so anything that connects gets a jolt of success. This fire sign is about freedom and excitement, and both esbats in this sign tend to feel good.

Sagittarius Full Moon: If there is an area in your life in which you feel restricted or just lackluster, this bright Full Moon will make it glaringly obvious. Before you lose your temper and start firing Sagittarian arrows in all directions, take a moment to breathe before working out how to address the matter. Knowing there's an issue to be addressed is a large part of the battle, so take your time.

Capricorn, the goat

Capricorn New Moon: Capricorn is all about hard work, achievement, and toughening up, so a New Moon in the sign of the goat has us strategising a demanding new project, strengthening our resolve, and standing on our own two feet (or four hooves). An auspicious time to embark on anything that requires commitment and discipline—Capricorn won't let you waver.

Capricorn Full Moon: At this time, we must remember to celebrate our hard-won successes and achievements. We can be our own toughest bosses, so if you are teetering towards burnout, think about whether you would feel comfortable treating another person this way. Take a rest as you trudge up that mountainside, and be refreshed by the view.

Aquarius, the water carrier

Aquarius New Moon: This visionary New Moon may find you coming up with schemes so bold and unconventional that they seem to come from outer space. Depending on your own sign, Aquarian characteristics might make for an uneasy mix, so hold tight during this magic carpet ride. A key theme is social responsibility, and this New Moon could generate ideas that see you serving your wider community.

Aquarius Full Moon: Air signs are associated with the intellect, so if you have a problem that needs solving, ask this Full Moon to inspire you. Aquarius's mad-professor mutability will be amplified at Full Moon, for better or worse. Wild plans will reach fruition if you've managed to earth them sufficiently, but eccentricity could spill into erratic or obtuse behaviour. Have patience.

Pisces, the fish

Pisces New Moon: The Moon in this sign brings the hypnotic, watery qualities of King Neptune to Earth. Your magic will be especially imaginative and psychically attuned now, as Piscean moonbeams conduct our wishes to the heavens. Bathe in Neptune's waters and emerge refreshed. Initiate artistic ventures and see what rises to the surface as the Moon waxes.

Pisces Full Moon: Whether a romance, a creative project, or a long-held dream, this Full Moon will bring something special softly to its peak. Release neuroses and delusions, as well as any residual sadness from incidents long past. This is potentially a serene time, but there may be confusion and illusion: sound and vision can be distorted in the deep.

RETROMANIA: WHEN PLANETS GO BACKWARDS

"Is it Mercury retrograde?" is a common wail amongst the magically inclined whenever anything goes awry. If you do nothing else, look up when the planet Mercury is in retrograde and note the dates. It is advisable that you avoid doing anything major (like signing a contract), buying anything with moving parts (like a car), or making any decisions that you want to be permanent (like getting married) during this time. If you can't avoid the above, get backup in place and hold on to your sense of humour.

Mercury is a small but significant planet that rules communication, expression, messages, movement, intellect, logic, travel, contracts, postage, and anything written down, so when Mercury retrograde hits, the world seems to turn topsy-turvy. It may seem unlikely, and admittedly a lot of chaos can be manifested just by people's anxiety about Mercury retrograde. Still, all too often purchases do need returning during this celestial cycle, cars do break down, technology does go haywire, the internet does misbehave, your partner does misunderstand you, "completed" projects do need revisiting, and you will need extra time for everything from your hair to your commute.

What Is a Retrograde Cycle?

Retrograde motion indicates when a planet appears to be moving backwards in the sky. It is just an optical illusion, but symbols and appearances in magic are potent. While it can be all too easy to blame chaos on Mercury retrograde, sometimes it really is too uncanny to ignore.

All planets undergo retrograde cycles from time to time, and it's interesting to think about the different qualities the planets embody and how those qualities are affected when their parent planet goes into apparent reverse. Working by lunar phases is all very well, but if a significant planet is in retrograde, you might want to tweak your plans, build in some contingencies, or simply wait.

Astrologers often advise against making drastic decisions about our appearances during Venus retrograde, what with this planet and deity ruling physical attractiveness. We definitely want Venus behaving herself if we're about to go for a wild new look. When Mars is retrograde, we feel it too: this action-man planet is in charge of courage, motivation, energy, and strength, so when the Red Planet takes a nap during a retrograde cycle, it's hard to get anything off the ground.

These are just a few examples, but the key thing to remember is this: retrograde cycles are nothing to be afraid of, just something to be aware of. They can even be amusing if you patiently observe how everything plays out and bear in mind that life will normalise when the planet in question stations direct. Let's face it: it's a relief to have something external to blame inexplicable chaos on (while always keeping in mind our own sense of personal responsibility, of course). It's also useful to remember that *everyone* is experiencing their own version of retrograde madness, whether they acknowledge this or not.

The Benefits of Retrogrades

Retrogrades do come with gifts, believe it or not. You'll find them easier to spot once you apply witchful thinking—which often means detaching ourselves, subverting what appears to be happening, and seeing what we can do when we view it from a fresh angle. For instance, retrogrades give us the perfect opportunity to do anything with a *re–* in front of it: reflect, revise, rethink, recover, repair, reconsider, relax. I had the chance to *re-*turn to this book and *re-*vise it during Mercury retrograde, and I'm grateful I had that opportunity.

Many people also find these periods to be creative times, conducive to thinking outside the box. Understand them and use them well. Don't let anxiety get the better of you. Be patient and do some research. Amid the madness and frustration, there is plenty of information out there from reputable astrologers who can guide you through these phases.

The WISE WOMAN'S CALENDAR: The WHEEL of the YEAR

Pagans live by each turn of the Wheel of the Year, which divides into seasonal sabbats, solstices, and equinoxes—equal day, equal night, equal dark, equal light. Actually, everyone does this, even if they don't consciously acknowledge it.

By more deliberately observing these ancient shifts, we naturally find ourselves turning to the agricultural calendar, which guides those who turn the soil as to when it's best to sow and reap, for example. You might not be a Pagan or a witch, but you've probably made reference to the nights drawing in after the longest day (Summer Solstice), and dancing around a maypole is unlikely to be an alien concept. Even card-carrying atheists have been known to green the house for Yule, at the very least with a Christmas tree.

Rather than observe traditions out of sheer habit and with no thought to their origins, it's much more meaningful—and fun—to do it because these moments call both to your soul and the earth like a joyful rallying cry. You'll start to see the whole year as an ongoing dialogue between yourself, the earth, the sky, and the elements. Having a better understanding of the roots of these age-old holidays will help you enjoy the festivities too, however you celebrate them culturally.

The word *pagan* originally means "of the country," and in many senses it describes the way of life for most people before the Industrial Revolution, when old traditions began to fade. *Pagan* was subsequently used as a pejorative term to describe a kind of rural lack of sophistication and a fondness for observing what was left of the nature religions. However, the term was reclaimed in the twentieth century to indicate a specifically religious way of life with nature worship at its core. The spotlight this has thrown onto the Old Ways has awoken an interest in many who are keen to find greater depth and meaning in their lives. This more often than not takes the shape of going back to nature—in small or significant ways.

The Sabbats

The sabbats are points of power that demarcate the year: times when the veil between the Seen and the Unseen is especially thin. It is easier at these times to communicate with the other side, or just to recognise the natural cycles of our planet and the microcosm and macrocosm. As above, so below; as within, so without. We reflect Mother Nature in more ways than we can imagine, and discovering that is one of the joys of witchful thinking.

The Wheel of the Year also symbolically reflects the traditional female life cycle—from maiden to mother to crone, before her rebirth again—not to mention that it relates to the lunar phases, the ebb and flow of the menstrual cycle, and the simple turn of a day. I have detailed how I see them below. (The following dates refer to the Northern Hemisphere. The Southern Hemisphere experiences sabbats in polar opposite; i.e., when it's Beltane in the UK, it will be Samhain in Australia, and so on.)

Imbolc: Around February 1

This is the first of four ancient Celtic fire festivals, the subsequent festivals being Beltane (May Day), Lughnasadh (Harvest), and Samhain (Hallowe'en). The name *Imbolc*—Candlemas in the Christian calendar—is believed to mean "in the belly" in Old Irish, referring to pregnant ewes.

This moment represents the psychically pregnant and sometimes anxious hours of the morning just before dawn, dark but never empty. It connects with the dark of the moon, when all is potential, and with the end of menstruation, shortly before preovulation (the crone-maiden phase). Imbolc is presided over by the Irish goddess Brighid and deities that connect to hearth and home. It's worth noting that Brighid (pronounced "breed") is a rare pre-Christian deity in that she was later Christianised as Saint Bridget, a patron saint of Ireland. While Saint Patrick is hailed for having chased the "snakes" (Pagans and Druids) out of Ireland, Bridget or Brighid connects us with a past steeped in ancient magic.

At Imbolc, we think of snow, but also snowdrops: life is stirring even if we can't see it. Despite the wintry weather, Imbolc is a time of light and warmth if we want it to be. We can light a fire in the grate, or at least a candle or two, and warm our hearts in the presence of family. In a quiet moment, it is special to read some of the Irish poet Seamus Heaney's verses celebrating Brighid, for she herself is a goddess of poetry. It's also a good time to clean the house to make way for the new. Brighid is queen of new milk and cows, so leave out a fresh glass of milk on Imbolc eve. You might also tie a piece of cloth—maybe a milk-white hanky—somewhere outside. Tradition dictates that the cloth will absorb Brighid's blessings as she walks the earth that night.

As well as being associated with poetry, Brighid is connected to blacksmiths, presumably because of her association with the element of fire. A spark being struck from cold, inert metal perfectly represents the first glimmer of life after winter—and there is no place better to witness the transformational properties of heat and fire than in the forge. For thousands of years, blacksmiths have been credited with powers that go beyond the natural, and iron has long been believed to have the ability to ward off negativity. Many old protection charms include iron nails or filings. Light a candle to Brighid and, if you have one, place an iron horseshoe close by to represent the protective magic of the forge.

Spring Equinox (Eostre): Around March 20

This is the beginning of spring: a time of freshness, fun, and light—and life—returning. This time means equal dark and equal light, rebirth, expectancy, and promise. Here we think of the sunrise, pre-ovulation, and the bright new moon.

The Anglo-Saxon goddess Eostre holds sway at this time. Yes, that name does sound like "Easter," and indeed "oestrogen," one of the main female sex hormones in charge of, amongst other things, egg production. This gives the concept of Easter eggs a different slant. The deity Eostre traditionally had the head of a hare, hence the Easter Bunny. Hares are often equated with witchery and the moon. Witches were said to be able to transform into them, and many country folk in England would eschew hare pie just in case.

Eostre is all about cracking out of the dark shell, sloughing off that which has been outgrown, and emerging into the light. Everything is coming into alignment and celestial balance. Some say that at the moment of equinox, you can balance an egg on its end and it will stand up like a Weeble.

With both Spring Equinox and Autumn Equinox, our focus is drawn to equilibrium. Consider whether there is anything in your life that is out of balance and whether negative thoughts are crowding out the light. Alternatively, you may be so fixated on being positive that you're ignoring shadows that could benefit from your attention. Go deep and emerge renewed. Crack your way out of that egg.

✳ WITCH TIP ✳
MAKING EGGSHELL POWDER

Use the irrepressible "new life" energy of this time to make protective eggshell powder, a witchy tool also referred to as *cascarilla*. Eggshells are magically significant because they literally protected an embryo as it developed.

If you eat eggs, save your shells, wash them, peel off the inner membrane, and dry the shells in the sun. Once dried, crush them finely with a mortar and pestle or coffee grinder while repeating an affirmation that reflects your intention. This could be as simple as chanting, "Divine protection, blessed be." Now transfer the powder to a container with a blessing and an acknowledgment to the mother hens who laid (and sacrificed) the eggs in the first place.

Eggshell powder, like salt, can protect boundaries, cleanse energetically, and banish negativity. It may also be used to protect a new idea while it is still in development. I blend mine with a pinch of salt and pepper and even a teaspoon of bicarbonate of soda to neutralise any residual egginess and also to add to the cleansing energy.

Sprinkle this in the bath or around the home, pop some in a locket, and even dust your hands with it, imagining your aura strengthened and your energy refreshed.

Beltane: May Eve and May Day

Beltane is, arguably, the sauciest time of year. It is a time of ovulation, midmorning, and the moon waxing to full. This is when the Goddess and God unite, blessing the earth with growth, warmth, and the return of the green. The seeds we planted at Imbolc are peeping up after being nurtured in the soil of contemplation, anticipation, and right timing. Beltane brings blessings of abundance to our crops, whatever form they may take.

This is a time to celebrate life at its peak, in all of its joyful sexuality, vigour, and fertility. Focus here on abundance, creativity, growth, and flow: these qualities are very much in tune with Beltane energy. Fertility does not have to refer only to human babies, but also to adventures, missions, and ideas.

There is an abundance of May-related folklore, such as washing your face in the morning dew to ensure unearthly beauty for the rest of the year, as well as using dream divination to discover the identity of your next lover. Bring in a May bough of rowan, holly, or protective hawthorn, tie it with colourful ribbons, and attach it to your front door. Light a purifying bonfire (or just a candle) and tell it your wishes, prayers, and dreams. Beltane is famously a time to honour the fairy folk: the Fae or, as they say in Ireland, "the Gentry" or "Gentle Folk." A "gentle place" was said to be one inhabited by fairies, and one would do well to know where those places were, not least because anyone building on or otherwise disturbing such a site might meet a rather ungentle demise. The Fae can be seen at this time by those of great sensitivity, but I tend to leave the Gentry to their own devices. Though they may be but little, to paraphrase Shakespeare, they be fierce.[16] That said, I place something sweet outside with a blessing of thanks for any unseen good works on May Eve, when the Fae are said to be "abroad." Milk and honey is a good call, perhaps in a pretty cup and saucer sprinkled with fragrant rose petals or accompanied by a few pieces of candy.

Summer Solstice (Litha): Usually June 21
The sun reaches its highest position in the sky. Ovulation and full-moon mother energies swell, and we bask in the heat of the noon-day sun. *Sol* means "sun," and *solstice* means "sun stands still": this is the day with the longest daylight. To some it marks the official start of summer, while to others it is Midsummer. It is a lovely time to

stay up late, commune with the natural world, light a fire, and be thankful.

The *balefire* is an old English term for a ritual bonfire, and people would jump the smoldering remains for good fortune and fertility, while the smoke would be used to bless the livestock and the crops. This kind of folk magic would have been considered an essential act to appease and honour the elements and nature gods. With your efforts, celebrations, and the time and energy you gave to these rituals, your livelihood would be assured for another year.

Traditionally a pastoral tradition to protect, bless, and purify, we can still use the symbol of fire to bless our lives whether we live in the countryside or at the top of a tenement. If you can't have a Litha bonfire, carve your wish or blessing onto a candle or write a wish on a bay leaf and safely burn it. The bay-leaf fumes might even give you some insight on this magic night: the oracle at Delphi in ancient Greece famously swore by them.

If it isn't safe to light a fire or even a candle, then get a battery-operated candle, draw a picture with fiery colours to represent the balefire, or even just search on YouTube for a video of a candle and use that as your focus. This will help you connect psychically with all balefires across time and space, link with others, and amplify your intentions. Focus on what you wish to release, intend your plans for the rest of the year, and then, if you can, jump or step safely over your candle or picture to signify the leap into the new phase—purified, energised, and sealed with protection.

Lammas (Lughnassadh): August 1

This is high summer: ovulation to premenstruation, starting to slow down, waning, early afternoon. The earth and sun are in union, and the first harvest of grain is ready to gather in. This is a time of bounty, abundance, and gratitude. Lugh is the Celtic god of sun or light, while the word *Lammas* comes from "loaf mass."

Do some baking and share the results with your loved ones, the birds, the elementals, and all helpers known or unknown. Lammas is another connection between the old agrarian calendar and the Church in the form of the harvest festival. Loaves made using the new crop of wheat would be blessed and shared, and food was collected for those in need.

Make a corn dolly to represent the Great Mother (or Grain Mother), and pop some fresh mint in your purse for prosperity. Using honey at this time of year is also special. In addition to its well-known health-giving and protective properties, this liquid sunshine is uplifting in its sweetness, and its golden glueyness is redolent of wealth that "sticks." Honey also connects to the Divine and the life-giving sun: sunlight pours into the blossoms of the trees and shrubs, all of which have their own magical significance. The bee goes from bloom to bloom, and honey is the exquisite result. It is pure sunlight, augmented with real flower power, in a form we can eat, drink, and put on our skin for healing. It's no surprise that mead—made of fermented honey—is considered the drink of the gods. A little honey water mixed with sparkling wine or sparkling water is a nod to this if mead isn't your thing but you still wish to raise a sweet cup of thanks to the sun.

Autumn Equinox: Around September 21

This is the moment the sun appears to cross the celestial equator southwards. Some Neopagans refer to this time as Mabon.[17] This phase connects with the energy of premenstruation and is a time to take stock, store what we need, and prepare to shed that which no longer serves—waning moon, late afternoon.

This is a time of harvest—fruit rather than grain this time—and thanksgiving for the blessings and nourishment of the earth, for the gifts of the Sacred Masculine (the sun and the grain or seed), and for anything else we have grown and nurtured to fruition. Apples abound: cut them widthways to reveal the pentagram, anoint with lemon to prevent browning if you're adding cut apples to an autumnal display, and as always, share your bounty with nature. This is a time of plenty but also of preparation for the winter ahead, so think preserves, pickles, and pies.

Dark and light and day and night are once more in balance, but from here on in, the nights become perceptibly longer and the days cooler. We find ourselves wanting to rest and turn our gaze inwards, so don't fight this. Now we can attend to our inner shadows and work through any blocks or anxieties before heading with serene confidence into the dark part of the year.

As the leaves fall, look around for treasures. You can collect fallen oak leaves and weave them into an autumnal wreath, either keeping them natural and drying them or maybe painting them gold for abundance. Alternatively, you could dry and powder them for use in spells or charm bags imbued with oak energy. Mix a pinch of this powder with a cup of sea salt for a fortifying bath if you're feeling insecure.

Pick up a few acorns if you can, while ensuring there are still plenty around for the squirrels. Associated with witches across time, an acorn makes a tactile talisman. Glaze it with clear or gold nail polish to secure it in its cup, and put it in your pocket for luck, protection, and even youthfulness. People in Nordic climes kept an acorn in their window to protect against lightning strikes and appease Thor, god of thunder, as he is said to revere the oak. If you aren't fortunate enough to live near an oak tree, treat yourself to an acorn charm to connect with the season and attract good fortune.

Samhain (Hallowe'en): October 31

Samhain is an Irish word, pronounced "SOW-en." This point is also known as All Souls' Night and the Celtic New Year. Premenstruation to menstruation, moon waning to dark, and the magic hour or twilight—this is a space between the worlds and is the most potent point in the year for most witches and Neopagans.

Samhain marks the end of the harvest season, and once more we light the balefire (or a microversion of it) to represent purification, protection, warmth, and light to illuminate the darkness as the sun continues its retreat. But we also want to embrace that darkness and what might be willing to come forth as the veil lifts. We do this with care, discernment, respect, and plenty of psychic protection. Don't dabble or start anything you don't know how to finish. I would echo advice to avoid blunt instruments such as Ouija boards, and also don't invoke anything you don't understand or feel safe with. In fact, I'd go so far as to say no horror movies, at least if you're a sensitive like me. Be careful what you open yourself up to—and what you plant in your imagination.

Hallowe'en is not about spooking yourself silly with slasher movies, dressing up as a corpse, or extorting candy from the neighbours. The original nature of this special time has been warped, but it is actually a time to celebrate those on the other side and to communicate with them if we wish. If nothing else, we can honour them by writing them a letter and burning it. (If you can't have a fire, use a steel saucepan.) We may also make a toast to them and leave the first pieces of, say, an apple cake baked for the occasion, as apples symbolise love and immortality. Give them their own place setting or set your offerings somewhere private; the Irish traditionally believe the departed come and "eat" with us at Samhain, but they don't want to eat in our earthly presence. Choose something you know they liked, whether it be their favourite candy, a drink they loved, or a packet of smokes. Anything that connects strongly to the way you remember them is ideal. The life-force energy of the gift will be consumed even though the physical remains will still be there the next day. In your offerings, remember the fairies and elementals or any other light beings or deities you wish to thank and include in your party. (Yes, it's a party—just with *real* ghosts, rather than people dressed up.)

Apples abound at Samhain, hence the old Hallowe'en game of apple ducking or apple bobbing: essentially trying to catch apples floating about in a tub of water with one's teeth. This can be traced back to the Roman invasion, when the conquerors brought apple trees to British shores and blended their celebrations with those of the Celts. People have been getting soaked every Hallowe'en since.

Samhain is also a good night for scrying, or divining the future, and the following practice is simple to set up, especially if you have been bobbing for apples already. Go to the tub of water you used for apple ducking, light a candle, and then focus on a question. Once you have your thought in mind, pour the wax from the lit candle into the water. The wax forms can be very revealing.

✳ WITCH TIP ✳
A CHEERFUL APPLE CHARM

Chop your apple horizontally, revealing the pentagram, and give the other half to a loved one. Think about a positive change you would like to see in yourself or your life.

Take a cocktail stick or toothpick and carve your wish into the flesh around the pentacle. Add any relevant symbols, glyphs, runes, or sigils you feel will power up your intention. Then eat it!

This is a good working for a waxing or full moon, as it is about increasing something in yourself or your life and making an aspect of yourself flourish. If it is a waning or dark moon, I'd suggest choosing an intention that focuses on releasing or banishing. Carve in the symbols or words as before, but instead of taking it into yourself, bury it with a blessing in the compost or under some leaves outside. It will nourish the earth and the creatures as it rots down, taking that which no longer serves with it and transforming the old into new and useful energy. We might not feel especially enchanted by the idea of rotting fruit, but there's magic in entropy and decay—don't let anyone tell you different.

I adapted the above charm from an archaic English folk spell.[18] The original working was used to bewitch another being—a badly behaved pig, to be specific—but I prefer the idea of working this kind of improving magic on one-self first. Unless someone really *is* being a pig.

Winter Solstice: December 21

On the longest night and shortest day, darkness and stillness hold sway, conceptually reflecting the dark of the moon, menstruation, and night. Here, we pause. This time is also known as the hibernal solstice, hence the term *hibernation*.

The days lengthen after this solstice, and the light returns. Many ancient traditions are celebrated, perhaps unconsciously, at this time: Yule itself is a pre-Christian Scandinavian festival, for example. The Yule log was burned in Thor's name, and fires were lit to symbolise and encourage the return of the light, mimicking the sunlight. We deck our halls with evergreen leaves, and indeed many of us have a Christmas or Yule tree too. Whether it is real or plastic, the symbolism is very real.

My family always had an artificial tree when I was growing up, and we loved it like an old friend, bringing it down from the attic every year with great excitement. I still use an artificial tree, charged with the good vibes of festive seasons past. While I realise it is a big part of many families' traditions, it saddens me to see real trees chopped down and sold only to be cast out on the street by New Year. Perhaps it's the animist in me, but unless it's a real tree in a pot that can be placed back in the garden after Twelfth Night, I'm sticking with my fake plastic tree.

Now is the time for us to rest, eat, drink, and make merry, but we also remember those less fortunate, sharing our abundance in any way we can. That might be shopping for someone who can't get out, sharing food with creatures outside, donating to food banks, or making gift boxes for children in need. There are always ways to work with the generous energy of this time of year.

Winter Solstice was originally on the twenty-fifth of December—yes, Christmas Day—before the introduction of the Gregorian calendar. Pre-Christian devotees would worship solar deities and enact the rising of the sun (later the "son" of God) and the return of the light (of the world) that was to come. It's a time to acknowledge the triumph of life over death, hence the evergreen boughs and wreaths. But while this time has long been seen as a party season, if you feel like you just want to hibernate, that is very much in tune with this season too. If you have snow outside, add some to your bathwater to soak in its quiet, pure energy. Alternatively, make a snowball while concentrating on something that worries you and throw it as far as you can, knowing that as it melts it will take that troublesome energy with it.

The long winter nights give us opportunity to reflect, think of our ancestors, and strengthen the ties we have with those on this side of the veil too. You can use this contemplative time for candle meditations or for making Yuletide creations. A wreath for your door, decorated with dried fruits, ribbons, pictures, and frankly anything you like, is a perennial and uplifting symbol of renewal and eternity. Return the wreath to nature after removing any nonbiodegradable items on Twelfth Night (January 6).

New Year: December 31 and January 1
This is not part of the Wheel of the Year, but I feel it merits inclusion as a point of power, because we all feel that collective new-start energy as January approaches. This is one of the few times of year that *everybody* works magic by setting intentions for the future and casting out the old.

I write down the "greatest hits" of the Old Year, going through my diary to jog my memory. If you think you've had a bad year, this practice may inform you otherwise. This is a lovely time to gather precious past moments like a bouquet and give thanks before deciding how you would like to shape the coming months.

It can also be interesting to look into one's magical journal or Book of Shadows, if you keep one, to see what you were wishing for at the start of the previous year. Some of your intentions may have come to pass. As for those that haven't, have your intentions changed, or can you make sense of why this year might not have been the right time for them? Look at all the magical pots you've got cooking on your metaphorical stove and see what needs a stir and a little spice, what might need to be frozen for another time, and indeed, what is ready to be enjoyed! Acknowledging these is an act of magic in itself.

EVERYDAY PLANETARY MAGIC

You can inject extra magic into your life—and extra life into your magic—by working with the days of the week and their planetary correspondences. This could mean making sure your hot date is on a Friday, a day blessed by Venus, or it could have you confronting that troublesome neighbour on a Tuesday, invoking the energy of dynamic Mars, god of war and justice, to back you up. Every day, and indeed every hour of the day, is ruled by a different planet, so it is wise to use these correspondences to your advantage.

I find that the day of the week on which I was born feels lucky too, so I ensure any events or meetings take place on a Thursday, also blessed by generous Jupiter, planet of success. Have a think about the day on which you were born and whether things tend to go right on that day. Either way, it's also nice to check in daily with the various planetary deities and elements, to say hello and acknowledge their influence. This will also mean that when you do invoke their qualities or request their assistance, you feel familiar.

Monday

Ruled by the moon, Monday is a reflective day of feminine and maternal energies, intuition, domesticity, emotions, and sensitivity. Tune in to your feelings and allow the moon to guide you. Wear white and silver, moonstones, or white metals, and sink into a meditation that links with the lunar phase; you can find these on YouTube or in some meditation apps. Don't like Mondays? You're not alone. The erratic and shifting lunar moods can make one feel in need of stability and rest. Hold fast, it will soon be…

Tuesday

Enter Mars, planet of war, passions, energy, sexuality, and motivation. This is a good day to show your strength and initiate projects. Just don't let that Martian aggression take over: use your power for good. More warlike associations come from this day's Norse connection. Tuesday was originally "Tiw's Day" or "Tyr's Day": the Nordic god Tyr ruled combat, law, and justice.

If something needs a push, light a candle and ask for assistance from Venus's favourite boyfriend. Venus and Mars are known as the Cosmic Lovers, in case you didn't know. Think romantic Stevie Nicks and combative Lindsey Buckingham from Fleetwood Mac: they can't live with each other, can't live without each other. However, when they unite—either on the stage or in the skies—it's magic.

Wednesday

The so-called hump day is presided over by Mercury, quicksilver planet of communication, wit, and clarity. This makes Wednesday a great day to sort out your correspondence, get in touch with others, or make a speech, for you will be especially eloquent. Alternatively, if you need help in the expression department, call on Mercury for support. This is also known as "Woden's Day," a reference to Norse god Odin, if you'd rather tune in with him. The vibe is coolheaded and intellectual, so use these energies to usher in a fresh breeze of reason and rational perspective and to blow away any cobwebs that might be clouding you mentally. Stay grounded amid all this head energy by going for a walk or doing deep breathing.

Thursday

Thunderbolt Thursday brings brightness, bounty, and brio. Jolly, generous Jupiter holds sway here, as do Nordic deity Thor and Greek god Zeus, both gods of thunder. These influences make this the perfect day for anything from a business meeting to a party. Jupiter ensures easy productivity, showering blessings on all proceedings.

Tune in to Jupiter and Thor vibrations if things need a push in the right direction or a bolt of energy—though, as always, be careful what you ask for. Once, when we were trying to move house, the buyer pulled out, jeopardising the entire chain. We had another potential buyer in the frame, but he was playing games and refusing to commit. I called on Thor to step in, and he was certainly listening: we unexpectedly received an offer from said game-player that very night. However, the buyer eventually let us down, causing much expense and aggravation. Sometimes you're better off going with the flow.

Friday

Friday is a very female day, alight with queenly energy and ruled by the Nordic goddesses Frig, Freyja, and Venus herself. This is a day to be sociable and get to know people better. Let the luxurious goddess vibrations inspire you to have fun; whether you're partying or pampering, Venus will make sure you sparkle. I choose this day to honour all aspects of the Divine Feminine, depending on which facet I feel drawn to at the time. Venus is the main event for me, but Friday links with all female deities. Commit to a simple candle meditation to tune in, choosing the goddess Fortuna for luck, Athena for wisdom, and the Morrigan or Hecate for hardcore protection and justice. Don't forget to ask them what they would like from you in return, and don't be surprised if you are put to work.

Saturday

Saturday, normally associated with being a fun day, is actually ruled by stern Saturn, who brings tough lessons and hard work. If you're not at the office, this is a day to tackle household chores, homework, gardening, and admin or paperwork that doesn't get the attention it needs during the working week. Either that or you're doing the serious work of going shopping. Magically speaking, Saturn's energy makes this a good day for protection and banishment, especially during the waning or dark moon. Saturn earths us, so take the time to walk in the garden or the woods and consciously allow the earth to absorb anything you no longer want. Don't worry about handing over toxic energy; just envisage it being pulled into the soil, where it can be transmuted into something more useful. Let it go, and let it change—because that's what energy does. As Shakespeare put it, "There is nothing either good or bad, but thinking makes it so."[19]

Sunday

Tune in with the radiant vibrations of magnificent sun god Sol on this traditional day of rest, and charge up with positivity. It doesn't matter if the sun is behind a bank of thick cloud or the rain is falling: we know the sun is there, permeating all areas of life. Set intentions for the week to come, and acknowledge the gifts of the week past, perhaps with a gratitude journal or just a silent toast. Meditate on the qualities of the sun and what they inspire—warmth, life, joy, fun, positivity, growth, purification, relaxation—and light a yellow or golden candle to give thanks. If you have any ideas, projects, or relationships that need saturating with sunshine, today's the day to place them in the light and power them up with positivity. Connecting with the life-giving energy of the sun on a Sunday, a day that is typically slower moving and freer of distractions than any other, is appropriate for this kind of work.

Joining Forces

Now that you are better acquainted with the days of the week and their heavenly influences, another thing you could do when working magic in this way is combine other appropriate deities with the daily planetary rulers. The Morrigan and Mars, two fierce, warlike deities, would make a good team on a Tuesday, for example. Unite Mars and Venus in a ritual or dedication if you wish to soften Mars's tough edges or if you have love on your mind and want to invoke the blessing of the Cosmic Lovers. Selene, the moon goddess of completion and solution, is the perfect lady to turn to on Moon-day, as is Bastet, the cat goddess who rules the home, as cats tend to do. Build up your spiritual team and see how you can work together.

WEATHER MAGIC

Magic and weather have always been connected. Witches were traditionally believed to be behind a good or ill wind at sea, and shamanic rain-dance ceremonies were vital in times of drought. These were matters of life and death rather than, "I want sunshine for my garden party," or, "Oh no, my tan's fading."

On a personal level, I have never been tempted to ritualistically command certain conditions: nature has her own plan, and I respect it. All the same, my family and I can usually ensure the right weather on special days if we just ask nicely for it. My wedding day in November was beautifully bright, and we were blessed that evening by a golden moon in a crystal-clear sky. I live in England: you know what kind of weather we have, let alone in November. It's always worth asking. Nicely.

Cloud magic can be employed by cloudbusting—that's right, it's more than just the title of a Kate Bush song. Try willing the clouds to disappear: you can use this practice by imagining the clouds as something you don't want and visibly dissolving them. Again, I prefer to leave clouds be, as I assume they are there for their own reasons, although I do like to gaze at them to see if they assume shapes or symbols. It's an enjoyable meditative practice and a simple form of scrying or peeping.

I do like the idea of working magically *with* existing weather conditions, especially ones that resonate with you. Witchful thinkers are adept at making the most out of any circumstances, so even if you hate the rain, there's a way to find some love for it and use the energy constructively by working a healing visualisation. For example, as raindrops fall, imagine purifying diamond-white or transformative violet light saturating the planet with healing energy and concentrating in areas that especially require it—as always, according to free will.

Alternatively, if you're enjoying a sunny day, consciously feel the heat and imagine the world bathed in divine cosmic rays, blessing and energising the planet. Fog and mist can be used in the same way: visualise fog as a cloud of colour—pink for love, violet for positive transmutation, green for healing—and see it caressing the land with soft, kind vibrations. See thick snow as a blanket of loving energy encasing the earth, eventually melting into it and nourishing it with peace, healing, and harmony. There are so many ways in which we can connect with what is powering down from the sky and work with it consciously for the betterment of the planet.

✳ WITCH TIP ✳
STORM WATER AND LUNAR DROPS

When the moon is high and clear, or when there's an electrical storm, put out a bowl of water to absorb and charge with moonlight or to catch the lightning-infused rainwater. I love doing this, because—brace yourself for yet more Thor thoughts ("Thor-ts"?)—sometimes you need maximum son-of-Odin vibes.

Once the water is collected, I pour it into a dropper bottle with a little thank-you, and I label it. It can be used for boosting a ritual or when calling on the beneficent energy of Thor or Jupiter. Drop some into bathwater, place it in a vaporiser, or dab it behind your ears when you need to be at your most zappy.

If you want to dissolve something—or someone—from your life, write it on a slip of paper in water-soluble ink during the waning or dark moon phase and then drop it in a glass of storm water and watch the words disappear.

Then pour it away into running water: a river is great, the sea even better thanks to the purifying salt, but down the drain with the tap running is fine too.

Have a think about the kind of weather you tend to have in the area in which you live, and, if you feel called, consider how you could work with it. Build up a communication with it, find the love for it, and let it love you right back.

THERE ARE SO MANY WAYS IN WHICH
WE CAN CONNECT WITH WHAT IS
POWERING DOWN FROM THE SKY
AND WORK WITH IT CONSCIOUSLY
FOR THE BETTERMENT OF THE PLANET.

WORKING WITH CRYSTALS

Crystals are marvellous talismans to keep close at all times, depending on our needs. Different stones give us strength in different areas of our lives and ensure a healthy flow of energy for all manner of occasions. I see these gems as little friends, all working to and for the good of all, merging with our energy fields to support us in different areas of our lives.

I keep a citrine in my purse, because this stone is great for abundance, wealth, and positivity. It's a very jolly crystal—as you would be if you personified those qualities. I'm also a big fan of selenite, which connects with the full moon and also angelic energies, and I have a fondness for black stones, such as tourmaline, shungite, obsidian, and onyx. Don't listen to the propaganda: the colour black is positive and protective, and it creates a psychic shield as well as a buffer against electromagnetic frequencies. Black stones reflect unwanted energy straight back to the sender, and at the same time, black as a colour absorbs maximum light.

I wear crystals on my fingers, ears, and round my neck, but admittedly there's only so much jewellery one can wear at any one time, and it can be expensive or just not to our taste. With this in mind, you could sew specific gemstones into your clothes, something people have been doing since ancient times. Even the designer Victoria Beckham released a collection of garments with crystals sewn into secret pockets.[20]

Finding the Right Crystals

Look for stones that are ethically sourced, and support an independent shop over buying online. Apart from anything else, you may find it preferable to see what you are physically drawn to, something we can't easily do through our computer screens—yet. Resist handling stones and just take the first crystal that draws you: it will be the right one.

There are plenty of books that leave you feeling as if you'll be bankrupt once you've amassed the collection of all the items you "need." The right crystals, herbs, oils, and ritual tools can indeed be great friends to a witch, but in my book (and this *is* my book), you just need a clear focus and awareness of what it is you wish to achieve. Witchful thinking—and feeling—is all. Props are a bonus.

Magic is working with energy, and you can connect psychically with anything you choose. To this end, I believe you can still work with a crystal without owning it. Learn about it, understand its subtle energies, and really visualise it. Meditate on its energy and beauty, and concentrate intently on conjuring up a sense of the stone and its qualities. You are now connecting with the crystal energetically, whether the stone is in your hand or not. In doing so, you can invite those qualities into your life, where they can then go to work.

Cleanse, Program, Activate

To program a stone with intention or to give it a new purpose sympathetic to its core qualities, first cleanse it. Depending on what your individual crystal likes, you can do this by submerging it in salt water, resting it on a salt bed (a thick, dry layer of salt), bathing it with incense smoke, sunshine, or moonlight, or placing it on a piece of shungite, which will zap away old energy. Cleansing is important when you've just bought a stone, when you want your crystal to help you with something new, or just as a periodic energy refresh.

Do find out what your crystal prefers in terms of cleansing. Water will damage selenite, kyanite, kunzite, haematite, amber, or calcite, for example, while many crystals, especially amethyst, prefer not to be left in direct sunlight for more than half an hour. Salt beds can be corrosive, especially to softer stones such as fluorite, sodalite, and lapis lazuli.[21] Also, do discard the salt afterwards rather than using it in a bath: you don't want to immerse yourself in stale, unwanted energies.

Once cleansed, reset your crystal by holding it in your hand and telling it how you would like to work together. It can be as easy as saying, "I would like you to bring me prosperity" (or "luck," or "love," or "good health"). Meditate with it, blend your energy with it, and charge it lovingly with your intention.

There are so many gemstones to get to know, but here is a selection from my own crystal vault to hopefully inspire you. Explore them, enjoy them, respect them. They will be friends for life.

Amethyst: An early favourite for me, this is a protective, intuition-boosting stone and is healing for the head—whether that be a headache, insomnia, anxiety, or psychic troubles. Keep amethyst by the bed or under your pillow. It was thought to be so purifying by the Romans that they would drop a chunk into their goblet of wine in order to neutralise any poisons that had been slipped in when they weren't looking.

Aventurine: A sea-green crystal associated with love and riches, aventurine also has positive effects on everything from the nervous system to eye health. Crystal Vaults calls it the "stone of opportunity" and the "luckiest" crystal for manifesting, winning, and wealth,[22] which makes it a great one in combination with citrine.

Carnelian: As warm and robustly affectionate as it looks, glossy-red carnelian is a jolly stone full of loving energy. Stimulating to the sex drive as well as a sense of personal ambition—and maybe it's your ambition to have more sex—carnelian can bring a healthy sense of confidence to the user. Great for new directions, creativity, warmth, and willpower.

Citrine: This is a famous abundance and success stone. Twinkling and golden, citrine even looks successful. It activates creativity and self-expression—connecting with the solar plexus—and is a positive motivator, releasing negativity and enhancing focus and concentration.

Fluorite: A gentle stone, but don't underestimate it: fluorite is capable of clearing gloomy vibrations from the aura, scattered thoughts from the mind, and negative patterns generally. Having fluorite on hand can bring increased concentration and clarity, as well as the ability to make better decisions. Its qualities are magnified in water, so pop some pieces into the bath and slow your thoughts, align with fluorite, and listen to what it tells you.

Haematite: This black, metallic stone derives from iron ore. It is an emboldening crystal to shield the wearer from negativity, tone the blood (hence *haema*–), and act as a magnetic force. Cleanse it regularly, as this stone takes on all sorts of vibes and will hold on to them until you clear them. This was my favourite stone as a child, but every time I wore it, before long it would break or explode. I now realise it was doing such a good job of absorbing dodgy vibes that it could take no more. Now I understand how important it is to give stones a break and a cleanse.

Kyanite: Like little blue spears of light, kyanite is a fascinating stone. It is also a key tool for psychic work. Another one that doesn't hang on to negativity, kyanite never needs cleansing. Crystal Vaults describes this as an "extraordinary crystal of connection" for its ability to raise our vibration and link us to higher realms, not to mention bring depth to our meditations. Also worth noting is its value in communication with other humans: it can be useful to have on hand when dealing with "disharmonious people," as Crystal Vaults diplomatically puts it.[23] (Or, as I prefer to call them, "assholes.")

Quartz (clear): This stone, as its appearance suggests, brings clarity, purity, and precision: indeed, quartz is used in watch mechanisms. Clear quartz is also a great amplifier and can add oomph to your meditations or to the qualities of other crystals. It is believed to be the most versatile crystal, so if you don't know where to start or if none of the other crystals in the shop are speaking to you, choose one of these. Healing, cleansing, and deeply spiritual, clear quartz can connect you to your higher self.

Quartz (rose): This stone is associated with love—from self-love to romance, beauty, warmth, and healing. I bought an unpolished chunk of this when I was a kid and still treasure it. Rose quartz opens the heart, and some believe it prevents ageing. You can get it in polished heart shapes and pop it in your pocket or your bra, if you wear one, to have it close to your heart. If you do this, just be careful when you take the garment off and make sure to avoid crystals skidding across public changing-room floors or breaking on hard bathroom tiles. (Guilty.)

Selenite: Named after Selene, goddess of the full moon and completion, pieces of selenite are a little like moonbeams. Selenite sticks can be relatively inexpensive, considering what they're capable of. This stone is a great protector, so high in vibration it never needs cleansing, and if you place other items near it, it will clear their energy. Use selenite like a wand and wave it over whatever needs attention. Run it around yourself and imagine it rubbing out unwanted energy. You can also sit with it under your bare feet for fifteen minutes, imagining negative energy being whisked away.

Shungite: Protective, detoxifying, and healing, shungite is often described as having the ability to kill disease and protect from electromagnetic fields. Like selenite, it doesn't take on negativity and so never needs cleansing. Some find the energy deadening, but some of us are so sensitive that we actually need a bit of that. I had some dark dreams when I first introduced this stone into my life, but I emerged positively changed. This stone comes into its own in the right setting, and I am often forcibly reminded of what a wide-open door I am without it. It is the ultimate energy shield.

Topaz: This crystal aligns with opulence and luxury, strength and loyalty, focus, peace, and love—and that's just for starters. I have a fondness for blue topaz: it looks like a sparkling blue eye, lit from within. I have a topaz ring, which my mother gave me when I was a teenager, and a silver topaz pentacle for working magic and wearing on sabbats. It's such a powerful stone for manifestation that I tend to save it for when I am consciously making positive intentions. Topaz is also associated with my astrological sign, Scorpio. The other stone for us Scorps is opal, which my superstitious family won't allow in the house—so topaz it is.

When Crystals Break

Whether they take on too much and haven't been cleansed—like my poor old haematite—or their work with you is complete, take note of when and why your gems give up the ghost. Sometimes, as with crystal-chip bracelets, it's simply because the elastic they are strung on isn't exactly made to last a lifetime. But even in these cases, it's worth considering the time and place in which they "decide" to break.

My onyx bracelet recently broke as I was leaving my parents' house after a visit. My dad had been unwell, and after I'd rushed up to spend time with him, I reluctantly had to take my train home. As I was saying goodbye, little black stones started flying in all directions. I told my folks to keep them, as they clearly wanted to stay. My tongue was in my cheek, but I believe in divine timing and that nothing happens by accident. As I sat on the train from Liverpool back to Essex, I looked up the health properties of onyx and was amazed to note that it is a supportive crystal for those suffering with the very condition my father had just been diagnosed with. When that jewellery breaks, don't get mad. Make sense of it.

Is everything significant? More often than not, it is, but you'll learn to feel the difference. Magic speaks to us in symbols, so pay attention to more or less everything and prepare for "aha" moments galore.

Making Crystal Essences

If a crystal or piece of gemstone jewellery breaks in your home, collect the chips, cleanse them, and give them a rest. Then you can use them to make a crystal essence by placing them in a spray bottle with filtered water, sea salt, essential oils, and herbs of your choice.

Crystal essences are effective and fun to make, and they are also rather kinder to bathtubs than unblended essential oils, which can stain. You can buy crystal essences, but if you're like me you're going to get through them quickly. Much better to make a bespoke selection using your own creativity and the crystal chips that have adorned your wrists for months and so are packed with your energy.

If you'd like to make your own crystal essence but you're not sure how to start, here's one I made recently. My citrine-chip bracelet broke, so I decided to make a prosperity essence to draw wealth. Pick a new or waxing moon to create this blend. As for weekdays, Thursdays are aligned with Jupiter, planet of success and abundance, and Sundays tap into the rich, golden vibrations of the sun. You will need:

> 10 citrine chips
>
> 2 small pieces of tiger's eye and aventurine
>
> 100 millilitres filtered water, spring water, or rainwater collected during the waxing or full moon (You could place it in sunshine too, but just be aware it will evaporate if left for too long.)
>
> 8 drops bergamot oil
>
> 2 drops cinnamon oil
>
> 4 drops sweet orange oil
>
> 1 drop nutmeg oil
>
> 4 drops basil oil
>
> 1 bay leaf
>
> 1 peppermint leaf
>
> 1 basil leaf
>
> 1 cinnamon stick

You can substitute these herbs for the corresponding oils if you don't have them. There are no hard and fast rules here, so just use what you have or what you can easily obtain. Never allow undiluted oils to touch your skin, eyes, or clothes.

Before you begin, set your intention in mind, and keep it in your head, repeating it like a mantra, as you make this essence. Waft some incense over the stones or rinse in salt water to reset their vibration and clear old energy.

Place the gems in the bottom of a jug or bowl and pour half of the water over them. Carefully add the oils, and then pour in the rest of the water: this gently breaks up the oils. Stir while repeating your intention with power and positivity. When you feel the blending is complete, pour the essence carefully into receptacles and then add the leaves and cinnamon to infuse. It is now ready to be used.

Spritz the room, spritz yourself, spritz your bathwater, your radiators, your bed linen, or your purse, wipe down your ritual space with it, pour it into your oil burner, or anoint whatever requires anointing. Do keep it away from pets, though: essential oils can trigger allergic reactions or worse.

You can customise the above recipe to make different essences for different purposes. I have one for protection, using pieces of onyx and tourmaline; one to honour full moon energy, using moonstones, jasmine, and rainwater collected during a full moon storm; and one as a sleep blend, using lavender and amethyst.

Crystal Grids

I find the chips from broken gemstone bracelets very useful for making mini crystal grids for different purposes. Essentially, a crystal grid is formed when you have a specific intention and you gather the stones that will support that intention, arranging them in a shape that is conducive to the way you want things to go.

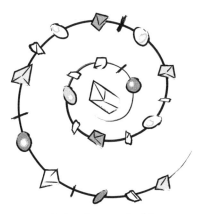

A simple crystal grid

You can use them to bless and protect a space, send energy to another person, or manifest something you want, for example. They focus our thoughts and, once the spell is complete, act as a visually appealing reminder of our intention. A simple and popular shape to follow when making a grid is that of the spiral: place the crystals in a spiral going inwards for something you wish to draw to you, and outwards if you are either pushing something away or reaching out to communicate to someone.

There is a plethora of books and websites dedicated to the subject of crystal grids, and there are templates you can use based on sacred geometrical symbols, such as Metatron's Cube (Metatron being an über-powerful angelic presence), the Sacred Spiral, the Pyramid, the Flower of Life, and the Seed of Life. However, before I knew that crystal grids were a thing, I remember instinctively creating one on the top of a manuscript for a book I had just written, to protect it and draw to it only positive energies. It had a powerful effect, so there's something to be said for making grids intuitively rather than rigidly following instructions.

Here is an example of how I might set up a simple grid. You don't need a template—just the appropriate crystals, a birthday-cake candle and suitable holder that will keep it safely upright, an athame or cocktail stick or toothpick to carve into the wax, a crystal point or wand, and, as always, your focused intention.

Let's say you want to make a grid to send a happy birthday wish to someone you love but can't be with. Appropriate choices would be rose quartz chips for love, citrine for joy and celebration, clear quartz to amplify, and any other relevant crystals that you have close at hand.

Prepare as you ordinarily would for a spell: take three deep breaths, meditate, cast a circle or bubble of protection, say a prayer—whatever works for you. Now put on some music, maybe "Happy

Birthday" by Stevie Wonder or something you know your friend enjoys, to link you energetically.

Cleanse all of the items in incense smoke, and then hold each crystal in your hand. Let them know what you're going to do and how you would like them to help.

Take the candle and carve the name of the person you wish to send loving thoughts to. Write a happy birthday wish and any symbols you feel are appropriate. Once you are satisfied, place the candle securely in your holder. This will be the centrepiece to your spiral grid. It can be placed on a table, if you know the grid will not be disturbed, or on a tray, if you think the surface you are working on will be needed for something else anytime soon.

We want to send the energy outwards, so with your intention powerfully focused, whisper it as an affirmation into each rose quartz and citrine crystal as you place them down about an inch or two apart in a spiral shape, spinning outwards from the light in the centre. Keep affirming that intention as you work.

Once they are in position, place the clear quartz pieces between each gemstone: these are your amplifiers or supporting stones.

Once everything is looking pretty, light the candle, take your crystal point or wand (or just your finger), and, still chanting or concentrating on your affirmation, carefully trace the spiral from the centre outwards, as if you are joining dots by linking all the crystals energetically into the spiral shape. Imagine light streaming out of the end of your wand or crystal point, creating a glowing spiral of energy, almost like a Catherine wheel firework. Now imagine the energy flowing out, directed by your wand, and reaching its recipient with ease. Allow the candle to burn down safely—stay with it, as birthday candles don't take long to burn down anyway—and keep the grid in place for as long as you like. Normally, I like to keep a grid in place for a lunar cycle or until my goal is reached, but if it's for a birthday, one or two days will be enough.

✳ WITCH TIP ✳
NATURE GIFTS

Keep a little pouch filled with crystal chips in your coat pocket: you'll always be prepared should you be inspired to leave an impromptu offering in nature. When I'm in the woods or find myself at a quiet crossroads or by a bridge, I like to leave a gift for the spirit of the place, for the elementals, or to the goddess Hecate, dispenser of justice, protector of witches, and deity of crossroads, boundaries, and doorways. These are all liminal spaces: places between realms. The veil is thinner in these spots, and many witches ritually leave spell workings at crossroads, burying items according to the magic they are working or presenting a gift to acknowledge Spirit. I always ensure I have my little bag of crystals, imbued with my own energy, for moments such as these.

If I intuit that a place holds trauma and could do with some healing and love—historic sites connected to the witch hunts, for example—I choose an appropriate stone or allow my fingers to pick one instinctively and then press it discreetly into the soil or the hidden nook of a tree with a prayer offered from the heart. Crystals come from the earth anyway, and there's something to be said for symbolically returning them once their work with us is complete.

As is the old witchy way, don't look back after you have placed your offering: just walk away. They say that if you've left a gift for Hecate and subsequently hear the barking of dogs, your gift has been received. The idea of not looking back is generally a healthy one on a number of levels. In magic alone, if we look back, we are indicating that we don't quite trust, we feel unsure, and we just want to check—rather than moving on and concentrating on the present, which is our point of power. I always think of this when I leave a gift in nature.

MANY WITCHES RITUALLY LEAVE SPELL WORKINGS AT CROSSROADS, BURYING ITEMS ACCORDING TO THE MAGIC THEY ARE WORKING OR PRESENTING A GIFT TO ACKNOWLEDGE SPIRIT.

SCENT FROM HEAVEN: THE FRAGRANT MAGIC OF ESSENTIAL OILS

I'm a great believer in how the power of scent can improve our lives. Perfumes are like potions, all with different properties and personalities, and of course, they are mostly made up from the essential oils of flowers, roots, herbs, and resins, all of which are magical.

Essential oils are highly concentrated compounds extracted from plants and flowers, and this extraction is usually achieved through distillation or cold pressing. You generally need a huge amount of source material. It is said to take ten thousand roses to make a 5-millilitre vial of rose essential oil,[24] which gives you an idea of the intense purity and high vibration of these essences.

Essential oils are like bottled light. They have a profound effect on our brains, and you can use them to create any emotional or spiritual state you wish. I have an ever-growing library of oils for different purposes, from cosmetic to occult. Forget air fresheners, and just use an oil burner or vaporiser: it's purer, healthier, and more economical to boot. As stated earlier, never allow essential oils to make direct contact with your skin. Instead, if you wish to apply topically, always dilute in a carrier oil, such as sweet almond, nourishing avocado, or the lighter grapeseed oil.

There are hundreds of essential oils, but here is my top ten go-to list:

1. **Black pepper:** Black pepper is superlative for scaring off negativity.

2. **Benzoin:** This sticky, chocolatey, resinous oil is comfort in a jar.

3. **Bergamot:** Fresh and zingy, this is essential (no pun intended) if you want to attract prosperity and a happy situation at work.

4. **Cinnamon:** Warm, enlivening, and evocative, this is another prosperity oil. Dab a little on your checkbook, wallet, or cash register and imagine riches flooding in as you breathe in that spicy scent.

5. **Clove:** Another festive spice oil, this spiky little friend is excellent for use in charms and spells that involve protection from gossip.

6. **Frankincense:** Like the best kind of protective father, keep this guy around to maintain a strong sense of security, psychic safety, and grounding energy.

7. **Lavender:** The mother of them all—comforting, relaxing lavender will heal mind, body, and spirit while reminding you of our intrinsic link to Mother Earth.

8. **Sweet orange:** Like working with actual rays of sunshine, sweet orange is superlative at changing the mood, lifting the vibration, and bringing cheer.

9. **Rosemary:** "Rosemary for remembrance"—seems there's something in the old saying, as this common herb sharpens our minds and memories and hones our focus.

10. **Rose:** Last but definitely not least. Earthy, warm Rose Maroc is my favourite, but Rose Absolute is heavenly. This is the queen of oils, positively vibrating with Venus vibes, celestial love, and heart-healing hoodoo.

Essential oils can be expensive, but when you remember just what it takes to create them, their cost isn't entirely surprising. However, when I think that the cost of a substance that will enhance my life, my spells, and my, well, *everything* is the same as that of two cocktails that I will either forget or regret—at the very least, they'll disappear quite quickly—it weighs up in the oil's favour. (Usually.)

If the oil you want is prohibitively expensive at this time and you need it for a charm, you can always use incense sticks with the same scent. Alternatively, use a cinnamon stick, a bay leaf, a clove, a little orange peel, or a grinding of black pepper. These items will be less concentrated than the essential oils, but it's more than fine to go back to the source.

Using Oils Without Using Them Up

One way I love to use expensive essential oils without charging through them too quickly is to keep a bottle close by and just inhale from it when I need to. If you want to concentrate or focus, a bottle of lemon or rosemary oil by the desk will do nicely. Take off the lid, inhale, hold your breath, and then breathe out. Alternatively, a whiff of protective black pepper while out and about can give you confidence and remind you the Divine has got your back if you're feeling unsure.

To ensure relaxation and sweet dreams, I keep a bottle of rose oil by the bed, and first thing in the morning and last thing at night, I breathe in the scent. With three deep breaths, I hold the scent in before breathing it back out, imagining pink light glowing within as I inhale. I'm convinced it makes me a *much* more loving person to be around, and it's a sweet little ritual to top and tail the day, sending me into the morning with a rosy outlook and guiding me into sleep at night.

Another way to keep the loving and protective energy of your favourite oils with you is to buy an aroma pendant or bracelet. These are easy to find online and are like perforated lockets containing a felt pad that you anoint with the oil or scent of your choice. The warmth from your body sends waves of fragrance travelling towards your nose throughout the day.

Notions and Potions

If you wish to delve into the fascinating study of essential oils and make your own products, I include details of my favourite essential oil bibles, including *The Fragrant Pharmacy*, by Valerie Ann Worwood, in the Recommended Reading section at the end of this book.

That said, I'd like to share with you two of my go-to everyday potions that you can easily make with water and a small selection of essential oils. Both have properties that will improve health (and beauty) and positively impact us on a psychological and spiritual level as well.

Sweet Speech Mouthwash

Fresh breath and healthy gums are all very well, but if your words are letting you down, may I recommend brewing up a bottle of Sweet Speech mouthwash? This magical mouthwash will both freshen your breath and uplift your speech. Like many homemade cleansing products, this recipe demonstrates how certain ingredients' physical benefits work together with their magical and psychological ones on a number of levels. It can also save money and cut down on plastic, as you will be reusing the same bottle. (Ensure you wash it between uses.)

Take an empty 500-millilitre mouthwash bottle, clean it in soapy water, and smoke-cleanse it with a little incense. You are about to fill it with a blend of your own. You will need:

> Sea salt
>
> 500 millilitres filtered water
>
> 2 drops clove oil
>
> 2 drops peppermint oil
>
> 2 drops lemon oil
>
> 2 drops sage oil

If you don't have the oils to hand, you can use the herbs, spices, and fruits, here using a chopped-up lemon and two teaspoonfuls each of cloves, sage, and mint.

First, bring the water to the boil in a pan with a handful of sea salt, then allow to simmer. If you don't have a measuring jug, just fill the old bottle up with water and then pour it into the pan.

Stir and let the salt dissolve, and focus with gratitude on the healing, purifying, and sanitising benefits of salt water. Then, essentially tell it what you would like it to do: in this case, cleansing and healing your mouth, but also imbuing your words with purity and healing.

After a minute, add two drops each of the essential oils, which have been selected with both oral health and advantageous speech in mind. For example, clove is historically and widely used for dental health, but it is also excellent at quelling gossip and protecting your words. Peppermint is perfect for oral freshness as well as clarity of expression. Lemon cleanses our energy on all levels, and sage is an antibacterial agent that also denotes wisdom and wise words.

Stir and breathe in the glorious fresh aroma, imagining the qualities that this mouthwash will enhance in you. Once you feel your ingredients are sufficiently blended, allow the mix to cool before pouring it carefully into your bottle. If you have used the herbs themselves, use a strainer.

Finally, label the bottle with care, adding any words and symbols that denote sweet and successful speech, as well as kind words that uplift and bless. These will act as a daily reminder of the importance of sweet speech. It's also worth noting that physically applying a word to a container of liquid alters its molecular structure: its vibration responds. (More on this later.) Careful labelling makes your "potion" more powerful.

Shake before each use, as the oils will separate, and murmur a little affirmation to activate the mixture's magical benefits. It doesn't have to be anything complicated, just something bright and purposeful like, "Please sweeten my speech today," "Bless my speech with clarity and strength," or, "May my words only bless, uplift, and bring truth." Anything along those lines will work nicely. Then, use it as you would any regular mouthwash, knowing as you swill that you are doing rather more than just freshening your breath.

Skincare Sorcery

Making your own skin toner or freshener is a great way of anointing yourself safely with (heavily diluted) essential oils and starting your day with their uplifting scent. It's also cheaper and usually healthier than shop-bought products—you'll know what's in it, for a start—and is free from alcohol, which dehydrates your complexion.

Once you've finished a 100-millilitre bottle of toner, for example, fill it three-quarters full with filtered water and add essential oils of your choice. I love lavender and tea tree for oily or combination skin, or try rose and geranium for drier complexions. Just add a few drops of each, as they are powerful. I personally add seven drops of lavender, three of rose, and two of tea tree for a skin-balancing freshener. As a rule, I am cautious with citrus oils, as they can sting sensitive skin. Do your own research, as you know your own skin best; there are countless recipes to draw on.

Experiment according to your own skincare needs. Instead of using water, you could brew a cup of horsetail tea, which boasts pore-shrinking abilities and contains skin-friendly silica, or you could add a tablespoon of witch hazel to the fragrant mix. In almost all cases—and this bears repeating—you mustn't apply undiluted essential oils to the skin, and always keep them away from your eyes. Mix with intention, breathe in the aroma, and enjoy.

PERFUMES PER SE

All scents, whether natural or synthetic, have an effect on our emotions and state of mind, so it's crucial to pick the right one. There are beautiful natural blends on the market, such as those created by Starchild in Glastonbury. As for designer perfumes? Well, they certainly have a place in my heart and on my dressing table if they are cruelty-free. It is easy to check with a little online research, and now more than ever there is less reason to compromise.

With your magical knowledge, even a bottle of high-street perfume can assume significance. Look out for scents containing rose and vanilla for conjuring up loving feelings, basil and bergamot for drawing money, and benzoin or black pepper for protection. When you employ witchful thinking, you know what to look for.

The Power in a Name

As for the names of perfumes, I think it's important to choose one with a name that is in keeping with the feeling we want to conjure or the way we want to be. I tend to avoid fragrances with names that connote anything negative, no matter how gorgeous the scent. You don't buy perfume every day, so when you do, it's an opportunity to snap up a potion that is perfectly appropriate, right down to the name.

The following story adds credence to this theory about names. The Japanese scientist Masaru Emoto discovered that water "reacted" to emotions, music, pictures, and even a simple word. He would write a negative message on a label, like "You're stupid," and stick it onto a bottle of water. He would then take a second bottle and label it with positive words, like "You are beautiful." These bottles would be frozen and then studied under a microscope. The results were unequivocal: the bottle with the insult taped to it contained warped and malformed ice crystals, whereas the water labeled with the positive message had responded by forming exquisite patterns.[25] Water absorbs, understands, *responds*. This is why I like my perfumes to have positive names—or at least not negative ones.

LOOK OUT FOR SCENTS
CONTAINING ROSE AND
VANILLA FOR CONJURING UP
LOVING FEELINGS,
BASIL AND BERGAMOT FOR
DRAWING MONEY, AND
BENZOIN OR BLACK PEPPER
FOR PROTECTION.

LET THE FLORIDA FLOW

Continuing on the subject of scent, Florida water (literally "flower water") has been used in hoodoo magic and shamanism for generations, as well as being used more generally as a household scent and a refreshing cologne in hot weather. The classic Murray and Lanman (now Lanman and Kemp) Florida water, manufactured in New York since 1808, is perhaps the most famous example of this enlivening essence. It positively bursts with orange, lemon, and majestic neroli with a touch of protective camphor, freshening you up as it raises your vibration. Some magical practitioners like to place it as an offering on their altar or keep it in a bowl, like holy water, to anoint themselves with.

I pour a few drops into my hands and clap them over my head—clapping, like any sharp noise, breaks up stagnant energy—before brushing it over myself to cleanse my aura. You can do this before a ritual or just when you get home from the outside world to reset your energy. I slosh a bit into my bathwater too, and once that fragrant steam starts to rise, it doesn't take much for it to permeate the whole apartment. It's not too expensive—hence the sloshing—and is usually easy to find in your local New Age or crystal store or, if you live in the United States, your local pharmacy. If you run out or can't get hold of it, lemon juice will do the trick.

I love the classic Murray and Lanman Florida water: the label is so elegant, and in using it, you are linking in with magical workers who have worked with it in the past. That said, if you can make blends yourself rather than buying manufactured versions, I always think they are more special, and they're usually less expensive.

Here's a basic recipe for you to work with (and customise) if you'd like to give making your own Florida water a try. If you only have a small container, adjust the amounts below accordingly. If in doubt, take your bottle and fill it two-thirds full with the alcohol, then pour this into the bowl to mix with the other ingredients. That way you'll know you haven't used too much base liquid. You will need:

> 5 cups vodka or rubbing alcohol
>
> 5 tablespoons of rose or orange blossom water
>
> 5 drops sweet orange essential oil
>
> 5 drops lavender essential oil
>
> 3 drops lemon essential oil
>
> 1–2 drops camphor essential oil
>
> 1–2 drops clove essential oil

In a large bowl, mix the alcohol and rose or orange blossom water with intention, and then gently add the essential oils. Stir together gently, and once you are satisfied that the ingredients are blended together, trace a pentagram over the top of the water to bless and seal. Then, pour carefully into receptacles. Add your own elements too: use different oils if you feel called to, and feel free to sprinkle in roots, powders, herbs, or crystals. A splash of full moon water, if you've collected some, can add extra energy, or you could use melted snow water for purity.

You can do this at any time, but I like to create my Florida waters on a Friday, the day of the goddess Venus, as she connects with flowers, scent, and beauty. The amounts given do tend to centre around the number five, which also chimes with this goddess (Friday is the fifth day of the week), but follow your instincts. If you feel you wish to add a little more lavender and a little less lemon, for example, then do. Just be aware that essential oils are very strong and, as I've said previously, must not make contact with your skin undiluted.

✳ WITCH TIP ✳
A SIMPLE SEALING RITUAL

Seal your home with positivity by conjuring a cleansing wash using a mix of Florida water, warm salt water, and a couple of drops of any other oils that take your fancy (step up, protective black pepper).

You can use this any time, but it's especially useful for refreshing your home's energy on new and full moons and for the turns of the Wheel of the Year. Play uplifting music to raise the vibration, and say a few words of incantation or affirmation as you clean your surfaces with it, depending on what you want to achieve. I also use the wash to clean windows, hard floors, and doorframes. Doorways are important, and we want to make sure what comes through them is positive.

Finish this ritual by dipping a finger into the mix and—you guessed it—drawing a protective pentagram on the door with a blessing. I draw invisible pentagrams on doors with my finger whenever I leave or enter. It's like a witch version of touching a mezuzah if you're Jewish. If you believe doing this adds protection to the things and places you love, then it does. Don't get obsessive-compulsive about it: the main thing to remember is that all is well. If that is your perception, you're doing fine.

PLANT MAGIC

Plant lore is a huge subject in magic, and it encompasses everything from age-old herbal remedies to secret floral messages, from vibrational plant essences to magical teas and tisanes. In the following sections, I will introduce some of my favourite "greatest hits" from the world of plant lore, starting with that essential resource, the Doctrine of Signatures—a fantastic illustration of how sometimes things really are as they appear.

The Doctrine of Signatures

The Doctrine of Signatures denotes that many plants have "signatures," or visible characteristics that resemble the parts of the body they heal. The historic understanding of this is that the Divine would have wanted humans to know what is available to them and to understand what the plants are for.

Many consider the Doctrine of Signatures to be a mediaeval idea; indeed, it was during the Middle Ages that the concept was first written down and illustrated, but the doctrine is far older. While its origins are debated, it is likely that countless herbalists and folk-medicine buffs understood it intuitively throughout the ages, and its relevance and wisdom is used to this day.

Here is a cornucopia of examples I'm particularly fond of:

+ **Avocados** contain folic acid, vitamin E, and healthy fats that are healing for the female hormonal system—when cut in half, this fruit mimics the look of a womb. The avocado also takes nine months to grow from seed to fruit.[26]

+ **Blackberries** are excellent for blood health—they look like a little cluster of capillaries—and can even help with thread veins.

- **Carrots** are known for containing eyesight-nourishing vitamin A: cut a carrot widthways to note the eye shape inside.

- **Comfrey**, with its bone-white flowers, is traditionally known as knitbone or boneset, and this is the herb we turn to when we've taken a knock. Stick to ointments rather than tea in this case, as comfrey taken internally can be a strain on the liver.

- Phallic plants like **courgettes** and **cucumbers** are associated with Venus, love, and male reproductive health.

- **Eyebright**, with its centre like the pupil of an eye surrounded by white petals, is still used in eye drops today.

- **Ginger root** resembles intestines and is a valuable remedy for digestive issues.

- **Lungwort**, a native of the borage family, features white speckles that mirror spots on the lung. It was traditionally used to remedy every respiratory ill from asthma to emphysema.

- **Mushrooms** are excellent for ear health, being full of vitamin D, although red toadstools such as fly agaric can be anything from psychoactive to all-out poisonous. Scarlet, being a warning colour, gives us that signal. Leave them to the pixies. (They have to sit underneath something, after all.)

- Yellow **St. John's Wort** flowers are a natural antidepressant that can bring sunshine back to our moods.

- **Walnuts** are rich in Omega-3 oils, polyphenols, and essential fatty acids known to be excellent for brain health.

I also love the helpful names so many of these herbs have: self-heal, toothwort (*–wort* means it has "worth"), milk thistle (sounds like a soothing balm for taxed livers). And as for brain-loving sage, you'd be sagacious indeed to keep this herb nearby. Not only is it marvellous for the menopausal symptoms of the wise (sage) woman, but it is good for respiratory health, enhances concentration, and can even alleviate the symptoms of Alzheimer's. As yet another example, yarrow was also known as bloodwort or woundwort, indicating its quality of being able to heal wounds and reduce haemorrhaging as well as speeding up the time it takes for cuts or burns to heal. Menstruating women are often advised to drink yarrow tea, as it eases symptoms and brings clarity.

This is a hint of what's out there, but I hope you feel inspired to look into this fascinating study further. Please note that it is not my intention to discourage you from seeking orthodox medical help: in an ideal world, orthodox medicine and the Old Ways work in synergy. If you are on medication, please research thoroughly as to whether there are any potential interactions to be aware of.

A final note of caution: the Doctrine of Signatures doesn't always check out exactly, so be cautious if foraging, and don't rely on symbolism alone if you aren't sure.

The Traditional Language of Flowers

Plant symbolism is more ubiquitous than many might immediately assume. We all know that a bunch of flowers can ease a troubled heart and deliver a message that goes beyond words. But flowers contain deep occult meanings too, and we must select our posies with care.

You might think that it's just "red roses = passion" and "white lilies = peace," but it's a bit more involved than that, especially when it comes to the giving of bouquets to a loved one. This might all seem a tad Victorian, but it's an art, and an interesting one at that. It also might save—or destroy—a friendship, so listen up:

- **Anemones** can speak of fading hope or the feeling of being forsaken. On the flipside, though, they can also mean anticipation. It's all about context and the blooms you accompany them with.

- Pink **carnations** are perfect as a Mother's Day gift: they denote maternal love.

- **Cherry blossoms** are lovely but short-lived, representing the transience of life.

- **Chrysanthemums** represent longevity, happiness, optimism, and love. Many believe they link to the psychic realm, so have a bunch of them in when the veil is particularly thin between the worlds, such as at Samhain or Beltane.

- For **daffodils**, give many or none at all. A single bloom foretells a misfortune, but a jolly bunch augurs joy.

- **Geraniums** are for determination and strength. They are cheery to have around, their positive vibe is protective, and they are traditionally known as witches' soldiers.

- **Gardenias** can represent concealed or secret love.

- Purple **hyacinths** aren't just fragrant beauties: they give the message that the giver is sorry about something and is asking for forgiveness.

- **Lime blossom** represents fornication, so don't thrust a posy of these into the wrong hands.

- **Orange lilies** might be stunning, but apparently they represent anger, hatred, and disdain. (I have to say, if I was angry with someone, they probably wouldn't be receiving flowers.) Note that lilies and members of the lily family are poisonous to cats.

- **Pansies** represent thoughts; the name comes from the French word *pensée*.

- **Primrose** signifies eternal love, as do amaranth, jasmine, and red tulip.

- **Red and white flowers** traditionally put people in mind of blood and bandages, so avoid that particular combination unless the recipient is an avid supporter of Arsenal Football Club.

- **Roses** alone have many meanings depending on colour. A lavender rose means love at first sight. Yellow is fine for a pal, as it signifies friendship, but otherwise it can mean betrayal or jealousy. Pink is for grace, desire, and joie de vivre. Red roses are, of course, the go-to for love and passion, and a white rose symbolises purity, spiritual love, and even secrets.

- **Sweet pea** is perfect if you wish to express gratitude, as are dark pink roses, campanula, and Canterbury bells.

- **Thistle** is a warning. I favour spiky flowers and plants for the fortification of boundaries, so pop a bunch in your vase to invoke protection and remind yourself of the divine shielding that is always there when you ask.

- **Yellow** might be one of the cheeriest colours in the spectrum, but a bouquet of yellow flowers tends to signify the end of a relationship. Some believe they even represent disdain or infidelity, so give these a miss unless you'd rather not see the recipient again.

This is a mere posy's worth of information to give you a sense of the subtly complex world (translation: minefield) of gifting flowers. If in doubt, maybe just stick with chocolates.

PLANT AND FLOWER REMEDIES

From admiring flowers and plants to ingesting their essences, whatever I'm going through, I always turn to flower and plant remedies. Many of you will at least be aware of the popular Bach combination tincture Rescue Remedy, which is reassuring and effective in times of stress or shock. Never mind "Got milk?"—a far more frequently asked question in my family home is "Got Rescue Remedy?" Rescue Remedy was created by flower essence pioneer Edward Bach, and it can be found in the houses, purses, and briefcases of people who might not otherwise be interested in plant lore. But there is a great deal more to flower and plant essences than this go-to combination.

Edward Bach was born in Moseley, England, in 1886 and trained as a doctor in London. In his research, he found there to be distinct connections between personality types and patterns of ill health. He had a deep understanding of how emotional imbalances can be the root of physical illness, and he combined his spirituality with his expertise in bacteriology, homeopathy, and vaccine therapy to ultimately become a pioneer of plant and flower remedies. Bach was generous in his approach and wanted as many people as possible to understand and utilise this way to wellness, never patenting or hiding his methods.[27] The world is now blessed with numerous manufacturers of flower and plant essences—including Vogel, Australian Bush Flower Essences, Findhorn, Healing Herbs, and others—all tapping into the flora of different areas of the planet and intuitively linking the remedies with human emotions.

The energies of plant and flower remedies are loving and powerful. Centaury is backbone in a bottle, chestnut bud is great for those of us who find we repeat the same mistakes, and white chestnut halts looping, anxious thoughts. Holly opens us up to divine love, while pine is heaven-sent for people who find themselves taking responsibility for things that have nothing to do with them. If you've been criticised for being too "my way or the highway," drop a blend of rock water and vine into your tea. If resentment and regret are dogging your days, try gentle willow. Australian flower essences are also wonderful: boab is essential support for those struggling with bad memories and trauma, slender rice flower can broaden our minds, and angelsword protects and heals our auras—the perfect companion while meditating. These tinctures also maximise the positive sides of the qualities that are being treated.

If you are fortunate enough to live in a place where an array of therapeutic flowers and plants grow in abundance, you might want to experiment with making your own remedies. A single essence can be created by placing flowers, herbs, or bark into spring water and alcohol—traditionally brandy—which is used as a preservative. You then heat the infusion, preferably in sunlight, to release the healing properties.

Here is a simple sun method for making a plant essence. You will need:

50 parts spring water for 1 part flower heads, and an equal volume of brandy or equivalent preservative

A bowl

Glass bottles to decant

A sunny day

On a bright, still morning, preferably with a cloudless sky above, spend some time with your chosen plant outside, ask permission to remove the flower heads you require, and then add the flower heads to the water in your bowl.

Leave this in the sun for three hours before removing the flowers. Now mix the water with the alcohol and stir gently but thoroughly.

Decant and store in a cool, dark place. If you aren't blessed with sunshine, you can boil the concoction instead for half an hour.

Making things ourselves is always preferable, although it is not always realistic or practical—there is certainly no shame in tapping into the widely available ranges of premade flower and plant remedies if you live in an urban area or the plants you need are not indigenous to where you live. Read up on these remedies, bearing in mind that it will take time to get to know them, and research how specific issues can be treated with these high-vibrational essences. A solution (in a little dropper bottle) will be at hand.

Flower Pow(d)er

Another way to harness plant energy is to create powders. This is easy to do, and you can use these powders to dress candles, infuse bathwater, enhance a spell, or even use them in arts and crafts: as usual, the only limit is your imagination. I started making powders when I realised I couldn't bear to throw cut flowers away once they'd started to wilt but, at the same time, didn't like the energy of dried (dead) flowers on display in my home.

Here's a method for making flower powders. Once those blooms start to die, remove the heads and either let them dry naturally or place them in the oven on the lowest heat for fifteen minutes, or longer if required. Keep an eye on them throughout this time: some flowers or plants may dry quicker than others. When they have dried sufficiently, allow them to cool and then crumble them with your fingers into a bowl. You can crush them with a mortar and pestle, but I prefer to use fingers as it's more gentle and personal that way.

While powdering the petals, you could talk to them or just think about how you'd like to work with them and the kind of properties you'd like them to bring to your magical work. Alternatively, just chant the words that are associated with them—such as "love," "grace," "harmony"—or maybe call in a blessing from Venus, say, if working with roses. Allow your breath to gently infuse the powder.

Once the process is complete, trace a pentagram over them as a blessing and pour them into a jar. You could also place an appropriate gemstone inside with a piece of tissue anointed with the corresponding essential oil before sealing.

This is a resourceful way to allow the energy and magic of a flower or plant to live on and be utilised, and it's particularly special if the flowers were a gift from a loved one. I have a tin filled with powdered rose petals from a birthday bouquet from my mother and an anniversary posy from my husband. These flowers are not only powerful energetically in their own right, but the fact that they were given by two people I love amplifies that energy.

You can do this with leaves as well as flowers. Use oak leaves for spells that require strength and stability and silver birch for female energy. You can also use lunar charms or ash for sacred knowledge and psychic dreams: place the powdered leaves in a pouch under your pillow with a little mugwort and see what comes. Herbs can be used too, and it's easy to find powdered or ground herbs for kitchen use, although your own homemade powders will always be more effective.

✳ WITCH TIP ✳
SAY "ALOE" TO FRESH, HEALTHY SKIN AND HAIR

You can tap into plant magic even if you don't have easy access to a hedgerow or a well-stocked herb garden. Acquire an aloe vera plant and use the leaves to give your skin and hair a natural boost.

To start, as always, ask permission or say a silent thank-you to honour the plant you are taking from. Then, gently snap off a frond, break open the leaf by scoring it down the centre with your thumbnail, and apply the gel directly to your skin. You can also scrape the gel out of the leaf into a clean pot and store it in your fridge, but remember that it is an organic material with no chemicals or preservatives, so it won't last long.

Fresh aloe soothes sunburn and rashes, and it is the only thing I will put around my eyes. Manufactured eye creams and gels build up under the delicate skin beneath your peepers and often create more issues than they solve. Aloe vera gel is rejuvenating but is also light, easily breaking down in your system rather than hanging around like an unwelcome guest. Think of the packaging you'll be saving too. You can also use aloe to moisturise hair and soothe the scalp: pat it onto your hair and allow it to absorb for about twenty minutes before shampooing it away.

If snapping off leaves seems like brutal treatment for a beloved houseplant, here's another of aloe vera's magical powers: it quickly regenerates. Break off a leaf and it will simply grow another.

Baneful Plants and Herbs

This would seem to be a good time to mention "baneful" or dangerous plants. It's worth remembering when foraging that although some plants and herbs can look remarkably similar, their properties can be very different indeed. With this in mind, I bid you take care.

Baneful can mean anything from sedative to hallucinogenic to fatal if ingested or touched, so if you intend to go down the foraging route, do plenty of research and always wear gloves, as toxins can enter your bloodstream through your skin. I would also advise always having a pot of charcoal tablets to hand, as charcoal can absorb and bind toxins in the body and possibly buy you some time if you're in great need of help. These can usually be found at your local health food store as a digestive aid. Needless to say, if you are ever in doubt, leave herb harvesting to the experts and support your local health food store by buying herbs from them—and always follow your intuition.

Baneful can also be beneficial when you are deliberately trying to get rid of something, from insomnia to fleas to unwanted animal visitors, but you do want to be sure of what you are using before you proceed. Many baneful herbs were prized for protection spells, as well as used for linking to the psychic realm, but the problems they can bring to the uninitiated can definitely outweigh the benefits.

Here is a small but dark bouquet for you to consider:

+ **Belladonna** (deadly nightshade) is infamous. The name is Italian for "beautiful woman," and it is powerful and potentially deadly—to be avoided, at least by the inexperienced. Life imitates nature, and while names like these remain part of the misogynistic spin that takes responsibility off men "ensnared" by "femme fatales," I don't mind if the inexperienced give me a wide berth, frankly. Belladonna is an effective sedative for the insomniac, but use too much and you probably won't wake up at all. I use it in its dilute homeopathic form when required.

+ **Datura** is a bloom beloved by the nocturnal gardener, being as it is a moonflower that only blossoms after dark. Despite its beauty, all parts of this plant are poisonous. Historically—and misguidedly—used as a hallucinogenic, datura was believed to induce psychic insights, but many who used the herb reported horrible experiences.[28] Admire from a respectful distance.

+ **Fleabane** is, as the name suggests, an effective flea and insect repellent: even birds have been known to line their nests with it to keep bugs away.[29] But this herb is poisonous to grazing animals like cows and goats.

+ **Foxglove** is adored by the fairy folk but best avoided by human folk. This beautiful plant was all over our garden when I was growing up. I loved to see it, but I was also very aware of its dangerous qualities, which can cause heart problems, delirium, visual disturbances, and many other problems besides. Leave it to the Fae.

+ **Hemlock**, notorious for killing Socrates, almost had me fooled in the past. I once thought I'd found a profusion of yarrow and started harvesting, but I had a nagging feeling that it wasn't what I thought it was. The flowers looked like yarrow; the purple-bruised stalks did not. After much obsessive checking, it turned out it was indeed hemlock, and I gingerly removed the flowers from my teapot. Listen to those nagging feelings if you have them. Mine, in that instance, saved me from paralysis and certain death.

- **Mistletoe** is, like many baneful herbs, considered protective. It is prized magically, especially by Druids, and can be hung in the home or burned to activate its shielding powers. While it is toxic in large amounts, it can be taken as a very mild tea to lower blood pressure: just add one teaspoon of dried leaves to one cup of boiling water. It can also be used in a compress to treat rheumatism, using the same tea.[30] However, it must be avoided by pregnant or nursing women.

- **Monkshood** can poison you just via touching. Used to poison arrow tips, this pretty purple beast goes to work fast. If, while foraging, you think it has made contact with your skin, be aware of the symptoms, which are initially nausea and diarrhea, tingling and numbness in the mouth, and burning in the stomach. Before long, the body weakens, and ultimately your cardiac and respiratory systems break down.[31]

- **Rue** or witchbane is a malodorous herb that will repel cats, as they don't care for its smell. Rue was also traditionally used to trigger miscarriage in pregnant women who wanted an abortion, although the side effects could be fatal to the mother. This herb is not called "rue" for nothing.

Flying Ointments

Baneful and psychoactive herbs such as belladonna, henbane, opium poppies, and even the lethal hemlock were traditionally used as active ingredients in mediaeval "flying ointments" or "witches' salves," said to be used as a hallucinogenic aid to what we would now call astral travel or lucid dreaming. These ingredients would often be the death of the user due to their toxicity.

But I believe this was the so-called flight that witches were said to be able to take: psychic, rather than bodily. We still often refer to flying when we are in an altered state of perception. The idea of flying may also have come from the old Pagan tradition of jumping over a broomstick to signify a new phase: a turn of the Wheel of the Year, say, or the newly bound union between two people (a handfasting). As usual, and as with dreams, when it comes to magic throughout history, we must question everything and view what is before us as symbolic rather than literal.

There is much to say on herb lore, and I recommend Scott Cunningham's *Encyclopedia of Magical Herbs* to those keen to learn more. Cunningham (I love that his name sounds like "cunning man") not only describes the physical benefits of the herbs and fruits therein, but also details their planetary correspondences and, of course, esoteric uses.

TO START, AS ALWAYS,
ASK PERMISSION OR SAY
A SILENT THANK-YOU
TO HONOUR THE PLANT
YOU ARE TAKING FROM.

WITCHFUL DRINKING

It's time to turn our attention back to the plants that can heal, rather than hinder, and that combine magic-making with tea-drinking: my two favourite activities. Herbs, plants, and flowers are, as you know, essential friends to the witch, and brewing teas is the ideal way to invite their magic easily into your world.

Like most people in the UK, the cup of tea is legendary for being the ultimate reward, remedy, and comforter. There's more to it than just the drink itself: it's the ritual of making it, especially if you use a pot. Use a mug or cup that lifts your spirits and stir in loving thoughts. Trace symbols into the steamy air above the surface or murmur a charm over the leaves as the tea brews. Every cup is an opportunity to cast a little spell, in my opinion. Water is easily encoded, so always take the opportunity to charge your cup with intention—a blessing in every sip.

Don't forget, as my grandfather always said when I made him a cup of tea, to stir clockwise. Clockwise, sunwise, or *deosil* follows nature's cycles. Anticlockwise, known as *widdershins*, is considered against nature's flow, although it is often used to close a magic circle after a ritual, to help with reversal spells or banishment, or just to harmonise with the waning moon.

With any blossoms or herbs that come from anywhere other than your own garden, ensure you energetically purify them by waving a little incense smoke over them or by placing a purifying crystal, like selenite, on top of the jar you store them in. They will have passed through many hands and many places before arriving in your kitchen. If you are lucky enough to have any of the following in your garden, as always, ask permission and say thank you once you have taken from a plant. I also offer a libation once I've made the tea, to acknowledge the circle of giving and receiving.

Here are a few of my favourite brews:

Awad's spiced tea: This is lovely at any time, but especially if you need some sweet heat. I've named it Awad's spiced tea because my late friend Awad El Zein, a wise and special man—certainly a "witch"—used to make it for me. Awad was a former war photographer who, after years in the field, decided he wanted to take photos only of plants and flowers. He was an expert in spice and herb lore, and he made the most comforting tea I had ever tasted.

To a pot of black tea he'd add a pinch of cinnamon bark, three or four cloves, and the same amount of rose cardamom. This was before the era of the Starbucks chai latte, although I now realise this is what some would call chai. I sometimes add a few slices of ginger to this mix: it's stimulating, warming, and excellent for the circulation as well as nausea. Have a cup when contemplating something you wish to "quicken" or put a little heat under.

Borage: I was shocked when a friend told me their garden was packed with borage, also known as starflower, and asked, "How do I get rid of it?" I assured them they were very fortunate and that no witch's garden would be complete without this special herb. They weren't a witch, to be fair, so they were more interested in exterminating it.

Borage is associated with bravery—something we could all do with a bit more of now and again. "I, borage, bring courage," goes the old rhyme. Its blue, pentacle-shaped flowers delight the eye and hint at their magical significance. A jar of borage honey is a good thing to have in the pantry: take a teaspoon stirred into a cup of black tea—also associated with courage—when the going gets tough.

Lavender tea: Lavender is the mother of herbs, although don't put the essential oil in your tea—just use the plant. You can use just lavender and hot water, or you can brew as you would a regular pot of tea, sprinkling in a teaspoonful of the dried flowers with black tea and milk to taste.

Lavender is good for so many things. It is a great relaxant and a tremendous healer. According to old lore, even gazing upon a lavender bush can lift depression, and a tiny dab of the oil on a burn prevents scarring. Drink this tea any time, but especially when you are winding down or if you've had a shock. It is a true spirit soother. I add half a teaspoon of rose petals to my lavender tea too.

Nettle tea: You can find this in shops, but I'm fortunate to live near a patch of land that explodes with nettles every spring, so I harvest my own before May, or before the tops blossom, as otherwise they can be bitter. But even when bitter, you could still use an infusion of the leaves for a hair rinse: nettle is known for bringing shine back to locks.

Once you have harvested your leaves, preheat the oven to a low heat and rinse the nettles thoroughly. Then carefully place them on a baking tray and pop them in the oven to dry out. Once dried, they lose their sting. Pour the dried nettles into a bowl and chop them up small: I have a nifty pair of herb-cutting scissors for this. Then pour them into a jar in readiness. Nettle tea is essential for allergies and hay fever, and it is packed with minerals, so it's a good one to have in your herbal arsenal. Springtime sniffles begone.

Rose tea with milk and honey: How romantic does *that* sound? You can buy rose teabags, which essentially contain rose essence or petals mixed with black tea, but personally I like to mix it myself.

If you don't have a rose garden, you can get bags of petals online, although it's preferable to support local independents if you know of an herbal supplier near you. Always ensure you are buying sustainably grown plants from a supplier who grows organically: we do not want to be sipping down on pesticide tea.

Add one or two teaspoons of petals to your pot or strainer along with the black tea of your choice and brew up a hot cup of loving goodness. Rose is a goddess flower and is associated with Venus, so have a cup when you want to amplify the love in your heart or comfort yourself after a difficult day. Milk and honey to taste—and these two ingredients have their own significance. Who doesn't want to live in the luxuriant land of milk and honey? As you know, symbolism is important, and when we align with the symbols of what we want—love, health, wealth, ease—we invite those things in.

Rosemary tea: Rosemary has so many uses. Easy to grow in a garden or in a pot on a balcony, this plant is very much the witch's friend. You can steep the washed leaves in hot water before allowing it to cool for a special iced tea that does more than refresh your body on a hot day: rosemary will freshen your mind and hone your focus too. It also tastes delightful and is packed with antioxidants and anti-inflammatory properties—a real all-rounder.

Those are the star turns in my personal tea chart, but here are a few more supporting actors worthy of mention:

Horsetail tea: Like nettle tea, this is good for health and beauty, as it's full of silica, which is marvellous for strong hair (hence the name), nails, teeth, connective tissue, skin, and bones.

Mugwort tea: This herb is an old favourite for lifting psychic awareness and enhancing intuition. It also combines well with the female-loving yarrow for this purpose. Take a cup of one or t'other or both before meditating or slipping off to sleep, and see what emerges.

Peppermint: Good for refreshing our minds and cooling our systems if we have a fever, peppermint is best known for helping with digestive issues. It is a soother for nausea, bloating, and also headaches. Magically speaking, peppermint is prized for drawing money, so keep a leaf or two in your wallet.

Spearmint: A milder, sweeter taste than peppermint, this member of the mint family is not to be underestimated: spearmint boosts our memory, can lower stress, and eases issues associated with hormonal imbalances, such as PCOS (polycystic ovarian syndrome) and hirsutism, by regulating the androgens in our system.

✳ WITCH TIP ✳
DRESS FOR SUCCESS

When you find you are getting to the bottom of the jar of herbs or petals and what's inside is too crushed and dusty to be used for tea, my advice is to dress a candle with that dust instead.

Scatter the bits onto a length of foil and add a little essential oil of your choice. Warm the sides of a pillar candle until they are slightly melted but not dripping, and just roll your candle in the powder and oil and they should stick nicely. Nothing is wasted in a witch's kitchen.

Enchant Your Cup of Joe

If you prefer coffee to teas or tisanes, you can still enchant your cup of joe—or anything you're about to consume—by tracing a pentagram or any other magical symbol you desire over your brew, charging it with light or intention, and, according to taste, adding spices.

Here are my top three ingredients to spice up your cup and perk up your percolator:

+ Stir a pinch of **cinnamon** into your morning coffee for positivity and abundance. Accompany with a spoken intention and a visualisation of golden light fizzing through the liquid—stirred clockwise for increase. Cinnamon warms the body and the mind, boosts our immune system, and is excellent at drawing wealth.

+ A tiny finger pinch of grated **nutmeg** also tastes good in coffee, whether stirred in or dusted on the froth of a cappuccino. Its magical gifts include attracting prosperity, magnetising good luck, enhancing psychic awareness, and imbuing protection: old lore has it that carrying a whole nutmeg can shield you from harm while travelling.[32]

+ Romantic, playful **vanilla** is delightful for sweetening your mood—or someone else's. Stir a pinch into your cafetière—don't bother with artificial syrups. If you can't get hold of a vanilla pod or don't have a French press, a dash of vanilla essence will do nicely.

If you use a water-filter jug, you can place crystals in the base to infuse your H_2O with extra benefits, although it is imperative that you ensure the crystals you choose are safe to use in this way. Some crystals dissolve in water and some are toxic. Thankfully, big-hitter shungite is not, and you can buy shungite crystals specifically for this purpose: I have about six of them safely powering up my water. A cup of coffee made with shungite water—with a pinch of spice mindfully stirred in, and maybe a couple of drops of flower or plant essence, depending on my needs—always sees me right.

Keep It Cool

If the weather is sultry or you just don't like hot drinks, there are other ways in which you can take herbs and spices into your body for magical purposes and general health. You could try any of these:

+ Tear some fresh **basil** leaves into your salad or pasta dish to boost the bank balance and bring protection.

+ Stir a **bay leaf** into your stew with your wishes, or a little sage if you want to boost your brainpower.

+ Sprinkle a teaspoon of **cinnamon** and brown sugar onto buttered toast to sweeten your life, warm your system, and draw wealth.

+ Add a dash of **elderflower** cordial and **rose** water to your sparkling water or wine for a romantic summer cup and to freshen your mood.

+ Add fresh **lemon** to any appropriate drink for cleansing. It is effective for purifying both the digestive system and the psyche.

+ Crush fresh **mint** to taste into a soda or a cocktail to awaken your senses and, again, attract wealth.

+ Sprinkle **rosemary**, **black pepper**, and **sea salt** over anything from baked bread to French fries. It tastes great, and this blend boasts the benefits of enlivening your mind and swathing you in protection.

Another tip for cold drinks is to take a cocktail stick or toothpick and carefully carve the name of something you'd like, or a symbol of that quality, into an ice cube. Then pop it into your drink and, as it melts, imagine you are taking that quality into yourself. As the ice changes state, so do you.

Sipping Spells

Using what you drink is a way of easily working magic with whatever is already in your kitchen. See what goodies you find in your cupboards and look up their magical and health benefits. Once you've ascertained what is good for what, decide what you want specifically from these herbs and spices and how you would like to work together with them. Mould that desire into a clear intention and then blend your focus with your ingredients as you go.

Like many witches, I also take note of the moon phase and consider how I can work in synergy with it. If the moon is waning but I want to increase my luck, I could consider banishing that which might be blocking my good fortune while I sprinkle, spread, or stir my concoction widdershins to reflect the decreasing lunar energy. Alternatively, if the moon is waxing but I want to lose some weight, stirring clockwise, I could word my intention to increase my body confidence, health, and beauty or to maximise the ease with which I reach and maintain my ideal weight.

Do it your way and have fun with it; these might not be rituals as we would ordinarily think of them, but they are certainly spells, and the effects can be delicious.

POTS OF PROTECTION

Staying with the potential magic contained within our kitchen cupboards, I'm going to share two of my favourite recipes for physical, as well as psychic, protection.

Most witchy kitchens are never without a pot of honey, a few bulbs of garlic, a bottle of apple cider vinegar, and a library of herbs and spices, so it is usually quite easy to conjure up a few "pots of protection" for the pantry. As always, the ingredients you use come with not only physical benefits, but magical ones too: the inner reflects the outer, and the protective qualities shield us on all levels.

I take a spoonful of both of these creations whether I'm shielding from a germ, a negative mood, or someone else's nonsense. As always, label with care. Words make a difference.

Golden Garlic Honey

For this I used a jar of honey that was already a third empty; this made it easy to add the ingredients. Alternatively, have a clean, empty jar at the ready to decant your ingredients into.

You will need:

> Honey (Use Manuka or tea tree for immune-boosting or use borage for bravery; the fear of illness in itself can weaken us, and is not wanted.)
>
> A garlic bulb

Separate the garlic cloves from the bulb and peel. Chop into halves or slivers depending on your taste, bearing in mind you are eventually going to be swallowing these down in a spoonful of garlic-infused honey. (It's nicer than it sounds.)

Once you have prepared the garlic, tell it what you are going to use it for and then drop the cloves into the honey. Stir with intention, chanting an affirmation of protection and health. Add a dash of apple cider vinegar if you wish, and then seal.

Every day for a week or so, give it a stir, repeat your affirmation, and allow any air bubbles out: the infusion will create gas as the garlic ferments. Some people find the garlic turns blue.[33] If this does occur, don't panic: the enzymes, amino acids, and copper compounds are reacting as part of the fermentation process. It is not dangerous; it just looks peculiar.

I take a piece of the garlic in a teaspoon of the infused honey as if it were a supplement, and I've bested a cold this way more than once. You can cook with it, but the heat damages the allicin, which is the active ingredient that strengthens our health, so take it raw if you can. The honey is pungent, but if you swallow the garlic without chewing, your breath won't be *too* offensive. This is why I recommend chopping the cloves into slivers—so much easier to down.

If you're worried about knocking someone out each time you exhale, chew fresh parsley to nullify the effects. The combination in itself is also protective: my mother would keep a bunch of fresh parsley in a pot surrounded by garlic cloves if there were unwanted energies lurking. Some witches keep a string of garlic bulbs hanging by the door for protection. There are myriad ways to use it. It's no wonder garlic was seen as effective against vampires, although these days we worry less about befanged creatures of the night and more about social parasites and energy vampires. Thankfully, as ever, we can rely on these wonderful herbs to work with us on all levels of being—mind, body, and spirit.

You can work with honey in all sorts of ways: adding cinnamon and nutmeg to a pot for prosperity and success, for example, or adding a little rose and orange blossom water for romance. Use your imagination and focused intent to charge, enchant, and expand the range of magical tools at your fingertips.

Four Thieves Vinegar

Another protection pot for your pantry is Four Thieves vinegar, a blend of natural ingredients so powerful that it can, allegedly, shield you from the Black Death itself.[34] Some of you will be familiar with the old story behind this elixir, though there are versions that differ through time and space to fit with cultural norms. What follows is the version I know.

During the 1300s, the bubonic plague, or Black Death, as it was known, was raging throughout Europe. In the French town of Marseilles, while residents were dying horrible deaths by the hundreds, four thieves—apparently unaffected by the fatal virus—were on a rampage, breaking into the homes of the dying and stealing their property. Initially, they were largely ignored, as people believed surely it was only a matter of time until the thieves caught the plague and died. But they didn't.

The four thieves remained in rude health and became richer and richer. Eventually, they were arrested and sentenced to death, but they were offered a reprieve if they could reveal the secret of how they had stayed healthy for so long. The answer was a secret blend of vinegar and immune-boosting herbs that they took regularly. They also anointed themselves with it, rubbing the formula into their hands, feet, and temples, as it proved an effective repellent to the fleas that were spreading the plague. Legend has it that the four thieves shared the recipe and saved their necks. They might have been ruthless villains, but their legacy has been keeping many people healthy for centuries since.

Four Thieves vinegar, if made with natural ingredients, can indeed be taken internally and used as bug repellent, but it is also beloved by hoodoo practitioners as a purifying wash for your floor, door, and front step, for example. I like to pour a tablespoonful into bathwater for a cleansing soak: it will make your hair and skin soft as well as dissolve any energetic attachments you don't want. As always, it depends on the intention with which you use it. You can find Four Thieves vinegar for sale from various outlets, but do check whether a specific offering is for consumption, as they are not always. As ever, I prefer to make things myself if I can: it is always good to know what is going into the pot.

Perhaps it's understandable that after six hundred years the recipe for Four Thieves vinegar has morphed and there now appears to be a considerable number of versions. There are a few staple ingredients, though: apple cider vinegar (which itself has been used as a cleansing, strengthening tonic for thousands of years), rosemary, thyme, black peppercorns, sage, and, more often than not, lavender. Some people just include four herbs—one for each thief—but I add whatever immune-boosting herbs and spices I have in my larder, if I feel called to. When you look at the herbs listed in any recipe for Four Thieves vinegar, they all have properties that are protective both physically and psychically.

Here is the ingredients list for my most recent batch. You will need:

A 500-millilitre bottle of apple cider vinegar
(with the "mother")

1 tablespoon thyme (fresh or dried)

1 tablespoon rosemary

1 tablespoon sage

1 tablespoon black peppercorns

1 tablespoon angelica root

1 tablespoon juniper berries

1 tablespoon dried lavender flowers

1 tablespoon cloves

1 tablespoon garlic-infused honey

    (see recipe above)

A Mason jar or other suitable receptacle

Mix the herbs together in a bowl with your hands and tell them how you would like to work with them and how you are going to create a blend for protection for physical but also psychic health. Affirm your intention as you breathe in the evocative scent.

Transfer the herbs into a pan and pour your vinegar on top. Stir and simmer, but don't allow it to boil. Feel free to adjust the amounts of herbs if you wish. I like to make it as potent as possible, depending on what is available to me at the time.

After a few minutes, turn off the heat and allow the mixture to cool before decanting into your Mason jar. Some people strain the mixture, but I like to keep everything fermenting together for as long as possible. Put it in a cool, dark place and stir daily, reaffirming your intent that its purpose is to protect, bring health, banish negativity, and attract only positivity—whatever you feel is appropriate to your needs.

Now that you have made it, it's time to put this ancient magic potion into use—but please, *never drink it neat*. It is far too strong and could damage the enamel of your teeth, your throat, and your stomach. Add a strained tablespoonful to hot water and sip, adding more honey if required. Splosh an unstrained tablespoonful into bathwater. Drizzle it on your salad. If you don't mind the smell, pour some into a bucket of hot water and wash your floors, windows, and doors with it at Imbolc or New Year. Dab it on ankles and wrists on a balmy night to keep bugs away, and anoint bedposts to dispel nightmares. Whatever plagues you can be banished by this beast of a brew.

If you can't bear the smell of vinegar, an alternative would be to make Four Thieves oil: swap vinegar for olive oil (which you don't have to heat) and use it for anointing everything from salads to pulse points. You can find Four Thieves oil for sale, but as these are created with essential oils rather than herbs, they tend to be more for anointing externally than for internal consumption. Again, *always* check what you are buying. If preferred, you can also create your own Four Thieves anointing oil for external use only with the corresponding essential oils of sage, rosemary, lavender, and so on.[35]

However you bring the protection of this historic philtre into your life, making and using it will make you feel empowered—even bulletproof. This remedy is not intended to replace any prescription medicines or conventional allopathic medical treatments. As always, I like to think of natural remedies working hand in hand with more orthodox preparations, when required.

I TAKE A SPOONFUL OF BOTH OF THESE CREATIONS WHETHER I'M SHIELDING FROM A GERM, A NEGATIVE MOOD, OR SOMEONE ELSE'S NONSENSE. AS ALWAYS, LABEL WITH CARE.

SMOKE CLEANSING with HERBS

Herbs and flowers and barks and roots are essential when we want to cleanse our homes on an etheric level. If you need a quick and effective purifier after a visit from an energy vampire, it's time to get smokin'—and I'm not talking about sparking up a doobie, man.

Smoke cleansing by using bundles of burning herbs clears negativity, cleanses ritual tools, and resets the energy of any items that come to you secondhand. The practice of energetic cleansing with smoke, known widely by many as smudging, has become a controversial topic as we improve our understanding of cultural sensitivity. The burning of white sage and the use of palo santo, for example, are indigenous ceremonial processes. We must ensure we are not buying into the commercialisation of sacred practices and devaluing traditions that are not ours to use. Doing this can also create a scarcity of sacred plants, so if you already have these items in your spiritual store cupboard, use up your stocks respectfully and then look for alternatives.

Depending on where you are in the world, that might entail burning a bundle of purifying rosemary, renewing juniper, comforting lavender, prosperity-boosting bay, or fragrant pine. You can also use a joss stick to burn incense: Dragon's Blood is a favourite for banishing negativity. Even burning a cinnamon stick will do. Take a moment of reverence to honour and thank the spirit of the herb you are using. Then ask it to clear your space and purify your energy field—or whatever you want it to do—before lighting it carefully and wafting the smoke wherever it is needed.

Not everyone gets on with the smell of burning herbs, so if you need an alternative, I recommend placing sticks of selenite around the home. It's relatively inexpensive in its raw form and clears energy swiftly. You could also ring a bell or clap your hands as you walk around your home: sound is an excellent way of clearing energy.

Whether you use smoke, selenite, or sound, try to cleanse your home energetically every month on a new moon to usher in fresh energy. If nothing else, ensure your working area is cleared if you're about to start a ritual or a spell. It's respectful to the work and the energies you'll be working with, and you'll ensure any energy from the last spell cast doesn't mingle with the next.

NOT EVERYONE GETS ON WITH THE SMELL OF BURNING HERBS, SO IF YOU NEED AN ALTERNATIVE, RING A BELL OR CLAP YOUR HANDS AS YOU WALK AROUND YOUR HOME: SOUND IS AN EXCELLENT WAY OF CLEARING ENERGY.

SOUL SIGNS, MESSAGES, AND GIFTS

How do you hear the soul? It's different for everyone, but for me it's about noticing feelings and observing how the outside world reflects the inner in the form of synchronicities. This can feel like the Universe or a guide confirming and validating your feelings and choices—like someone saying, "Yes, now you're getting it," or, "We're with you."

You may find apports, which are items that appear from nowhere and are associated with a loved one in Spirit or with an angelic or divine presence. White feathers are a common example. Set up a respectful dialogue with Spirit, decide on a symbol that you can communicate with, and see if it comes up for you. Don't forget to write down any synchronicities: you'd be surprised how much you forget.

A friend of my mother's jokingly told her and her pals during a conversation that when she died, she wouldn't be leaving white feathers around: she would leave Ping-Pong balls instead. They all laughed about this, but a few years later this lady passed away, and within a few weeks, those friends all discovered a Ping-Pong ball in their homes. That is an example of an apport.

Other, more common apports include candy or coins. I've had chocolates inexplicably turning up in my purse, which is always delightful. As a child, I used to find old coins around the house we moved into—coins like farthings, sovereigns, and Victorian pennies, currency that had not been in use for some time. Only recently I brought the subject up with my parents. They were completely unaware of the coins and had no idea where they would have come from. It was an old house, and many different families had lived there before us. I think someone in Spirit was playing a benevolent little game with me. I recently read somewhere that coins are also considered a gift from Venus; I have an affinity with Venus, so this pleases me immensely. But there are no absolutes, and if you associate finding a copper coin with your Uncle Charlie, or if the date on the coin correlates with your grandmother's birthday, then that is where the meaning lies for you.

Apports can be stones, either with a naturally occurring symbol on the surface that means something to you, or with naturally occurring holes going all the way through: "holey stones." Holey stones are considered gifts from the Divine and protective talismans for witches, and one is meant to be able to see different dimensions if one looks through them when the time is right. I have found hundreds of these—or they have found me. Tradition dictates that you should keep your holey stones rather than sell them or even give them away, as they are a gift to you. A stone that is holey is, if you take the witch view, holy. We're holy too. (At the very least, we do have quite a few holes ...)

Holey stones are also sometimes known as witch stones—my preferred name for them—or more commonly hag stones. For me, the name *hag* connects with patriarchal propaganda against witches (or just older women), painting us as ugly and frightening, so anxious were our oppressors to keep us disempowered, so I never use it. *Witch stone* works fine for me. Interestingly, the layperson back in the day would see these special pebbles as protection *from* witches. Whichever way you look at them, they hold a protective charge and are reminders of something bigger than us.

I see these and all "spirit signs" as a meaningful ongoing dialogue between myself and the Unseen. I am always thrilled to find them, and the more I acknowledge them, the more they pour into my life. Joy and excitement are qualities that connect with the heavens and bring more light to the planet. The loving unseen forces around us will ensure that whatever sparks these qualities in you will appear to you more and more.

It's nice to leave gifts for the Divine or Spirit too, not as a bribe or a sacrifice but as an acknowledgment and encouragement for further connection, if that is your wish. Just ensure your offerings are earth- and animal-friendly: flowers cast into a stream, crystals returned to the earth, and food scattered for the birds to safely enjoy will do nicely.

I SEE THESE AND ALL "SPIRIT SIGNS" AS A MEANINGFUL ONGOING DIALOGUE BETWEEN MYSELF AND THE UNSEEN. I AM ALWAYS THRILLED TO FIND THEM, AND THE MORE I ACKNOWLEDGE THEM, THE MORE THEY POUR INTO MY LIFE.

Magical Musing
Respecting the Soul in Everything

A Jewish friend once told me that her rabbi advised "treating everything as if it has a soul." Once you embrace the belief that everything has its own spirit, energy, and purpose, no action will be mundane or mindless and you will nurture a healthy reverence for all things, from the flowers in the vase to the stars in the sky. This ideology is known as animism, from the Latin word *anima*, meaning "breath, life, spirit."

This idea exists in various forms across cultures and spiritual paths, and there are many who embrace the concept of animism. The concept is one I've lived and breathed for a very long time. No one particularly taught it to me, so I live it in my own way, but my friend's rabbi's quote was the first time I had ever heard it articulated like this. It is a beautiful way to move through the world, and that which you treat as "ensouled" will certainly respond, reflecting your love and care back in ways that may surprise you.

Treat your home as a sentient entity that loves and guards you rather than just seeing all the things you need to fix or wish you could change. Treat your garden in the same way and watch it flourish; listen to it, as it will communicate with you. Treat everything with a loving awareness and you will become less clumsy, dropping or damaging things with less frequency, because you will be inherently aware of the spirit of the objects you handle every day. Your behaviour, voice, and demeanour will soften, and you will tread more lightly upon the earth, noticing everything anew. Try it, and be sensitive to the subtle shifts that take place.

PART 3

AS WITHIN, SO WITHOUT

Energy, Protection, and the Power of Our Words

SYMPATHETIC MAGIC

Sympathetic magic, also called imitative magic, utilises physical objects or symbols that resemble a being or event. The practice uses correspondences to represent that which we wish to attract: that which symbolises the other draws it like a magnet. This is also known as the Law of Attraction, an ancient and fundamental concept dismissed by some as a New Age fad. The occultist Agrippa was writing about it half a millennium ago, and it is very simple: like attracts like, and when you apply your "vehement imagination,"[36] that's when the magic can really happen.

There are examples of sympathetic magic that can be traced back to prehistoric times, in the form of cave paintings: hunters would paint images of what they wanted to achieve, e.g., a picture of them successfully slaying an animal for food. When we create an image or visual symbol of that which we wish to manifest, we are working sympathetic magic by means of drawing our goal to us with the magnetism of symbols. These visuals also provide focus.

Many of the workings and suggestions within these pages take the form of sympathetic magic. Just take a look at any turn of the Wheel of the Year. We draw light and warmth back to the cold earth when we light candles and fires at Imbolc. Likewise, we focus our intention on fertility when we dance around a phallic Maypole at Beltane; in celebrating our own sexuality, we reflect the earth in its most abundant state.

Poppets and Contagion Magic

One example of sympathetic magic would be a poppet, "voodoo doll," or effigy of a person or thing one wishes to influence. Poppets can be made from all sorts of materials: wax is popular, either carved or melted into an approximate shape, or you can make a rudimentary human shape out of fabric. Your poppet will have extra charge if you are using fabric that belongs to the person you are working the magic for—but please ensure you have consent, not just to take the material, but to do the work.

For your own good and that of others, I recommend using this practice with positive intention: stroke the effigy's head to heal someone's headache, talk to it, maybe tell it something you hadn't felt able to say in person, give it a kiss, or otherwise use it as a focus for sending kind thoughts and healing.

You could make a poppet of your cat or dog if they get lonely in your absence. The poppet doesn't have to be exact in terms of likeness, although you could stuff it or coat it with hair or fur from your pet. This is incorporating contagion magic: the idea that an energetic link exists between two beings and is facilitated by something tangible that belongs to one or the other. If you do this, be sure to take the fur or hair from a brush or from your companion's bed, never from the live animal. Once you have made your poppet, charge it with meaning and intention, and maybe allow your pet to nuzzle it. Keep it with you and, when appropriate, take it out, stroke it, talk to it, and use it as a conduit for psychic messages of love and reassurance. It is an easy and powerful way to connect with someone or something you are absent from and wish to keep safe.

A Witchful Warning

It is wonderful to use sympathetic magic techniques such as these with love and kindness in mind. However, if you want to make a poppet or effigy with a will to do harm or "teach a lesson," be assured any damage will return to you—many times over and in unexpected ways. Better to rise above negativity and let the situation fall away of its own weight. Leave any lessons that need teaching to forces higher and more powerful than us, and get on with your own life.

ENERGY CENTRES OR CHAKRAS

Energy is everything, so it's high time we discussed our energy centres. The main energy centres in our bodies go from the foot of our spine to the crown of our head. They are known in Sanskrit as *chakras*, and this is probably the most common way of referring to them. That said, I personally prefer the phrase *energy centre*: there is the argument that many Westerners routinely use powerful words and phrases from other cultures and religions without really appreciating their full significance, but I also feel that using equivalent words from our own languages helps us connect with their meanings more directly, as there is less of a linguistic leap for our brains to make.

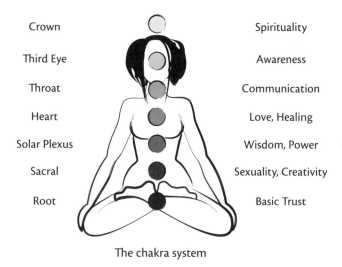

Crown	Spirituality
Third Eye	Awareness
Throat	Communication
Heart	Love, Healing
Solar Plexus	Wisdom, Power
Sacral	Sexuality, Creativity
Root	Basic Trust

The chakra system

As well as the energy centres or wheels situated along and above our spinal column, we also have energy centres that extend above and below us, and in our hands and feet. Beneath our feet is the earth star, which connects us to the grounding protection of the planet. Above our head is the soul star, which aligns with the Divine.

For an easy healing session for yourself or another, check which colour equates with which energy centre on the illustration, and imagining it flooding your physical and etheric bodies. See the energy centres lighting up like coloured jewels or glowing, vibrant flowers. The wilder you go with the intensity of the colours, the easier it is to visualise them, because you have to put your imagination to work.

Spend a few minutes doing this, and then, once you have filled yourself with a surge of energy and are ready to "come back," imagine the centres closing like buds.

Colour Healing

As you have seen in the preceding illustration, colour connects intrinsically with our energy centres, so it is time to immerse ourselves more fully in the colour rays and learn more about their correspondences. Colour work is a deep study and can take us into powerful areas of healing, for ourselves and others.

We all engage in colour magic, often without realising. When we light a pink candle to illuminate a romantic meal, paint a bedroom green to create calm, wear a colour that makes us stand out (or hide), or dye our hair because of the way that shade makes people perceive us, this is all colour magic.

Colour can enhance your mood, draw certain qualities into your life, or even act as a psychological shield. There is a theory that the wearing of red lipstick is an attempt to replicate the lips of the vulva when aroused, but there's more to it than that. Red is emboldening, providing a mask of confidence that may belie our initial reticence. We can trust in the transformational power of the cosmic colour rays.

Absorbing the Colour Rays

Colour rays beam down on us from the sun all the time—we all know white light contains the entire spectrum—so when you concentrate on absorbing specific colours into your cells, you can create changes in your mind, body, and spirit. My bedroom is rose red: a healing, comforting shade, warm and womblike, and deeply regenerating.

When you relax under a clear blue sky, intentionally imagine yourself breathing vivid blue light into your system, your aura, or wherever you feel you need it. Sunbathe and invite the diamond-white rays of the sun to imbue you with the full colour spectrum—just remember to wear a decent sunscreen and shades.

Lie on the grass or walk in a forest to absorb the harmonising green ray. I've never met anyone who feels worse after spending time in a wood, immersed in "the green." When you really tune in, heart and soul, to the green energy of a wood, the concept of nature worship makes complete sense. Forest bathing, or *shinrinyoku*, is a phrase coined by the Japanese to denote a time of calm contemplation, breathing in the green ray in a forest or wood to ameliorate stress and burnout. If you can't get to the natural source, colour lamps and even coloured glasses are known to be effective ways to attune to certain colour frequencies in order to effect a change of state.

Colour Correspondences

Here is a list of the magical, psychological, and energetic correspondences of some colours, many of which you will already know instinctively:

+ **Black:** protection, invisibility, mystery, power, occult

+ **Blue:** healing, spirituality, calm, harmony, grace, flow, communication (throat centre)

+ **Brown:** earthiness and grounding, health and stability, strength (earth star centre)

+ **Rose red:** love, warmth, healing, courage, positive energy, passion, sexuality, roots (root/base centre)

- **Gold:** wealth, opulence, prosperity, positivity, warmth, power (soul star centre)

- **Green:** health and healing, pure love, calm, wealth, nature, growth, forgiveness, resilience (heart centre)

- **Indigo:** spirituality, second sight, sensitivity, magic, psychic power (third eye centre)

- **Orange:** creativity, fun, sociability, stimulation, warmth, confidence (sacral centre)

- **Pink:** love, affection, softness, warmth, beauty, forgiveness (heart centre)

- **Violet:** prosperity, royalty, spirituality, enchantment (crown centre)

- **Silver:** the Goddess, celestial connections, space, femininity, psychic connection (soul star centre)

- **White:** Spirit, divine light, soul health, protection, purity (crown/soul star centre)

- **Yellow:** sunshine, happiness, wealth, success, strength, personal will (solar plexus centre, where your gut feelings come from)

I like to wear black—red occasionally, but mostly black. I'm a Scorpio, and those colours are what I feel comfortable in. They are associated with my ruling planets of Mars and Pluto, although I took to them before I was aware of this. I love black's protective nature, and I associate it with the energy of deities like the Morrigan and Hecate and the qualities of gemstones like onyx and obsidian. My mother also says wearing black gives her a "blank canvas" and allows her to add coloured jewellery or scarves as she sees fit. This is a good approach: if you want to align with the qualities connected with a specific colour ray—say you have writer's block and need the creative boost you know that orange can give you—you can wear a badge, piece of jewellery, or shawl to link with it. Not all of us have the cash or the wardrobe space—or the inclination—to buy entire outfits in every hue, after all. Colour blocking isn't for everyone, especially if you're a witch who likes to stay in the shadows.

Exercise: Colour Me Calm

On the subject of accessorising, here's a colour therapy trick you can try. Take a silk scarf or handkerchief in your chosen hue: let's say you have chosen blue to attract a sense of calm into your life. Hold the piece of silk gently but firmly, and concentrate on your intention as you do so. Imagine your thoughts and energy entering the fabric. Now "see" the blue colour ray beaming into you and unfurling throughout your entire being like a sparkling blue mist, eventually pouring out of your hands and into the silk and creating a circuit of heavenly blue light.

Meditate further on your intention, and when you feel ready, imagine the cosmic rays folding into the silk and sealing up the energy. Now close down the meditation. You can do this by literally saying, "I now close down this meditation," by maybe drawing the shape of the infinity symbol (a figure 8 on its side) or a pentagram in the air with your finger, or by stamping your feet or clapping your hands to ground yourself.

Keep the silk with you as a talisman, imbued energetically with your magnetic thoughts and the blue ray, and as a reminder of this meditation. When you feel yourself getting stressed or anxious, just whip out the silk and run it through your hands, pat your brow with it, or place it over your face or head and close your eyes. It will bring you back to a more peaceful present.

As with all of these practices, the use of your thought and intention is what truly activates the healing.

WHEN YOU RELAX UNDER A CLEAR BLUE SKY, INTENTIONALLY IMAGINE YOURSELF BREATHING VIVID BLUE LIGHT INTO YOUR SYSTEM, YOUR AURA, OR WHEREVER YOU FEEL YOU NEED IT.

PRIORITISING PROTECTION

A word you'll have noticed cropping up frequently in this book is *protection*. You may think that if you're working positive magic, you're not going to be attracting anything unwelcome. Most of the time, that may be true. You could also go out having left your front door wide open, only to return and find everything exactly as you left it—but you probably wouldn't risk it.

When meditating, practicing magic, or doing anything of that ilk, you are opening up your spiritual front door, so you want some control as to who, if anyone, comes striding in. You want to invite the kind of guests who respect and love you, lift your spirits, bring you gifts, and leave at an appropriate time, rather than the kind who pocket your valuables, block the toilet, drink all the beer, and never want to leave.

While like attracts like, there is also a theory that high vibrations can be attractive to lower energies, because they're drawn by the light and want to feed off it. Surely there are enough parasites to deal with in everyday life. Whenever you sense anything that feels unwelcome or sticky, whatever the source, give it short shrift. With this in mind, I'd also suggest that we look within as well as without: usually, the main culprit when it comes to the sabotaging of our own hopes and dreams is ourselves, after all. We are bundles of contradictions, anxieties, doubts, and shifting moods, depending on our circumstances, health situation, hormonal cycles, and what's going on in the skies, so bear this in mind when working to banish negativity. If it seems futile to try to be positive, at least work to neutralise negative feelings, catching them when they arise and banishing them with the phrase "No harmful power: turn this to good," or something similar. I learned this from ethics witch Marion Weinstein; she was the positive magic queen, but she was also nothing if not realistic.[37]

More frequently than we imagine, it is our *own* fearful, keyed-up energy making the planchette move or acting as a "poltergeist" and breaking or moving things around. I remember a friend telling me with alarm that a picture I had painted and framed for her had exploded on her wall: she came home to find glass everywhere, but no one had been near it. Curiously, it happened at exactly the time I was going through some heightened distress. The picture contained my energy and was clearly still linked to me.

Similarly, if the energy that can cause problems or even chaos is within us, so is the energy that can protect us. While I would always recommend connecting with protective deities and forces, I have also realised that one of their lessons is this: protection, if you want it, is within as well as without. Draw it up within you; strengthen yourself with the power of your own conviction; imagine yourself with bones of steel. This is a two-way street, and protective deities, such as the Morrigan, are likely to respect and respond to you more positively, I believe, if you don't just act like a victim, asking for help all the time. We have a duty to empower ourselves in our magic, our behaviour, and our focus.

Stay Discerning

While I am fairly down-to-earth about these things, I believe that just as there are mischievous, bored humans just waiting for the opportunity to cause trouble, there are entities on other planes that do the same. They are every bit as attracted by uncertainty, fear, nerves, or lower vibrations as they are by the bright, shiny high ones, as referred to above. In fact, I suspect they are even more attracted by fear, because that's when they can really mess around with us and have some fun.

If, when meditating, divining, or connecting with Spirit, these types start chiming in with "answers" to your questions—and it can be hard to tell who is really responding to you, no matter who they *say* they are—then the whole thing is, at best, a waste of time. At worst, it can be frightening and hard to control.

I generally advise against using Ouija boards or talking boards. It may be easy to achieve some kind of apparent communication with them, but it's never guaranteed to be what you think it is and, again, what is instigating the movement is often our own consciousness or some lower energy that is easy to reach and eager to play. We are all too easily fooled, because we believe what we wish to be true. Some people become obsessed with the use of these techniques, and I've seen strange things unfold as a result. This kind of dabbling, usually conducted for a hit of occult excitement, is best avoided unless you are confident you know what you're doing. Just as you don't necessarily understand electricity but you do know how to use it respectfully, if you see communication with Spirit in the same way, you won't risk a shock.

Before heading into an altered state, come up with a protective affirmation invoking the white light of the Divine, Spirit, or however you like to refer to the universal forces of love and protection. Learn this affirmation off by heart and say it throughout the day, every day. This way, you will ensure that you have it up your sleeve when you need it. Here is the one I use if you need inspiration: "I am now surrounded, filled, purified, and blessed by the dazzling white light of divine love and protection." Feel free to use it as-is or adapt it to make it natural and personal to you: it will be more effective that way. I recommend using words that give your affirmation or charm a visual pop, so words like *dazzling, shining,* and *sparkling* are going to instantly bring images of light to your mind.

I say this charm three times and imagine myself grounded: roots going into the earth, light travelling up them from the core of the planet and pouring into me, surrounding and sealing me, linking with and amplifying the light in my energy centres. Then, my friends, I am ready to rock.

You can use this technique when you go to a meeting, enter a space that doesn't feel friendly, or just have to leave the house when you feel out of sorts. Divine support and love is always there when you need it. You just have to remember to ask.

One thing to bear in mind: protection is there to liberate us, not restrict us. When we have sensible shields in place, we are free to proceed as we please. As sensitives and lightworkers, we can admittedly become so preoccupied with protecting ourselves that we close ourselves off, hide away, and forget that one of the main reasons for our existence is to shine. As always, balance is essential.

Psychic Attack and Invisibility Cloaks

We all need to toughen our psychic shells sometimes. It's not always enough just to be nice and hope for the best like Paddington Bear. "If we're kind and polite," he says, "the world will be right."[38] I love that for a mantra, and it's a good place to start, but we need to back it up with something beefier than a sweet smile, the occasional hard stare, and marmalade sandwiches for all.

Psychic attack is commonplace: it's definitely not the preserve of cartoon monsters or cackling wicked witches, despite what the old movies and stories tell us. We were misled when we were given the impression that negative influences and psychic attackers are so removed from us. It can happen to anyone, and it can be perpetrated *by* anyone. It comes in the form of negativity, fear, and vengeful emotions that spin out of control and roam unchecked.

You may say that if thoughts and words are so powerful, surely we're making stuff happen all the time. My response to that would be simple: we are. When one feels nervous and vulnerable, one is telegraphing those vibrations, which is why such people often find themselves to be targets of the very people they wish to avoid.

Sometimes—and it's normally when we stop listening to our inner voice or allow it to become clouded—we find ourselves on the wrong side of the tracks or in the presence of someone aggressive, dark, or just annoying. It is at times like these that I employ my invisibility cloak.

I know, Harry Potter, et cetera—but these ideas don't come from nowhere. They're in the collective consciousness, for starters, waiting to link with a mind that is on the same frequency—and everything has a frequency. It's been said before, but we really are like radio sets. The more in touch with your intuition you become, the more stations you pick up, and the more clearly you do. When you team up your intuition with conscious intention so you are deliberately choosing the station you want to tune in to, well, then you're getting somewhere.

If I see someone I want to avoid walking down the street towards me, I imagine myself cloaked in a bright, reflective aura that renders me instantly invisible to any negativity. Any potential trouble glances straight off, and I pass unseen. I sometimes say in my mind, "I am invisible to trouble." I believe it will work, and therefore it does—and I have had plenty of opportunities to test it, because for three years the people who lived in the neighbouring block were exactly the type of people you would cross the street to avoid. Tricky when you live on the same side of the street.

Give it a try with your head held high, not least because not holding your head high doesn't make you less visible; it makes you look more like a potential victim. Far better to imagine yourself in a gleaming cloak and stride forth with the kind of rock-star confidence that would make Madonna take notes and Freddie Mercury go off in a huff. Maybe visualise a few protective beasts of your choosing too: I like wolves and ravens for such purposes.

Exercise: The Auric Egg

A popular method of visualised protection is the auric egg: a giant oval of light that seals around you. Imagine it with a mirror finish if you need to reflect anything back to the sender, as a halo of divine light surrounding your auric body, or as a spiral of light (my mum's favourite). The more dazzling you can make it, the better. See the light expanding, and maybe even add glittering spikes to repel discordant energies or to consciously boost your psychic antennae, if you wish.

Daily invocation of the auric egg can also hone your awareness generally: your energy field is being given some loving attention, so it will eagerly respond with heightened sensitivity to the world around you. You can always incorporate a little dusting of eggshell powder, the magic dust I described in the chapter on the Wheel of the Year, for maximum "tough shell" protection.

I use these techniques before going out or before meditating or spellcasting. It makes me feel safe and secure and also links with the divine realm. All of these techniques are best when you find your own way of doing them: the magic is strongest when it is from the heart. But, if you are in need of inspiration, here's how I like to do it:

1. I imagine golden roots going down from the bottom of my feet deep into Mother Earth, through the layers of soil, clay, crystal, and magma, strengthening and grounding while drawing loving energy up into my body.

2. Then I imagine my crown opening at the top of my head like the petals of a huge white flower to allow in white, sparkling light from the Universal Source or the Divine. The light floods my body and aura with great intensity, washing away

any negativity, which flows out through my feet to transmute into positive energy in the earth.

3. I then imagine this radiant light sealing around me, filling any gaps with pure light. Then I'm ready to begin, well, anything.

Yes, you're "imagining" these things, but that just means you are "imaging" them: creating the image of what you want. This is active, not passive, and visualisation is a vital part of the process of manifesting something very real. Indeed, it is hard to manifest successfully without it.

Stop thinking that *imagination* means "whimsy," "not real," or a "flight of fancy," and start seeing it for the powerful tool that it is. Everything that exists sprang from imagination, so take it seriously and use it well.

Life Is a Garden: Keep It Weeded

A garden is a good analogy for our psyches, our energy fields, and our lives. It doesn't become or stay beautiful without planning, work, and determination: you need to keep it tended. Keep thinking about what you'd like to see in it and the kind of creatures you'd like to attract. If nothing else, it's a good idea to keep it weeded of any negative influences that have crept in.

Going within and imagining how life would look if it were our very own plot of land is a quick way to sense how well things are going and whether we need to do any pruning, mowing, digging, or planting. Is something positive blossoming, such as a new friendship or creative project? Let's make sure it has sufficient space, light, and water to bloom. Has a negative person or situation taken root? Time to get weeding.

It's sad but true that life can present us with a cavalcade of characters who are rarely as they seem—or how we want them to be. Our kindness can be construed as stupidity or naïveté, and sometimes people we treat well repay us with disrespect. These infiltrators to our spiritual gardens are often necessary teachers, if harsh ones. Understand why they've appeared in your life and then weed them out. Don't waste any more of your time with them than necessary, and certainly don't fertilise the situation with any more of your energy. Take the lessons and let them learn theirs. They now reside in your compost bin—and compost helps things grow.

A wise friend of mine, Pauline Godfrey, now in Spirit, used to wear a badge that said, "Kindness is cool." I'd go further and say it's also brave, intelligent, and tough. We've all experienced hurts and betrayals, but to still act with kindness and an open heart in spite of everything? To be so secure in yourself that you respond with love even when faced with hostility? That's profoundly evolved.

Keep being kind, but keep yourself and your energy—your garden—protected. Don't allow toxicity to ruin the flowerbeds. There's no use being persistently kind to others if you're going to be unkind to yourself—and you'll keep getting those "teachers" until you learn that lesson. Accept, understand, forgive if you can, wish them well, and move on. It's not up to you to fix anyone, because everyone has their reasons for behaving the way they do. Just pull up the bindweed and let in the sun. If you can't avoid irritants, or worse, right now, just say this to yourself: "I'm giving this as much of my energy as it deserves—which is none at all." Before long, your psychic garden will be filled with blossoms rather than blight.

It's useful to note triggering behaviours and ask, "Does this push my buttons because I actually do this myself?" Be unflinching with yourself. You'll be better off. As the pioneering feminist and social activist Gloria Steinem famously said, the truth will set you free—but first it will piss you off.[39]

FEELING "OTHER"

This is a feeling so many of us can relate to in our different ways, and yet we feel so alone with it. Sometimes we're supremely conscious of our "otherness" simply sitting on a park bench. Sometimes we feel rays of anything from curiosity to enmity when we're just getting on with our work. I'd advise a daily dose of auric egg protection when experiencing this kind of anxiety, but I would also suggest taking the time to consider this feeling of separation—even ostracisation. In doing so we may attempt a fresh understanding of it rather than packing it away into a part of our psyches that is hidden but that still hurts anytime it is triggered.

While it is not a feeling confined to self-conscious teenage years, it is generally at school where many people feel this first and most keenly and have the least understanding of it—especially if we are being outright bullied or alienated. Whether our persecutors even understood it at the time, a light inside us shone forth and they couldn't handle it. It didn't matter if we tried to be inconspicuous. Lights don't work like that.

Bullying can happen at different times, come in different forms, and be sparked by myriad reasons, but anything "a bit different" can be a target. Let's face it: those of us who walk this path generally *are* a bit different, naturally. You're just being you, but some people subtly perceive those differences and, not understanding them, take them as a threat. They will have their own reasons for this attitude, and those reasons have nothing to do with us. It can take a lifetime to recover from the scars of bullying and victimization, and indeed some of us never fully heal. But we owe it to ourselves to try to gain a better understanding of what we went through, with compassion and forgiveness for ourselves and how we responded at the time and for the other people involved. Not easy, I know, but it can be helpful to bear in mind that hostile behaviour can often be borne of projections. For example, if someone is acting as if they're better than you, could it be that deep down they think you are better than them? Before reacting, consider this and proceed with compassion rather than defensiveness.

Either way, that light, that "otherness" they couldn't cope with and had to attack—maybe you couldn't cope with it either and wished you were "normal" so you could blend in. This is standard stuff for sensitive souls, but if our coping and defence mechanisms go into overdrive, the effects can be binding. Project yourself back with a fresh understanding of what is happening here, and promise yourself you will no longer dull that shine to make other people feel comfortable.

I'd like to share some tips if you or someone you love is going through something similar—and these issues are by no means exclusive to teenagers:

1. Consciously build your psychic defences using the techniques in this book—and remember that you have those defences in the first place.

2. Be friendly but don't bond too fast. It's wiser to let friendships unfold naturally.

3. Galvanise your sense of humour. Learning to laugh at life is a good skill to have. This is not to trivialise trauma—some things cannot be treated lightly. But teenage life can seem so serious, not least because most of us don't have much in the way of experience or perspective.

4. To expand on that last point, pick your battles and make it your mission to rise above the rest. Your worth does not depend on another person's attitude towards you.

MAGIC WORDS AND AFFIRMATIONS

I want you to start talking to yourself. No, it doesn't have to be a sign you're going crazy: we're talking to ourselves all the time in our minds anyway. I just want you to get more intentional with it, because words and thoughts shape your consciousness and, thus, your life. They are magnetic and transformational.

You may recall my earlier story of the Japanese scientist Masaru Emoto, whose experiment with frozen water showed that water exposed to kind words created beautiful, healthy patterns while a bottle labeled with cruel insults contained warped, ugly crystal formations. The message from this experiment is that we must take greater care over our words to ourselves and others. Water is easy to encode. We are seventy percent water. Do the math. We know how negative language can damage us and, similarly, how a loving word can make us blossom, so take what you say—and think—seriously and watch the words you allow in from others.

Words form, shift, instruct, create. "In the beginning was the Word" and affirmations are nothing new, but it is amazing what you can do when you really put your energy into it. Our minds—our brains—are in charge of our bodies, the brain is flexible, and we create new neural pathways with persistent conscious thoughts, good or bad. Use this power and see how you can improve your health.

We are often told that when it comes to the Law of Attraction, we must really feel it for it to work. This rarely comes easily, but try to find a way to conjure a feeling of excitement for the result that you *know* is coming your way. Visualise it, draw it, create it, or write about how it will be and how fired up you are about it. The vibration of excitement is magnetic; if you can invoke those feelings when you make a wish, you may be surprised by how easily the result manifests into your life.

Rhyme and Reason

Clarify what you want, word it into a catchy, rhythmic, or rhyming affirmation, and repeat it until it impresses itself on your subconscious mind. Soon, you *will* feel it. It's no accident that many charms and spells are made up of rhyming couplets. It's not strictly necessary to use rhyme, but it gives them a rhythm and a flow—and makes them easier to remember. Music and poetry connect with other realms quickly and effectively, so when writing or chanting your intentions, make them rhyme and see if things flow a little more readily. You'll start to see hints that what you wished for is coming to pass: a coin in the street, a heart-shaped piece of confetti in your path, a name that keeps cropping up. What you want is on its way. Get ready.

Go Over the Top

I have always loved this singer's tip: if you are worried you won't reach the high note, imagine yourself going well over it and you will invariably reach the desired note with ease. I apply this to affirmations and magic: if I need an extra positive charge, I go way over the top with my language to leave no margin for error. So if I want to, say, be rich, I will say something like, "I now affirm that I am magnificently wealthy, my lifestyle is fabulously opulent, and riches and abundance now flood into my life unstoppably and in perfect ways." See what I mean? Those adjectives give you a dazzling visual too. As always, using the words "I am" rather than "I want" is more effective: "I want" has an air of lack, but "I am" aligns you with the qualities you desire now.

Saying "I have beautiful eyes" while you apply mascara, for example, can be a glamour spell if you are infusing those words with intention: they create changes, and those changes will be perceived by others. The word *glamour* originally describes a visually transformative spell that can change one's appearance and bewitch the onlooker. We can use glamour magic in our own way every day.

Admittedly, seeing ourselves as beautiful at all can be a stretch: so many of us are out of touch with our true beauty. Anything that encourages a positive reconsideration of ourselves is tops with me. Try intercepting that critical inner voice and using words that have the greatest emotional charge. If you feel it's more effective to tell yourself you are "stunning," "magnificent," or "majestic," then do it. Like a cat being stroked, we rise to these words, we respond to them—we *become* them.

It doesn't happen overnight—especially as many of us have been using the opposite kind of language with ourselves for years—but it will happen. Language works on a cellular level. Use it wisely and you'll see yourself as heavenly in no time.

The Mind-Body Matrix

You can talk yourself confident, entrancing, rich, youthful, peaceful, strong, and healthy. It's like giving yourself a bunch of flowers or paying yourself compliments even when you don't feel like it. *Especially* when you don't feel like it. Just keep going, because you will change your vibration until you *do* feel like it. This way of thinking and being has worked its way into the mainstream and is even being recommended by orthodox medical practitioners as the mind-body connection is becoming better understood.

When working with your body in this way, you must believe you will have instant results, but don't beat yourself up if you don't get them or if you see only a slight improvement at first. We have been trained to think we don't have this kind of ability at all, so cut yourself some slack. Persevere, and appreciate any incremental improvements. At the very least, assure yourself that you are creating shifts you aren't consciously aware of yet.

Putting Out the Call

When you speak to yourself in this way, you are putting out a call, and whenever you put out a call for anything—healing being a good example—you may find you are guided towards a conventional solution. Acknowledge what comes, and follow the signs. Magic doesn't happen in a puff of smoke and glitter: you may have an instant manifestation, or you may just feel drawn to a certain solution or down a different route. If in doubt, just add to your affirmations that you wish to be shown exactly what you need to do, clearly and perfectly.

There is another reason why this is an important witchful thinking technique: by talking to yourself in an uplifting way when you might otherwise be thinking negatively, you get into a habit of thinking and speaking purposefully. This will make it a great deal easier to manifest what you want, whether you are casting a spell or not. Keep your thoughts and words as conscious, meaningful, positive, and truthful as you can, and expect to see a difference in all areas of your life.

PLACEBO POWER

The placebo effect is magical in itself: it proves how much influence is in our minds, our will, and our belief—not to mention the written word. When I was a lot younger, I used to make placebos for myself with jelly beans, charge them with intention—whether to dissolve a headache or magnetise something I wanted—and place them in pretty envelopes with different "properties" written on the front. The more fun I had with this, the more placebos I would prepare for myself. Beauty, confidence, a good day at school, happy dreams, a successful date: you name it, I had a jelly bean for it. The action of taking time to prepare these treatments with lighthearted but definite intention and carefully chosen words made a tangible difference to me.

I know what you're thinking: theoretically, placebos only work if you're using them on someone who doesn't know they're fake. But the fact is, I felt the acts of deciding, naming, and then consuming could at least do *something*, and even effect a change of state.

If this playful idea chimes with you, give it a try and administer when required. The worst that will happen is you'll have eaten some jelly beans, which is never a bad thing—unless you're allergic to jelly beans, of course. Find something that works for you, if you feel inspired to.

✳ WITCH TIP ✳
THE ULTIMATE LOVE POTION

Words, words, words are all very well, but the most surefire way to create magic between two people is that most simple act (or is it?) of *listening*, because genuine listeners are so rare.

Most people are thinking about what they want to say next rather than giving you their full attention. Many humans, essentially, are self-absorbed, needy, vain, and insecure. This puts them at a disadvantage, because no matter how arrogant they are, they will always be at the mercy and manipulation of that person who gives them the attention and soft-soaping they crave. The good news is that you can use this knowledge and power for good. Listen well—with love, sincerity, and appreciation, for the right reasons and not just for your own agenda. I guarantee you will be considered particularly lovable.

There's an old tale of a charming man who was invited to all the best parties because he was such a great conversationalist. In reality, he barely spoke; he just knew how to listen.

"WHY AREN'T MY SPELLS WORKING?"

Traditionally, we are told we can expect results from a magical working in "three days, three weeks, or three months." If you still aren't seeing any manifestations—bearing in mind that they don't always appear in the way you expect—then try again, do something different, or have a think about whether it's really right for you at this time.

The Universe is a good listener, so be patient rather than repeating yourself every day: this only sends out the signal that you didn't believe in what you were doing in the first place. Just send it out with confidence and certainty. You can always weave in a request like, "Show me what I need to see," or, "Show me a clear sign in the coming days."

Sometimes that sign is immediate. Once, I had to perform a banishing spell to gently remove a persistent admirer from my life. As soon as the work was complete, I opened the curtains and the first thing I saw was a black van parked by my gate with "Romeo Removals" emblazoned on the side. I had to chuckle, and I was reassured that the wheels were in motion.

We all have to accept that we don't always know what we need, so another reason a spell might be ineffective is that the Universe has something better in store. The success of your original spell might have meant you missed out on something far better in the long run. It's often difficult for humans to see the bigger picture, so while we know we can weight the dice, we must still trust that the Divine knows best and has our back. Therefore, I repeat: be patient, be positive, and stay perceptive. You may even have already received what you need—you just might not recognise it yet.

When You Get What You Want

While we must always work magic with a fervent belief that it *will* work, it's always a thrill when we experience the pleasing results of a well-planned spell. Unfortunately, many of us don't notice when our work is effective, not least because spells don't always manifest as we expect, and sometimes the results develop incrementally. Apart from anything else, we are often too busy moving on to the next thing that needs fixing to really notice when we've had a little—or big—win.

Make an effort to notice the signs that things are shifting, and when you do feel you have successfully pulled something you want into your realm, don't just tick it off and move on. Take a moment to celebrate, be happy, and give thanks. You're doing this yourself, but you're also getting a little cosmic help—or a lot of it. So take a moment to be grateful, and write your appreciative feelings down in a journal: nicer than a cellphone app and easier to look back on. You could even make a simple offering, perhaps of candlelight or incense: both of these create a bridge to the other world and attract the attention of the Divine. Choose colours and scents that correspond with the nature of the result you have achieved. For instance, use a green or gold candle and sandalwood incense if you've received a windfall. Blue wax and rose incense connects with peace and healing. Black candles and frankincense are appropriate if you want to acknowledge the protective forces around you. Alternatively, just use a white candle and a fragrance of your choice: the acknowledgment and the intention is sufficient, so don't panic if you can't get your hands on anything too specific. With witchful thinking, thought and focus is all.

Giving Back

Think about what connects with your deity or guide and, if you are able and have the time, do some volunteering accordingly. For example, if Hecate has helped you, you could volunteer at a dog shelter or offer to walk someone's pooch when they're at work. Alternatively, if you have invoked assistance from Isis, the queen of magic words, you could help out at a library on an adult literacy program, or you could just conduct your own private work, meditating, chanting, and sending out magical healing energy to those who need it. Has generous Jupiter removed obstacles from your path? Donate to a charity or give a gift to a child who would really appreciate it: there are charities that collect gifts for children who wouldn't otherwise receive anything at Christmas, for example. If Old Father Saturn has stepped in, maybe give back by volunteering at an old people's home, spending time with residents and engaging with their stories. You will learn from these precious wise ones, and they will brighten in your presence. These are just ideas to get your cogs whirring.

The main thing is that you give back in your own way—whether tangibly or in terms of energy or thought. This is active gratitude, and it keeps a healthy energy dialogue going between the two worlds. Enjoy the reciprocity.

IT'S OFTEN DIFFICULT FOR HUMANS TO SEE THE BIGGER PICTURE, SO WHILE WE KNOW WE CAN WEIGHT THE DICE, WE MUST STILL TRUST THAT THE DIVINE KNOWS BEST AND HAS OUR BACK.

ENERGETIC PERCEPTION: SPIRIT LIGHTS AND ORBS

We can sense psychic energy, build it, and use it. Some believe we can even see it, and that brings me to the subject of orbs. An orb—a circular shape that looks like a light anomaly on a photograph—is believed to be a capture of psychic energy or paranormal activity. Sometimes you can catch them in motion, like a little comet with a trail. Many believe them to be either angels or loved ones in Spirit.

Orbs in photographs are often white but can be different colours, and they sometimes appear to have patterns. One thing is for sure: they love a good party. I, for one, have many photographs of jolly gatherings where we appear to have lots of company in the form of orbs galore. I'm always pleased to see them, and I'm rather disappointed when I don't.

Orbs are hard to see with the naked eye, although I accidentally saw quite a few of them flying about when I was taking a picture on my phone recently. I was in my bedroom and wanted to take a picture of my cat. The light was dim, so it was a slow exposure, and just before it finally "clicked" a rush of orbs flew across the lens in front of me. At first I wondered if they were dust particles, but they were too large, and while I captured them on a couple of subsequent photos, they were not visible on others. It's the room in which I do a lot of my spiritual reading and meditation, so it makes sense that the vibration is attractive to psychic energy.

Spirit lights are more perceptible to the naked eye, and I see them regularly: so much so that I thought I'd better have my eyes checked, but thankfully there's nothing wrong with them. Just ghosts, then. Some people interpret the lights as a sign of angelic presence. Whatever they are, I feel they come from a place of love.

When you see a spirit light, say hello, thank it, salute it, or blow it a kiss. That's what I do. Spirit is keen to attract your attention, but it can never force communication. It's always up to you. Appropriately, as I write this, I can feel a feathery tickle on my cheek: a sign I have company.

If you take the presence of spirit lights as an invitation to converse or connect, remember to call on the Divine and your spirit guides or guardian angel to place a cloak of protection and love around you before attempting any communication. In fact, I do this before any meditation or ritual or just before I go to sleep. It is a lovely way to change state and stay safe.

SOME PEOPLE INTERPRET
THE LIGHTS AS A SIGN
OF ANGELIC PRESENCE.
WHATEVER THEY ARE,
I FEEL THEY COME FROM
A PLACE OF LOVE.

PYRAMID POWER

We witches do tend to be fond of pointy things. There's something about them, from the cartoon witch's hat, which points straight to the heavens while focusing our psychic energy, to the traditional Cone of Power, an energy shape used to channel and direct intention within a magic circle. Then there are crystal points, athames, magic wands for really important pointing, and now, enter the pyramid.

Pyramids connect with the energy of the earth, and they can play a positive and practical role in our lives. I don't love the fact that the pyramids in Egypt were opened and plundered: what one person might see as archaeological "discovery," another will understandably view as grave robbery. As we now know, the twentieth-century explorers who discovered the mummified remains of the teenage pharaoh Tutankhamun came to sticky ends shortly after opening the tomb.[40] Either it hadn't occurred to them that these sarcophagi would be energetically protected, or they unwisely didn't take magic seriously enough to worry about it.

Orgone Energy

The word *energy* appears frequently in this book because it is at the heart of everything: it *is* everything. This life force energy is also known as *orgone*, *chi*, or *prana*, and it can be amplified within the shape of a pyramid. The writer and occultist William Burroughs was a prominent advocate of orgone energy research,[41] while Hollywood star Gloria Swanson kept an orgone pyramid underneath her bed and swore she felt its "tingling" effects[42]—perhaps she was having an org-asm. Joking aside, orgasmic energy is often used in magic to "ensoul" sigils or lend power to manifesting. It's easy to think of different ways in which an orgasm—building to a climax before a release—can be used as a potent tool for spellcraft.

You can get crystal orgone pyramids, but a popular option is the copper frame pyramid with a wooden base. The copper pyramid never needs cleansing—although that doesn't mean they won't need dusting. (I know; I found that disappointing too.) They come in various sizes: I have one just big enough to place a jar of moisturiser under—and I'll tell you why the heck I would want to do *that* in a moment—but you can find pyramids large enough to meditate and even sleep beneath.

Pyramid Purification

Pyramids charge and purify our atmosphere with negative ions, neutralising the broth of electromagnetic frequencies that surrounds us, so it's healthy to have them in the home or the office. Anything that is placed beneath the pyramid will become purer and higher in vibration. Some people place the pyramid over an area of pain and report positive results. Others have, in the name of experimentation, placed water underneath the apex and felt energised after drinking it. Foodstuffs placed underneath take an inordinately long time to go off.[43] This sheds light on the fact that the ancient Egyptians would place food in the tombs of their kings and queens to sustain the deceased on their journey to the underworld: the pyramid shape of the tomb ensured those perishable gifts would stay fresh for as long as possible. The bodies themselves stayed in fairly good shape too.

We can use pyramids to cleanse and supercharge everything from crystals, sigils, and ritual jewellery to tinctures, potions, vitamins, and face creams. It's also an idea to meditate with a small pyramid on your lap, or you can write down whatever you want to manifest and place the paper under the pyramid.

If you really need tangible evidence that pyramids work, place a dead battery or a dull razor blade under the pyramid overnight: it'll be as good as new in the morning. You can have lots of fun with pyramids, and the effects never cease to amaze me.

DISTANT HEALING

If your hands sometimes get inexplicably hot or you see hazy energy around them in low light, you may have a natural gift for healing— although in truth everyone is capable of directing healing energy. When my hands get suddenly hot, my body is telling me I'm holding on to energy that is bursting to go somewhere and do something, so when this happens to you, think about who, what, or where might benefit from some distant, or absent, healing.

My grandfather was a hands-on energy healer: his hands would not actually touch the skin, though, just hover over it. From my own, less-experienced point of view, I'm more comfortable with distant healing, not least because there is less distraction and pressure. If the person you wish to send positive energy to is open to such things and isn't going to think you're harbouring some kind of a messiah complex, discuss it with them. Ask if they are comfortable with the idea of you doing this, and if they are, tell them when you are going to do it so they can make sure they are relaxed and receptive— although this is not essential. The possibilities with distant healing are infinite: time and space are irrelevant.

Being a Channel

You'll be drawing down divine energy, directed from the cosmos and from the earth, and *this* is where the healing is coming from. You are the channel, and Spirit is utilising your own energy—with your consent—to go where the healing is needed. Add to the divine energy with your own love and intention, by all means, but know that the healing is ultimately coming from another place. Also know that by doing this you are not taking on another person's pain, but working with the Divine with the intent to dissolve it and help the recipient's body heal itself, according to their free will and receptivity and always for the good of all. Don't expect credit or thanks for this work, and don't publicly trumpet that you are doing it: this is not about you or your ego. This is about doing the work and assisting the energy in where it needs to go.

Keep It General

Trust that Spirit knows best and keep specifics out of it. You may wish to send healing to a friend with a headache, but the tension could be caused by an emotional issue you know nothing about, perhaps something even they haven't made the connection with yet. It's also a good idea to send general positive healing energy to doctors, hospitals, medical staff, and scientists to give them energy, strength, and ingenuity, for the good of all and according to their free will and whether their higher selves accept the energy. If they don't, then it has not gone to waste: you have still created a positive charge.

Be general, as if you are handing over a gleaming ball of pure golden light and allowing Spirit to shape it in the way it sees fit. It may be directed in specific ways, or it may just cocoon your friend, a location, or a situation in love. It will know what to do and, wherever it goes, it will do some good.

If there is someone you know who is suffering badly and is ready to leave the earth plane, again, it is best if we are not too specific about how the healing energy is used: the recipient's higher self and spirit team (angels, guardians, guides, and assembled light beings) will know what to do. Your healing energy could be used, as directed by Spirit, as palliative care to ease the psyche, soften pain, assist in the journey, and release any energetic attachments where necessary to lighten the onward journey.

Healing Aftereffects

For those of you wondering whether it is possible to give—or receive—"too much" healing, from the healer's point of view it is possible to become drained and in need of replenishment after an intense session. However, for the recipient, my instinct is that, as with vitamin C, the person or situation takes what it requires and resists what it doesn't. I like to imagine excess energy being absorbed by the earth to be used accordingly. Nothing is wasted and, unlike with prescription meds, you cannot overdose. This is my personal feeling on the matter, but it's one that makes sense to me.

When I was younger, I'd end up with headaches and fatigue after sending healing. Now I'm more careful: I don't overdo it, I make sure I stay grounded, and I ensure I'm visualising the energy coming not from me but rather from the Divine *through* me.

Method for Directing Healing Energy

There are many books on energy or spiritual healing, Reiki, of course, and other forms of bodywork. I recommend finding a guided video that you like, because it's easier than trying to remember words from a book. All the same, here is a rundown of the method that works for me:

- Take three deep breaths to prepare your body and mind, and imagine yourself rooted to the earth and surrounded by a cloak of divine light.

- Call in your posse. This could be spirit guides; angels of love, light, and healing; and any healers on the other side, known and unknown, who would like to work with you. You may personally know people in Spirit who could help. Invite them all in to assist, direct, or amplify your work, if they wish.

- When you feel grounded and surrounded, ask the Divine Power to use you, under grace, according to free will and for the good of all, as a channel of healing. Ask that your guides assist with this and that the guides of the person you wish to send healing to will allow the energy to be accepted.

- Then imagine two divine hands a few feet above your head (at the soul star centre) opening up and allowing a waterfall of diamond-white light to pour into your crown and down into the heart centre. Now imagine golden light coursing up from the earth, through your roots, and into your body to mingle with the diamond-white light at your heart centre.

- The healing energy forms a glowing globe, which pulses and grows bigger with every breath. See the light being fortified by the healers around you.

- Now see, with great clarity, the face of the person you are sending healing to. See their face, clothes, expression, and how and where they are sitting. Ask permission from this person's higher self to allow this pure healing light to go exactly where it is needed, should it be accepted.

- Now return your thoughts to the ball of light, which is now big enough to engulf an adult human and their energy field. Give it another boost, asking your gang to power it up so it is shining brighter than ever. Imagine it imbued with waves of green healing light (or blue, or whatever you feel is needed).

- See it rising with you up through the roof and travelling to where it needs to be. Once this glowing light reaches the desired location, it sinks down into the room where the recipient is sitting. See it surrounding your friend entirely (unless you have a strong feeling for it not to do so). They are now receiving healing energy. Visualise them looking happy and relaxed or even saying, "I feel so much better." Make it as clear and easy to believe as possible.

+ Stand with the assembled healers in front of the healing light, charging it with love. Watch the beams and waves of colour and light pulsing through the globe of energy, going wherever it needs to go. Spend as much time on this as required.

+ Finally, see the magnificent light sealing securely around your friend, infusing their being with health and positivity. They look happy, relaxed, at ease, better than ever.

+ It is time to allow them to rest and integrate the energy. Gently imagine yourself back in your room. Remember, we are working outside of the realms of time and space, so you don't have to imagine yourself coming back the way you went, unless you want to. Wiggle your fingers and toes, stretch, and feel that you are "back" in your body.

+ Now, thank the healing posse one and all, the Divine for using you as a conduit, and the recipient and their guides for accepting and assisting in this healing.

After this meditation, take your time and slowly ground yourself. Move around, stamp your feet, put on some music, or have a cup of tea and something to eat. Try to relax, drink lots of water, and don't do anything too demanding for the next few hours. Better still, have a bath and go to bed: you may have interesting dreams.

MEDITATION FOR PERSONAL AND UNIVERSAL HEALING

When I was a teenager, I used to think it was all very well for monks and yogis to be so peaceful in their isolation: they weren't exactly dealing with the real world. But I now understand that their dedicated lives of meditation actually work towards increasing the peace and harmony of the world. They draw down more light when they are in a peaceful, high-vibrational state, as do we. When you meditate, you are sending out peaceful, positive ripples. If nothing else, you are not creating any negative ripples. And don't kid yourself that you aren't sending out ripples. You're rippling, all right. All the time.

If you have ever stopped yourself from meditating because you think you're being selfish, then quit that way of thinking right now. Not only do we all deserve that time to just be still, but it is worth remembering that when you do something that raises your vibration, the benefits go way beyond the self. As my mother told me, when you give healing, you get a dose of healing yourself, and I believe meditating works the same way. So do yourself, and everyone else, a favour. The world needs you happy, light, and peaceful, radiating good energy like sunbeams. It does not need you beleaguered, grumpy, self-righteous, and practically wilting the flowers with your negativity. Turn off your phone, get comfortable, pop on an eye mask, and just shut out the world for a bit. If you have time to scroll down the feed on Instagram or Twitter for twenty minutes, you have time for this.

A Reminder to Be Mindful

If meditation isn't working for you for whatever reason, or if you feel too agitated to sit peacefully, do something menial—like washing the dishes—and think *only* about what you are doing. This is mindfulness. Appreciate the scent of the soap, the warmth of the water, how clean you can make even the dirtiest cup. Think about the elements that everything consists of: the water, the fire that heats it, the earth in the crockery, the air in the bubbles, the prisms on their surface.

All of this will bring you back to a state of being present and prevent your mind from wandering into darker areas. I know this is something many of us have read about and perhaps practiced thousands of times, but if you're anything like me, you sometimes need reminding to be mindful.

When you meditate or are in a high-vibrational state, you are doing yourself good, and not just in that present moment: you're building the momentum for more positive, harmonious moments going forward. But you are also doing beautiful witchful work for those around you—in your home, in your community, for the whole planet.

✳ WITCH TIP ✳
"WHAT DOES THIS MEAN?"

If a ritual, meditation, or dream has left you with more questions than answers, try to avoid asking another person their opinion and trust your own instincts, at least at first. Only you know what it can relate to, because only you know every corner of your life, what is happening in your mind, your plans, your memories, and your overall take on things. Another person will take the isolated instance you have given them, offer a generic explanation, and possibly send you down the wrong track according to their own reference points. Ask your higher self, be patient, and trust what comes via your own intuition; in fact, this method will help you improve your intuitive powers.

You can apply this to oracles too. When new to an oracle deck, for example, as you first pull a card, pause and study it. Feel its energy and write down what you think it represents to you *before* you consult the instruction booklet. It's a great way to develop your awareness and self-trust.

WHEN YOU MEDITATE OR ARE IN A HIGH-VIBRATIONAL STATE, YOU'RE BUILDING THE MOMENTUM FOR MORE POSITIVE, HARMONIOUS MOMENTS GOING FORWARD.

DIVINATION TECHNIQUES

Divination is the art of prophecy, and this book wouldn't be complete without a nod to a few techniques. Whether you use cards, crystal gazing, runes, or pendulums, divination is something humans have instinctively used since childhood for guidance and fun, whether by flipping a coin to find an answer or by pulling the petals off a daisy to find out whether "he loves me" or "he loves me not."

But telling the future is not just a parlour game or a joke: as many of you can already attest, divination is at its best when developed as a useful skill. Yes, some people are more naturally attuned to their psychic side than others, but like anything, practice and commitment is important, and we can all develop the ability if we try.

There are many techniques from different cultures and ancient family customs, and these can be "taught" or picked up intuitively. Pyromancy is a good example: as the heat and darkness envelops and relaxes our senses, we easily find ourselves reading the fire in the grate from the shapes that arise and any strange cracks or sputters we hear. We can also instinctively "read" the behaviour of incense smoke as it shifts and sways, taking our wishes and thoughts up to the heavens. We can sit quietly with another person's piece of jewellery—with their consent, if they are living—and listen to what it tells us: this is psychometry, an art in which my mother was adept. We can ascertain the way a situation might turn by casting runes or bones from the kitchen onto a surface and interpreting the symbols that present themselves. On a warm, dry day, we can lie back on the grass and see what images appear in the clouds as an answer to a question or a thought.

Divination is a book in itself, but here are a few methods to try, if you haven't already.

Augury

This is the ancient method of interpreting the behaviour of birds. These days, we're unlikely to read much meaning into the flight paths of birds—unless they career right into our window—but almost everyone can instinctively appreciate the significance of a dove or a robin. "Robins appear when loved ones are near," goes the saying, connecting our red-breasted chums with those in Spirit. Goldfinches, on the other hand, link with the prosperous energy of Jupiter. The sight of any bird close by can be a comfort or an omen of dread, but one way or another they usually have a message. Some people feel nervous when crows and ravens appear, although witches are fond of them. Celtic deity the Morrigan comes accompanied by ravens and crows, as does Norse god Odin.

Swans, pigeons, and sparrows are beloved by Venus, as are collared doves; the last, to me, denote Spirit being close. As ever, your intuition and your own associations will play their part in your interpretations. Research this subject if you feel called to, and if a specific bird appears in your dreams, take note.

Books and Songs

This is a fun and easy way of divining an answer that my family and I have always loved: think of a question and then allow yourself to be guided to a book on the shelf. Open it at a page and see what message is there for you. In the old days, people would do this with the Bible—possibly because this was one of the few books you could find in almost every home—but use any tome you feel drawn to.

Another way to do this would be to ask the question, respectfully request a clear answer, and then switch your iPod to shuffle or turn on the radio or TV to see what song or sentence comes up. Don't feel you need to give the Universe time to prepare. We are talking about connecting with a dimension where time and space are meaningless and things can happen in the twinkling of an eye. This is hard to get our heads around, I grant you, but we just have to trust it. The Divine is always on time.

Candle Divination

Have a question in your mind, and then stare gently into the flame of a candle, allowing yourself to drift softly into an altered state. Having candlelight to focus on can be helpful if you tend to get distracted. See what thoughts appear in your mind. The behaviour of the flame, smoke, and wax themselves can also be telling, as author and candle-magic expert Madame Pamita explains: "Reading a candle can get quite intricate, but you can do a simple reading by looking at your candle in the following way:

Pyromancy: A steady burning flame shows a strong spell. A flame that is burning high means that emotions are high (not necessarily a good thing, depending on the spell). A flame that is weak or goes out shows lack of energy or passion.

Capnomancy: No soot or smoke on a glass-encased jar or vigil candle means the spell has a clear path. Heavy soot or smoke indicates spiritual blockages and how far the soot goes down from the top to the bottom of the glass indicates how long it will take to overcome. Grey or white haze on the glass indicates that spirit guides wish to help with the situation.

Ceromancy: Look for symbolic shapes in the wax remains and read them like tea leaves. Common shapes are hearts, which indicate love, and tears, which indicate sadness, but you may see symbols related to spirit animals or even people in the wax remains of your candle.

Dowsing (Pendulum)

You can divine yes or no answers to questions by using a pendulum, a necklace, or even a ring on a piece of string, depending on the way the weight swings. People have traditionally divined the gender of children this way. Just be aware that the strength of your subconscious desires can also cause the pendulum to move in the way you want it to rather than present a truthful answer—which is quite magical in itself. Ask it to show you yes or no, or give it options to choose from: the direction of swing differs for everyone.

If you really want to be sure, write a "Yes" and a "No," or different options relevant to your questioning, on separate pieces of paper. Then turn them over so you can't see which is which, and dowse over them. Shuffle them around with your eyes closed between questions so you can't cheat.

Dowsing (Rods)

You can also dowse with rods to find sources of water or anything else that might be underground that you'd like to reveal: they will move "by themselves" when you pick up on water or energy lines. Traditionally, dowsing rods are made of copper or a wood such as hazel, but you can easily use old coat hangers.

Scrying

The word means "seeing," "peeping," or "gazing," and this can involve the use of a black mirror, a crystal ball, or just a bowl of water. Allowing your mind and eyes to relax and then gaze can cause visions to appear, although this takes practice. If nothing happens yet, just treat it as a meditation and be patient.

Tarot

Tarot is an immense subject in and of itself. Some say you must only be gifted a set of cards, while others don't mind buying their own.

Either way, I advise cleansing your deck with incense smoke before use and adding a little blessing or greeting. See them as friends: a new and treasured addition to the family. Use them as much as possible, not just to learn and practice, but to bond with them and impress your vibrations upon them. Wrap them in silk or velvet, maybe with a crystal or two if it feels appropriate, and place them somewhere safe but accessible when not in use.

The cards are tools of guidance; the real work comes from your own intuition. Learn the classic interpretations, but I strongly suggest sitting with each one without your book of instructions and writing down what *you* feel it means. Tap into the collective unconsciousness, the timeless wisdom from countless minds. Give yourself time with this.

Tasseomancy

This is the art of reading tea leaves: *tasse* means "cup" in French. Make a pot of tea with your question in mind. Pour the tea—don't use a strainer—and once you have drunk it, swirl the leaves with a little of the remaining liquid.

Place the cup upside down onto its saucer and turn it clockwise thrice. Lift it and see where the leaves have settled, and into what shapes. The website Crystalinks has a helpful list of the symbols you might encounter,[44] and as with everything, there is plenty of literature out there to guide you further. If you aren't a lover of tea, coffee grounds also work nicely.

Here are a few examples of what might turn up in your cup:

+ **Anchor:** stability, peace, strength, constancy

+ **Acorn:** at top: success; at bottom: good health

+ **Bell:** spirituality, unexpected news

- **Book:** a sign you will find your answer in something written; open book: good news; closed book: you need to look into something

- **Cross:** protection

- **Gun:** anger, sex

- **Hat:** head, consciousness

- **Heart:** pleasure, love

- **House:** security, success

- **Ladder:** promotion, rise, DNA

- **Ring:** a phone call, an engagement

- **Star:** health and happiness, success, Goddess energy

You can get specially designed fortune-telling cups with painted symbols inside, or you can just see what your instincts tell you. If a symbol means something personal to you or someone you know, but means something different in a generic book of symbols, go with your gut and what you know. Rely on your instincts and be confident in your findings.

Follow Your Hunches

This was just a handful of divination techniques, but as ever you must learn to trust yourself and what feels right to *you*. This technique of self-trust works across all areas—even when working with herbs and spices in your pantry. Fancy putting a pinch of angelica root in your tea but aren't sure why? Look up the benefits: you may find it is exactly what you need. One of the great things about this method is that rather than making you reliant on an external source, it encourages you to increasingly go with your hunches, which will become stronger and clearer in response.

A Witchful Warning

Don't get *too* reliant on divination. The idea is to sharpen your awareness rather than to look for reassurance to the extent that you can no longer make a decision on your own. Also, remember that we are not talking about destiny here: divination points you in the direction you appear to be heading as things stand, but this doesn't mean you are doomed to go that way if you are prepared to make a concerted effort to change direction. Similarly, it doesn't mean you will automatically have the success indicated if you don't do your bit. You are always in charge of your life.

AS EVER, YOU MUST LEARN TO TRUST YOURSELF AND WHAT FEELS RIGHT TO YOU. THIS TECHNIQUE OF SELF-TRUST WORKS ACROSS ALL AREAS, AND WILL MAKE YOUR HUNCHES STRONGER AND CLEARER.

Meeting Freya Ingva, Diviner and Tea-Leaf Reader

Tasseomancer Freya Ingva had been studying the language of symbols for many years before naturally bringing her research together with her love of tea-drinking. Before long, she was reading the leaves and deciphering the symbols. She tells us more about how a cup of tea, when combined with our intuition, can unlock deep truths:

Freya Ingva: For me, a tea ceremony is about sharing a moment outside time, where we open a space for something magical to happen. To truly make sense, the symbols must be felt, not simply read. However, one way does not exclude the other: one needs to start walking before one can run, so to speak. Size, position, clarity of a symbol can alter its meaning, as this can also change in relation to what else it is found nearby. Incidentally, the possible combinations are too many to be learned from a book. Symbols need to come alive to convey their message, and they do so through our intuition.

Archetypes provide a great starting point, as they offer universal patterns we can all relate to. There is definitely more to them than a few lines on a page.

OUR INTUITIVE BODIES

When we think of intuition, we think of our minds and our spirits, but most of us disregard the art of noticing what our *bodies* are telling us. The exception to this would be acknowledging gut feelings in emergencies or a sinking feeling in the heart or stomach.

You know that old phrase, "By the pricking of my thumbs, something wicked this way comes"? I can honestly say that the more I look to my intuition as the years go by, the more my body responds with clearer signs and messages—and sometimes I actually do get a pricking "nerve" sensation in my thumbs. Insights and warnings don't always come as perfectly formed thoughts or an external sign. Our energy fields and nervous systems work together and are powerful communicators. Body, mind, and psyche are not separate; indeed, it is often suggested that the gut is our second brain, so it makes sense to listen to our bodies.

You might feel fizzing energy in your body while meditating, perhaps in your solar plexus, in your heart centre, or maybe around your third eye. Observe not just the sensations, but where they are focused. This will help you to interpret the messages more fully. Your psychic awareness may be waking up, or you may be receiving an energy overhaul. I take note of all of these prickles and tingles, and I suggest you do too.

We all know that shuddery "someone walking over my grave" feeling. I think this indicates that our auras are shaking off negative energy. Essentially, our etheric body is doing its job. If you're dreaming about something and you feel a rush of energy, don't shrug it off. If something excites you on a cellular level, work with it.

On the other hand, when I think about logging into Facebook, I can feel my energy drag unless I consciously "put up my shield" first, usually by visualising myself in a bubble of light. We all have this sensitivity, but it is often masked by the distractions of everyday life. Don't be frustrated if your body gives you a signal (like nausea) that all is not quite right. We don't want to numb ourselves so we can take in more rubbish; we want to fine-tune ourselves so we always sense exactly what we need, never mind what's right for anyone else. The alternative means being tossed about on an ocean of other people's energy or plunging ourselves into situations that aren't right. Then we wonder why we are anxious and depressed.

Tell your body, mind, and spirit that you are listening and that you value the messages that come through. If you get a gut feeling—maybe you can't rationally justify why, but you feel anxious—let yourself off the hook and say thank you. Your awareness and intuition is working hard for you.

✴ WITCH TIP ✴
NOTICE WHAT YOU NOTICE

Sometimes you're about to leave the house and, as you go, something you'd normally ignore catches your eye. Then, an hour later, you realise you need that exact thing. This used to happen to me a lot. Now when my eyes fall upon something or I think, "Should I take that with me?" before I go, I just pick it up and I take it, and I'm always glad I did. I now recognise this to be my instincts subtly but definitely letting me know what I need.

SETTING INTENTIONS: USE IT or LOSE IT

Now, when I say, "Use it," I mean, "Use your power and use it for good"—specifically, as many witches like to say, for the good of all and under grace, in the perfect way. It's about the language we use to set our intentions, and we are setting intentions all the time, deliberately or not. If you're thinking at all, you're setting intentions.

We need to be specific. We need to take care. We need to let Source know that while we might want to lose weight, we don't want to lose it at any cost—losing a limb will drop a few pounds. We also don't want to have a windfall under any circumstances. Word it carelessly and that windfall might come in the form of an inheritance from the death of a loved one. You get the idea.

I once put it out there during a difficult week that I wanted to cancel everything and rest. Two hours later, guess what happened? I seriously injured myself and could do nothing *but* rest, in opiate oblivion, for many months. But I got my wish—express delivery. That was a literally painful reminder of how careful you have to be, especially when your words are charged with emotion. Emotion contains strong, heady magic. You can make stuff happen fast if you put feeling behind your words, so watch it, my friend.

"For the good of all," "in the perfect way," "under grace": these are my mantras when I set intentions, cast spells, or wish upon a star— and respect for other people's free will is, as we have established, essential. Again, it's about being mindful with words or thoughts. Everything that exists begins with them, so be scrupulous and ensure that you are not inadvertently risking the good of others or manipulating or disrespecting the free will of any other being with your own intentions, wishes, thoughts, or deeds.

One of the universal laws every religion seems to agree on is the law of cause and effect. Thoughts, words, and deeds are causes, so always have one eye on the effects you may be creating.

Get It Writ: Physicalising Your Intentions

Writing in a journal is a great way to physicalise a wish or intention, and you will have the added benefit of being able to check back later to see if it has manifested. By the time the wish is realised, you might have forgotten you'd actually made the wish, so it's encouraging to be shown that everyday magic works. Often people write down a list of, say, qualities they'd love in a partner or a property they're dreaming of, just to focus their mind. They then find this list years later in an old box and discover that they've magnetised exactly what they had written down.

Another element of this method's success is the Law of Detachment: by writing it down, you are getting it out of your head and onto paper. Read it through, and then put it away and hand it over to the Universe. You can also storyboard or script your life as if it's a motion picture. No film gets made without a storyboard: if it did, it would likely lack focus and direction. Similarly, authors rarely commence a story without drafting a chapter breakdown first. It's a way to see your intention through to the end and make sure it doesn't lose its way or just get abandoned altogether. You can see and imagine the whole, right down to completion. The chapter breakdown or the storyboard is the backbone of all that follows.

Rewrite History

You can use writing as a transformational practice by writing down your memory of a situation, burning it (safely), and then writing an ending you prefer. Put as much detail in as you can, make it real, think about it, feel it. Perceptions and memories—our own and those of others—change over time, so take control and make sure those changes go in a positive direction.

You can direct the future as well as the present and the past. Write glowing reviews of your upcoming work. Write about the glamorous adventures you haven't had yet, creative ventures you wish to embark on, or the qualities you'd like to embody. Even write your own obituary. Set wheels in motion and imprint these intentions into the surprisingly malleable clay of Future You. This is what witches sometimes mean when they refer to working backwards and forwards in time. Neuro-linguistic programming (NLP) uses similar techniques to uproot old perceptions of the past, often with liberating results.

Planting Seeds

Write down how you want a situation to develop, fold up the paper, and plant it with a new seed in a flowerpot on an appropriate new moon: New Moon in Gemini for matters of communication, say, or New Moon in Sagittarius if you want to take that adventure-of-a-lifetime trip but don't know how yet. You can find more advice on working with different new moons earlier in this book. These little spells are easy, inexpensive, and discreet, and you can visualise the magic growing with that brave little seed, imbued with the energy of your carefully chosen words.

Automatic Writing

Another way to use writing magically is by trying the technique of automatic writing. This is a meditative practice that, in essence, involves putting pen to paper and letting whatever comes, come. It works well first thing in the morning, before the rest of the day encroaches, when you are still a little sleepy and have a foot in both worlds, as it were. Doodle, scribble, don't inhibit yourself or try to control the results—no one has to see this but you.

Many have found this to be an effective therapy tool. It can help us get out of our own way and release judgment, and you might be surprised by what emerges. Anyone who has read Julia Cameron's *The Artist's Way* will know of her "morning pages" practice, and I love that Cameron has ensured this technique—by whatever name—is being used and loved as a tool for creativity and self-knowledge by so many.

Often used as a technique by psychics—the channeling possibilities here are obvious—this practice is also a superb aid for creative spirits who need to shift a block or allow their thinking to become more flowing and inspired. A writer friend of my parents sat down with a notepad every morning after breakfast and just allowed the words to spill from his psyche onto the paper. Whether they were coming from within or elsewhere, he often came up with winning ideas, because he was giving his mind the opportunity to become clear, still, and receptive. Give it a try: sit down with paper and pen or pencil, breathe deeply, allow yourself to relax, and then let the words or images flow.

The Magic of Chance

The techniques of automatic writing and drawing were famously used by the surrealists, who knew a thing or two about the magic of chance and letting things happen randomly. All "randomness" actually turns up for a reason, even if it's not immediately obvious, and especially if it takes you by surprise, which often means there is a message trying to reach you. And if the reason is *not* obvious, and you want to get specific, ask, "What do I need to know?" Then pay attention to the signs, the sights, the sounds, any messages, and your dreams. Life takes on a new dimension once you start paying attention.

By all means, buy a special notebook and pen for this practice. Honour it and try it regularly. Don't allow yourself to be disturbed, and don't police yourself. Just sit down, relax or go into meditation, place pen to paper, and allow the pen to move. You might even find the answer to a problem rushing out in a tumble of ink, and you may discover that this is an easy and direct way for your guides to communicate. Set your objective before you start, if you wish.

The same goes for automatic drawing: just scrawl and scribble. It doesn't matter if you think you're good at art. Be as unrestricted as possible: this is a personal exercise, and you want to be free to see what comes through. Again, the results might hold a message, a symbol, a face, or a feeling that is relevant to you or needs acknowledging.

Cut-Up Poetry

Another practice I use in my artwork is Dada poetry, or the cut-up technique. It's a simple creative "game" initiated at the turn of the twentieth century by surrealist Tristan Tzara and used by artists and writers from William Burroughs to David Bowie to blast through blocks and bend minds in turn.

You take a magazine or newspaper, cut words out individually, shuffle them, and then rearrange either in the order they present themselves or more consciously. The results can be hilarious, strangely wise, prophetic, or downright obscene. One of the things I love about this technique is that odd synchronicities can occur and pertinent messages can appear. You never know what's going to come through, especially when you have a mishmash of words from lots of different articles so they don't obviously relate.

Treat these games and techniques like an oracle, and be open to the possibilities.

✳ WITCH TIP ✳
MAKE THAT MOVE

Got an idea you can't get out of your head? Action it, or someone else will. Ideas are just floating about in the collective unconscious waiting for the right person to bring them into reality, and they won't wait long.

Believe me, I know. Every time I went away for a break, the germ of a book kept coming into my head. I felt excited whenever I thought about it, but I put it on the back burner because I had other projects to complete. And guess what? Eventually, I would hear that an almost-identical book was about to be published by someone else.

The idea just wanted to be born. But I wasn't the only person who could have birthed it, and it needed to arrive when it needed to arrive. I rolled my eyes, sent goodwill to both book and author, and accepted it was an idea whose time had come. But next time inspiration strikes, so will I.

WORKING WITH SIGILS

A sigil is an image that communicates meaning and symbolises a desire and an intent. The use of sigils was popularised in relatively recent years by chaos magicians, many of whom were and remain inspired by the creative occult practice of the English artist Austin Osman Spare, who worked extensively with sigils and was making all sorts of strange things happen, artistically and magically, until his death in 1956.[45] Again, this practice taps into the idea of physicalising that which we want to manifest. I like using writing or drawing in magic because, when we do so, we are conjuring something up out of "nothing" and concentrating the energy. I also like the idea of designing a symbol that, once charged, can be hidden in plain sight to work its magic. You don't have to be good at art to do this.

When my father became ill a few years ago, I made a range of colourful protective sigils and hid them around the house in little boxes, under rugs, or inside books. He recovered well, but, being of deceptively tough stock, perhaps he would have done anyway. Still, it didn't hurt, and it made me feel like I could at least do *something* positive at this worrying time.

Example of a sigil

You can make a sigil out of your own name and create your own trademark with hidden layers of meaning, or you can use the letters in your family name and turn them into a crest, imbuing it with power, strength, loyalty, good times, and all of the qualities you would like to bless your family with, in all directions of time and space.

Making a Sigil

Here are some simple guidelines. You will need two pieces of paper and a pen—black or, if you wish to use correspondences, coloured—and an intention.

You can write down your intention in a conventional Law of Attraction style. If you want more money, you could word it thus: "I am rich, under grace." Alternatively, if you want to be more formal, write, "It is my will that money flows into my life with ease, under grace." Make sure you write clearly.

Cross out the vowels, and then do the same with any repeated letters. So, if you are using the first wording above, the letters you're left with will be:

$$M R C H N D G C$$

Now's the time to stir the creative cauldron: you are about to let your inner artist loose. Using the letters that are not crossed through, design a symbol that pleases you. Go with your intuition; there is no right or wrong way to do this, but magic is always more effective when you are having fun with the process. As you draw, keep your objective clearly in your mind or chant it as an affirmation. You are imbuing this symbol with the energy of your wish. Draw a circle around it to contain the working.

$$M H D C$$

Example of creating a sigil

It is now time to activate your sigil. I sometimes just give it a kiss, place it under my orgone pyramid overnight, or burn it and release the smoke to the ether. Austin Osman Spare would memorise the image of the sigil and then hold it to his third eye and concentrate on visualising the image he had memorised. Another popular way to activate and release a sigil is to focus on the image while exhausting yourself physically or bringing yourself to orgasm. Your choice.

Now that the spell is done, look out for evidence over the coming days that your working has created the shift you desire.

WITCH & WISDOM
Art Witch Laura Keeble

Mark-making in its many forms is magical, and art is the ultimate in manifestation work: something wasn't there, and now it is. I could think of no one better to talk to about this than Laura Keeble, an acclaimed British artist who uses subversive strategies to create pauses in perception. Famously, Laura made a replica of Damien Hirst's diamond-skull artwork titled "For the Love of God" and left it outside the White Cube gallery with the trash (titling her work "Forgotten Something?") after the close of his 2007 exhibition there. Hirst was duly impressed, to the extent that he bought Laura's work. Let us hear from Laura and give our creative cauldrons a stir:

Laura Keeble: Bringing an idea and making it a reality is what artists do. Their belief that an image in their head or an idea needs to be created into something tangible is full of intention and direct, proactive energy. Whatever the purpose, it always contains a process of ritual in preparation and being "in the zone," similar to spell or intention work. The thought or idea becomes an intention, and that energy is directed into creating an object or an action. Artists have absolute focus and belief in their need to create this magic, and so it happens.

I also feel that ideas are channeled. Often I have thoughts that pop into my head like a sort of "eureka" moment, normally when I am doing something mundane or repetitive like vacuuming or sewing, which is similar to being in a meditative state, in that I am not really using my logical brain. I then need to create or bring life to the idea.

I prepare what I need, have my space ready for creating in the way that I feel comfortable and familiar (my magic circle of protection), and then go through an intense process of creating the actual form. It's obsessive in the need to make it happen, and I reach the meditative, "in the zone" feeling whilst doing it. This, to me, is intensive magic-making. I feel I am connected to Source and energies in a very direct way. Whilst making the work, I am adding intention in every movement, and when the work is complete, I know that I have not only manifested the original idea, I have also created an object that is magical and holds that energy. Its power is constantly projecting out to wherever it needs to go.

Belief in yourself and your idea or intention is the only thing a magical practitioner needs. Magic work can be created from anything around you; if you believe it's important and powerful to you, then it is.

Magical Musing
A Note on Spare Time and Awareness

You don't get to be a wise woman by filling every spare moment gawping at reality TV or scrolling social media, although admittedly both can be interesting from an anthropological point of view. I find my sense of awareness gets skewed and dulled if I allow myself to get sucked into the virtual world too often, but it is oh so easy to do. Thankfully, it is also easy to pull yourself out of it. We can do this by feeding our minds, reading, leaving our phones at home when we go out for a walk, dawdling in galleries, staring at the sea, and listening to the birds at twilight. None of this is time wasted.

The pioneering metaphysical writer Florence Scovel Shinn observed that we're all too used to relying on the reasoning mind when we would be better off handing situations over to our intuition.[46] Try it. Next time you lose something, calmly ask yourself where it is and then see where your nose leads you. I do this if I can't find my husband when we're shopping at the supermarket. I've usually become distracted in the cake section while he's zoomed off to look for something else. Instead of getting my phone out, I ask my feet to find him, and they always do. He can always find me too—although that's probably because he knows I can usually be found by the cakes.

Another way to test your burgeoning intuition is to jettison your alarm clock and ask yourself to wake at a specific time. I am just one of many who find this works every time. Keep relying on those instincts as much as possible; cultivate and trust them, and they will get stronger and clearer, especially if you ration your exposure to internet use, gaming, and trashy TV shows. I'm not saying stop altogether: sometimes we need a switch off, and there are some wonderful—and witchy—films and programs that both entertain and inspire. It's dangerously easy to get into the habit of just killing time. As with all areas of life, balance is key.

Challenge yourself to swap the time you spend scrolling for learning something new. Be a voracious self-educator; being wise has nothing to do with formal education. Pick your subjects and read, learn, observe, and take pleasure in the process. It never stops: life is the ultimate university, and planet Earth the eternal dean. We just have to pay attention, take notes, and understand with hearts as well as minds. And when we create space for ourselves away from our digital lives, we allow the beautiful inner world to awaken.

PART 4

EQUAL DARK, EQUAL LIGHT

Facing the Dark, Finding Your Light,
and Embracing the Crone

DON'T BE AFRAID OF THE DARK

We have been taught since childhood that "dark" is frightening. There are many reasons why this is untrue, and, like so many of these things, when we unpick it, we see the agenda behind it. The agenda is usually misogynistic, racist, or both.

With the Chinese yin-yang sign, the dark side is considered feminine. Darkness is receptive, nurturing, and reflective. Much can be done in the dark that cannot be accomplished in the light, and I'm not just talking about developing photographs. The dark is the life-giving earth. It is also the grave. The darkness is the crone, the bleeding time of the menstrual cycles, timeless wisdom, the pause in winter, rest, release, and repair.

It's also worth remembering that black and dark colours are associated with witches and their familiars—usually black cats. This brings us to the ridiculous superstition about black cats being unlucky. This nonsensical belief has tragically caused many black cats and kittens to be rejected in shelters, abandoned on the streets, or worse. But in some cultures, black cats are considered lucky. Ultimately, as we witchful thinkers know, if you decide something is lucky—or unlucky—it is.

Black clothes were useful to those practicing magic, not least because their lives, historically, were an exercise in inconspicuousness. Many outdoor rituals would be conducted in the dark; the witching hour and the full moon are undoubtedly times of increased cosmic power, but full moons were also rather useful because they allowed you to see what you were doing and where you were going when you were out on the fabled "blasted heath." But black clothes were and remain favoured, because black is protective. This could just originate from being inconspicuous, of course—there is usually a practical element to these customs—but there is generally an occult significance too.

All this does put paid to the notion of "dark or black = unlucky and negative." Quite the opposite, I would say. Darkness and light are part of us. Every day has darkness and light; it is natural to the cosmos and the seasons, so it's going to be natural to us too. We generally spend nine months in the dark of the womb before making our grand entrance. Seeds germinate in the darkness of the soil. We repair and reset when the sun goes down and we take to our beds. (No phone or computer screens before sleep, please: that blue light and associated emissions affect us in untold ways.)

Understand Your Shadow

We *all* have a dark or shadow side. In fact, it can give us great strength and insight, but women in particular have been brought up to pretend it doesn't exist or, at best, to repress it. People wonder why so many women suffer from nervous breakdowns, postnatal depression, hormonal imbalances, and illnesses almost certainly sparked by harbouring unreleased anger. Our minds, bodies, and spirits are one.

Get to know your dark side. Give it your attention and the space to express itself safely, and you will see how it can transform into something that truly serves a positive purpose. In the meantime, just try to understand it. Find out what it is, what triggers it, and how you can offer it healing.

It took me ages to come to terms with the fact that if I don't watch it, I have a tendency to be possessive, territorial, mistrustful, and guarded—the astrologers out there may have guessed that I'm a Scorpio with Capricorn rising. The flipside of this is loyalty, protectiveness, and discretion. But don't worry about finding the flipside for now: just patiently allow your shadow to reveal itself to you—no judgment, no disappointment—and bring yourself into balance. You'll soon find that if you do have a wobble, you won't be shocked or embarrassed by yourself, you'll just think, "Well, yes, that's me. I'm all of these things at the same time, and that's okay. I'm mature enough to understand what's happening, and that it will pass."

If you are feeling particularly down, angry, unwell, or emotional or are on heavy meds—or have just had a few drinks—I'd advise a break from any magical practice or divination: the effects may be muddled at best. You want your energy to be aligned and focused, so wait for clarity, and in the meantime, raise your vibration with self-care, in whatever form that takes for you. Spend time in nature; spend time with animals; listen to music that makes you smile; have a "potion" bath swirled with oils, crystals, salts, and intentions; wear your loveliest clothes; bake a cake; plan a trip, a get-together, or a party; or make a *really* good pot of tea. These things do the trick for me, anyway.

EVERY DAY HAS
DARKNESS AND LIGHT;
IT IS NATURAL TO THE COSMOS
AND THE SEASONS, SO IT'S
GOING TO BE NATURAL TO US TOO.

GOOD VIBRATIONS: CHANGING STATE WITH A SONG

We all have songs that are forever installed on the great jukebox in our hearts. A song can put us into an altered state, whether we play it, sing it, or simply listen to it. You can go to a concert and come out feeling like a new person: euphoric and excited or soothed and calm and ready to take on life again. That's magic right there. You have to open up to it, of course. Witchful thinking is much more effective if you are in a receptive state rather than feeling closed off. We have to meet life halfway.

I believe that songs are spells, music is magic, and the makers of it gifted conjurors, whether they connect consciously to other realms or not. A genuinely great piece of music has the ability to change our mood, take us backwards in time, and even make us do things we never thought we could. If that's not sorcery, I don't know what is. When you consider how we can shift our consciousness with sound waves, frequencies, binaural beats, and chanting—and raise our endorphins by singing with others—it's no surprise that the right piece of music can create positive change.

Note down songs that speak to you or uplift you; make a list of tracks that have the power to catapult you from glum to glad, to soothe you to sleep, or to remind you of what's important; and turn to them when you need to perform a little mental alchemy. It's as easy as pressing Play.

I love to finish rituals by putting on a special track that propels me into a positive place to round things off. In case you were wondering, it's "The Only Star in Heaven" by Frankie Goes to Hollywood. It raises the vibrations and seals the rite while keeping things light. Doubt and anxiety are magic killers, or at least magic warpers, so when I play this after a ritual, it pushes any potential wobbly thoughts away with a blast of 1980s synths.

Magic, for me, isn't solemn and po-faced. It is celebratory. It's about raising energy. We do it because we want to be happy and fulfilled, ultimately. That will mean different things to different folks, but the nature of sympathetic resonance—and sheer common sense—tells me that I'm more likely to attract fulfillment if I act accordingly. To my mind, any music that lifts your spirit, inspires you to be strong, and effects a change of state within you—whether it's by Clannad, Mozart, or David Bowie—is magic for *you*. Use it.

A GENUINELY GREAT PIECE
OF MUSIC HAS THE ABILITY
TO CHANGE OUR MOOD,
TAKE US BACKWARDS IN TIME,
AND EVEN MAKE US DO
THINGS WE NEVER THOUGHT
WE COULD.

NAVIGATING AND INTERPRETING LIFE'S JOLTS

Beyond the anticipated shifts and losses in the course of an average lifespan, our souls can use jarring incidents to wake us up and force us into awareness. Those jolts can be tough, but they're necessary. You'll need to sit with them for a while to understand the lessons they present: they don't exactly arrive gift-wrapped.

Jolts can take you to a fork in your personal road. Everything is a choice, including how you respond. You could choose acceptance and understanding, no matter how hard that might be at first, or you could opt for "why me?" whining and self-medication. Don't ask, "Why me?" Ask, "Why has this happened to me? And what do I potentially get out of it?"

These may sound like strange questions to ask yourself if you're ill, injured, or damaged in any way, but delve deep, because you will find an answer. It may surprise you; it may anger or disappoint you; but as long as you don't face it, you will spiral and circle and never find closure or truly understand yourself. Worse still, you risk attracting it again and again—or variations on the same theme—until you damn well understand what the lesson is. This may be infuriating to hear, but I would never suggest anything like this if I hadn't been through instances like this myself many times and come through them with a new sense of understanding.

Historically, the Japanese used to mend broken pots by filling in the cracks with seams of molten gold.[47] For many, this has become a metaphor for the soul, and it's easy to see why. That old chestnut about problematic situations being character-building is true, and, depending on the time needed to recover, this can take years, even lifetimes. Still, if you dig deep and sit with your thoughts, your circumstances will make more sense and you never need be a "victim" again. This is vital, not least because adopting a victim complex is a slippery slope. We are what we think about every day, and no matter how justified your anger and hurt may be, they can become self-fulfilling. Reject all invitations to pity parties—including your own.

Luckily, if we wake our awareness and stop ignoring our hearts, bodies, and souls—this is a big one—those jolts can become fewer, softer, and easier to understand. I can't promise you will nix problems completely, but reframing them will assist you in ultimately seeing them for what they are: opportunities for growth and ascension.

This is at the heart of the witchful way: honing your awareness to minimise the need for jolts and, in the meantime, trusting yourself to feel your way through them with perspective and patience should they arise. We all break and we all have cracks, and some are deeper than others. But they are part of our stories, and they show we have lived bravely and fully. When we face our cracks rather than suppressing or hiding them, and when we carefully, lovingly put ourselves back together, we have the option to fill those fissures with gold and become more beautiful than ever.

LUCKILY, IF WE WAKE OUR AWARENESS
AND STOP IGNORING OUR HEARTS,
BODIES, AND SOULS—THOSE JOLTS
CAN BECOME FEWER, SOFTER,
AND EASIER TO UNDERSTAND.

THE TRUE BEAUTY of AUTHENTICITY

I have a theory: now that fewer of us are automatically taking on the traditional role of housewife, more energy is being poured into distracting us with the latest product to help us block nature and prevent wrinkles, sagging—you name it, there's a new thing to be anxious about every week. While we're busy being anxious, we're not getting in the way and trying to actually, you know, *do* stuff. Stuff that makes a difference to the world. "Don't worry your pretty little heads about that. Don't you have a salon appointment to go to? Aren't you looking a little chubby? I can see a couple of hairs on your face that shouldn't be there."

Ta-da. Paranoia takes hold and we're swiftly tidied out of the way while we deal with the "ugliness" that seems to matter so much because, like it or not, we intrinsically know that the people in charge only really give us space if they find us attractive. And it's men—generally, straight white men—who currently hold the strings. That grip is loosening.

The point is, deep down we are just trying to survive. Many of us have been conditioned to feel that if we aren't physically attractive, we will not be welcomed or accepted—not only as a romantic prospect, but in life. That is a profoundly fearful situation for women. When we bear this insidious programming in mind, it reminds us to feel compassion rather than all-out judgment when we see yet another image of a woman who has gone to town with plastic surgery.

I love wearing makeup, but I largely see it as part of my self-expression: I have fun with colour and love how it makes me feel. I wear it whether anyone is going to see it or not. It's disturbing, however, when we see even young girls with lip filler and Botox, proudly displaying improbable pouts and rigid foreheads on social media.

We don't know what their real faces actually look like. There'll be little resemblance to their own relatives because of the work they've had done, although they will look strangely similar to everybody else with Botox and fillers. I do think it has to do with belonging, fitting in, and acceptance.

Are we so afraid of not looking sufficiently like a reality-TV star that we would obliterate our own facial characteristics in order to feel more secure and acceptable? This, to me, is both sad and sinister. We all bring our own enchantment, but it gets stuffed down, both physically and psychologically, when we try to emulate someone else. I believe we are already in an era in which looking like yourself as a woman is becoming a radical act.

When I see someone being completely herself *for* herself, beaming back at us on Instagram or TikTok amid a feed of people who haven't looked like themselves—or any natural human being—for quite a while, I feel relief. When we are real, natural, and unafraid to be ourselves, our minds are free to make a difference in the world. This is both wise *and* beautiful.

WHEN WE ARE REAL, NATURAL, AND UNAFRAID
TO BE OURSELVES, OUR MINDS ARE FREE
TO MAKE A DIFFERENCE IN THE WORLD.

THE POWER of DECIDING

"Fake it till you make it" are some of my favourite magic words. This phrase commands us to take what we want to feel and use it to imprint our subconscious, which is basically power awaiting direction. It doesn't take long, but you have to commit, and it is worth it. When you feel more at ease with yourself, you are less defensive and insecure, so your dealings with others become easier, kinder, warmer, and luckier. It's the most marvellous kind of snowball—even better than the kind made with Advocaat liqueur and lemonade with glacé cherries on top.

Think of someone you know who just seems lucky. It's unlikely they spend most of their time moaning, comparing themselves to others, or looking for fights online. Deliberately change your attitude to one of gratitude and positivity: it is a daily choice and a decision, not just the way some people are hardwired. The difference will be immediate and significant.

Start by making a conscious effort to notice the simple but essential things you take for granted. For example, look at the food and drink you prepare and consume at mealtimes. Instead of just cooking it absentmindedly before shoveling it into your mouth like an automaton, think of where it came from and the people involved in the chain of getting it from its origin to your table. I quite like adapting the Christian idea of saying grace for this: it reminds me to take a moment of appreciation, although I prefer to do it in my head and use my own words.

Looking Outwards
Outward thinking is essential to our mental health. Depression has been known to ease when we stop focusing on ourselves. Writer and healer Betty Shine observed that the auras of people with depression

visibly sank inwards, pressing down on the head, but then lifted and radiated outwards again when thoughts were directed away from the self.[48] When we think about and care for others instead of obsessing about ourselves, and when we sustain this new way of being every day, we release this pressure and start to look, feel, and *be* lucky.

Remember, working with energy is what we're doing—energy is what we're made of—so it's vital to work with it the right way rather than allow life to happen and be buffeted about by it. Don't punish yourself or start stressing if you lose concentration and find yourself going down the wrong track: pulling yourself back and onto the right track is as quick as a thought.

Authentic Decision-Making

It's all about decisions. If you don't like what's happening, make a decision to change things. It doesn't have to be a complicated or expensive change, just a start—and you're allowed to change your mind and make another decision if you don't feel it's working out. Yes, we should stick to our guns and see things through, but many dreams die, years are wasted, and resentments flourish because we stick rigidly to a decision we made. It may have seemed—or was—right at the time, but maybe we didn't have all the information, or maybe things have changed, or maybe *we* have changed. If your job or relationship or location makes you feel like you're dying inside, then it's definitely time to make a new decision.

You're allowed to change your mind. You don't need permission to do so, and if you wait for someone else to tell you it's time you moved on because it's better for your health, you may be waiting a long time. Life is as big or as small as you decide. Decide to love it, enjoy it, participate in it, embrace it—it will embrace you right back. And it's all about the things we give our awareness to: choose them with care and according to your heart and soul and gut, not what is trendy or what you think will make you look good or what the people around you want. There's a lot of talk about being authentic these days. I think this taps into that.

Square Pegs and Round Holes

Admittedly, if you have been, say, in the wrong job for years, it can be hard to even know a new decision needs to be made, because of the drudgery that has numbed you and muted the messages from your heart. It can be difficult to hear what your soul is crying out for when it's being drowned out every morning on your commute by the screech of the tube train or by the motivational self-hypnosis tapes you doggedly listen to with gritted teeth because you are so on the edge. This was me some years ago. I was in the wrong job, but I thought *I* needed to change—to squeeze and force square-peg me into round-hole job.

This was ridiculous, of course, but Wrong Job was so in my face that I couldn't see the truth that was in front of me. I didn't think, "Wrong job." I thought, "Wrong me." The fact is, we were wrong for each other. It's always a two-way street.

Sometimes there's nothing like immersing yourself in the wrong situation to focus the mind, although, like a bad relationship, it can take far longer to escape than it should. Every time I plunged into square-peg mode, usually motivated by money, I became deeply unhappy, angry, and inevitably ill, both physically and mentally. I was not myself—I wasn't even allowing my real self to peep through—so my soul was reacting, big time.

This may sound overblown to some, but I know others will understand exactly what I am saying. I'm sharing it in order to say that if this is what you are feeling now, you are not mad: you are brave for toughing this out. Nevertheless, you need to understand that if you are feeling these things, then you need to make some changes, as soon as you feasibly can.

The thing is, I never asked my soul—never even thought to listen to it—until I gave myself space to hear it. Once I started to hear it, I heard it more and more. Nowadays, what my soul needs, wants, and feels comes first, and I'll never betray it again. Still, there are always gifts to be found in all experiences. We are sculpting ourselves all the time, and I very much came out of those situations with a viscerally clear sense of what I wanted, who I was, and who I definitely wasn't.

✳ WITCH TIP ✳
CHOICES, CHOICES

You are free to do anything you choose—so how do you choose? If you're a creative spirit, you may be good at lots of things, but this can lead to a tendency to try to do everything. Doing this means that, more often than not, you'll end up achieving little more than a migraine and a chronic sense of confusion, anxiety, and guilt.

I used to start writing and then think, "But I'm not making art." I'd start making a piece of art and harbour guilty feelings because I wasn't spending enough time practicing music. The only way forward is to stop and say, "What does my *soul* want to do right now?" I wish I'd worked that out sooner. It is so simple, and it makes all the difference. No more guilt, no more burnout, just fulfillment and focus.

FALSE MODESTY AND IMPOSTER SYNDROME

For many of us growing up, it was an unspoken part of our training to be humble to the extent that we actually felt slightly suspicious of confidence. "She's a bit *confident*" is a loaded comment that many girls from my generation and before will have heard from time to time—and it wasn't meant as a compliment. It reeked of, "Who does she think she is? What gives her the right? *I* don't feel confident or good enough, so why should she?"

These messages go deep—"mustn't be too much"—and we receive these messages long into adulthood. When I was about to release a novel after years of writing nonfiction, I was shocked when a friend suggested it was arrogant to do so. There it was again: get back in your box. It was acceptable to write about other people's lives, but to presume that anyone would want to hear *my* story, fictionalised or otherwise, was apparently beyond the pale.

Here's the thing: most of us have enough self-doubt to contend with without having to steel ourselves against other people's restrictive attitudes, which, as ever, have nothing to do with us. Sadly, many of us habitually do restrict and do keep ourselves down for fear of being "arrogant," and we end up totally reliant on the approval of others, from our looks to our work. That is a precarious place to be. Approval is nice, but witchful thinkers depend on no one: *we* must know when we have reached our own standards, and we must be happy when we do, never mind anyone else.

Who are we to try something new? Who are we to bravely share our thoughts, experiences, and gifts, to not fit in neatly with other people's assumptions about us? Actually, who are we *not* to? Being defined by others is not the witch's way. We are who we decide to be. We take what works and we reject what is no longer a positive force in our lives. That includes people.

Be Honest with Yourself

If you find yourself having resentful feelings when you see someone else apparently living their best life, sit down with a cup of tea and be gently honest with yourself about why that might be. Look over your previous interactions and your relationships with peers, former authority figures, and your parents for clues.

If you feel you've been subtly oppressed or judged, not just by society but by loved ones—whether teachers, friends, family, or partners—then it's healthy to admit this to yourself. Doing so doesn't mean you don't love or appreciate those people, but you have to face the truth for your own good. Often, we want to protect loved ones—even the memory of them, if they are no longer with us—but this can be at our expense. Remember, like everyone, they contain multitudes, and not all of their subpersonalities are particularly evolved, kind, or gracious. That will most likely have something to do with the messages *they* internalised, and so on and back it goes.

These patterns are set up in our formative years, when we are generally unquestioning of authorities and tend to view parents and teachers as godlike figures we want to please. Again, this is to do with survival: we naturally seek approval from those we rely on to care for us. But you're not a child anymore. It's safe to chip away at these layers and set yourself free, with love and respect to all. You don't have to tell anyone you're doing this work; what matters is that you are doing it.

Have you had your light extinguished by an authority figure? Face facts, try to understand this person's intention (it may have been to protect you), and send them thanks, if appropriate. Silently assure them—and yourself—that these beliefs are no longer needed, and then consciously wave that person goodbye. Imagine them surrounded by light and disappearing into nothingness. See yourself giving them a physical push if need be. Imagine them exploding like fireworks, if you need an even more forceful image. Whatever gets you there.

Exploding the Imposter Syndrome

The above issues may stem from generational or cultural patterns, so if you can't relate to the imposter syndrome or any of these get-back-in-your-box feelings, then believe me, I am happy for you. However, if you do, please know that dealing with this is important soul work. Too often, women and girls across time have been warned not to boast about our worth, and many of us went further and became unable to even acknowledge or recognise it at all. Where does that leave us? Not of much use to the world, that's for sure.

And so to the important intention of bringing forth that light within. That light is you, it's your essence, and the world needs it. Wise ones know who they are, and we are lost if we lose sight of that. How can we know anything if we don't know ourselves to start off with? I repeat, we contain multitudes, and that's as it should be. Just don't forget that it's the same for others too. I've always said that people are lots of things all at once. Walt Whitman put it more succinctly with the ol' "I contain multitudes" line,[49] but it's all the same and it's all good.

Embrace those multitudes.

WITCH & WISDOM
Dream Expert Linda Yael Schiller

The writer Clarissa Pinkola Estés (author of Women Who Run with the Wolves*) suggests that nightmares about pursuers can represent a buried part of our psyche trying to catch our attention. I was keen to know what Linda Yael Schiller, psychotherapist and author of* Modern Dreamwork: New Tools for Decoding Your Soul's Wisdom, *thought, and her suggestions for how we can work with our nightly visions for personal development. Read on, dreamers:*

Linda Yael Schiller: More often than not, our dreams do represent a part of ourselves, other than a premonition of events. The gestalt point of view in dreamwork would say that every character in a dream, even every object or landscape, represents a part of ourselves. Therefore, we could ask, "What is the monster part of me?" or "What is the part of me that is chasing down another part of me?"

The key to letting you know how far you have got with your healing is the emotional effect, or emotional narrative, of the dream. The dreams that leave us upset or wrung out indicate that we have not yet resolved or fully healed the traumas that have generated the nightmares.

The more work we do on ourselves in therapy or in dreamwork or in healing in a variety of ways, the less our dreams will haunt our lives, and nightmares will become less intense and less frequent, will have a better ending, and ultimately may go away altogether. Yes, old traumas rise up in our unconscious desiring to be processed and healed, and if we have not yet done that in our waking life, they will rise up in our sleep, as the "censor" part of our brain is asleep then, which allows the dissociated elements to rise up into dream consciousness.

Write out your dream. Give it a title. Give it a rating of 1 to 10 on the "upset" scale. Then go with your associations. Allow yourself to be surprised; don't assume you know. Working with others helps: they can see the "back of our heads" when we can't. Then work with the dream to add resources the characters in the dream need to resolve their dilemmas, or rescript the dream to end differently. I tell my clients that this is where we woke up, not necessarily where the dream ended. Then rerate the distress level and see if you have a new title that has emerged. With trauma, get help from a professional if the distress is affecting your health and well-being.

DOING WHAT COMES NATURALLY

It can take years to find your heart's desire and your heart's ease. Some people never try. Humans make things complicated, but life and nature are quite simple and logical, and believe it or not, they are on our side. We're supposed to enjoy life on Earth.

I loved music and art as a kid, but because they came easily, I didn't value them and went on to make myself do things that *didn't* come naturally. It took decades to understand I should have just listened to what was singing out of me when I was young: I'd already found what I was supposed to do with my life. Let's lose that complex that says we are only really worthy if we are struggling. Always ask yourself what is at the root of this way of thinking, and then stick two fingers up at it by doing the radical work of being absolutely yourself.

I'm not saying we shouldn't challenge ourselves: the sense of achievement we have when we improve at something that we love but that doesn't come easily is priceless, and I would never discourage that. What I'm saying here is this: we should remember to take what comes easily and naturally to us seriously too—because all too often, we just don't. Essentially, if something makes us feel happy and alive, we should nurture it and see where it takes us rather than expend endless energy getting frustrated with something that makes our soul wilt and is frankly something we're only doing because we think an authority figure—or just our inner school ma'am—might approve.

Reviving Your Heart's Desire

Think about the things that lit you up when you were younger. Write them down, and ask yourself if you still do any of these things now or whether they feel remote. If they feel unreachable or silly, it's possible that people who don't even figure in your life anymore, like teachers or bullies, made you think they were a waste of time. No blame—just understand, accept, release, and move on through. Once you identify these subjects or activities and the feeling around them, it's a lot easier to return to what your soul is probably crying out to do—or has gotten tired of crying out to do and has gone to sleep. Wake it back up. It's never too late.

Often, we trip ourselves up because we're used to trying to make things "perfect" (hi again, schooldays). Or worse, we worry it will never be perfect or even good, so we don't bother starting. But your soul, your mind, your body, your life need you to unlock yourself. As the saying goes, we're here for a good time, not a long time.

NO BLAME—JUST UNDERSTAND,
ACCEPT, RELEASE, AND
MOVE ON THROUGH.

THE TRICK OF TREATS

Give yourself a present on a regular basis. (Fellow fans of the David Lynch series *Twin Peaks* will relate to that one.) It doesn't have to be a Tiffany bracelet: it could just be a cup of coffee. It could be sitting outside to gaze at the stars. It could be a candlelit bath, a walk, a chance to draw, an afternoon's treasure hunting in the local thrift stores. It could be five minutes of nothing—but deliberate nothing. All of these things are gifts.

It's important to get into the habit of treating yourself like the best friend you've ever had, because you *are* that friend. You're the one who makes it all happen. If you make that friend in you feel valued and loved, you'll make even more good stuff happen. Alternatively, if you make your inner pal feel worthless and jaded, well, don't expect life to improve.

If I want flowers, I don't wait for someone else to buy them and then feel disappointed when they don't: I buy them myself. If I want a drink in that swanky new café, I'm not waiting to be taken. I'm going in, and I'm going to have a lovely time, even if I just order a cup of tea. Who knows what might happen, who I might meet, what article I might read, or what idea might pop into my head while I'm in there?

A Change in Atmosphere

When you're showering yourself with gifts large and small, tangible or otherwise—a walk, a nap, a blow-dry for no reason—the atmosphere around you starts to bristle and sparkle, attracting more good energy. You're changing your own personal weather system. That's the kind of magic we can all conjure up. If you put yourself last because of some martyr complex that might not even be yours anyway, you don't need to be a genius to guess how that works out.

When you *decide* you're worthy of treats, the Universe has a tendency to fall into line and present more goodies because of that very important decision—and you are your own authority. You don't need anyone to sanction any of this. Like attracts like; treats attract treats. Never think you don't deserve it. Be lighthearted about it and know you are worthy of anything anyone else has. It's not a competition. Good stuff is getting ready to unfold into your life, so lay out the welcome mat and allow it in. Resentment has the opposite effect, by the way.

A key part of what follows is learning to recognise gifts. Allow compliments, for example, and let them take root inside you rather than resisting them because you feel embarrassed and unworthy or you don't want people to think you're being arrogant by just saying thank you. Take a compliment as you would any gift: graciously. Then hold on to that loving vibration and expand it. Sincere compliments contain healing vibrations—indeed, they could be the very thing that turns a person's day around—so give and accept them freely.

IT'S IMPORTANT TO GET INTO THE HABIT OF TREATING YOURSELF LIKE THE BEST FRIEND YOU'VE EVER HAD, BECAUSE YOU ARE THAT FRIEND.

"PLEASE ADJUST YOUR SET": CREATING NEW CHANNELS

Notice when things are going good—specifically, when you get what you want. It's human nature to become so used to things being a certain way that when they do change for the better, after the initial elation, we tend to revert to our original pattern of thinking. It's hardly surprising: this is the neural pathway that has been established, especially if we've complained about our situation repeatedly.

Modify your settings accordingly once you achieve your will. If you don't, it will be as if you're wearing shoes that don't fit. It's too easy to snuggle back down into old furrows, no matter how unhealthy they are, rather than dig fresh ones that better reflect our more positive situation, but we must. Move on with awareness, and embrace and appreciate those longed-for changes when they come.

It takes time for the mind to catch up, but it's important that it does. Otherwise, you'll attract that old negativity again, because it fits those long-worn paths that have been created by undisciplined habitual thoughts.

Carve new channels with determination, and watch out for the shifts.

✳ WITCH TIP ✳
LIGHTEN UP AND LAUGH

When something or someone is starting to get on my proverbials, I say to myself, "I choose to find this amusing." It helps me detach and gain some perspective. Humour is a healer and also a preventative: it stops irritations from worming their way under our skin.

Next time someone fires a passive-aggressive arrow your way, instead of adding it to your inner logbook of hurts, just chuckle—it will confuse them—and try to understand how small that person must feel to act this way. As you laugh, an energy shield goes up. Imagine those arrows bouncing straight off.

Laughter also releases endorphins and can prompt cellular changes—that's why it feels so good when we *really* laugh. It can also make us more beautiful, lifting the face and creating pretty crinkles around our eyes. When I was little, I thought there was nothing more attractive than laughter lines, and I was impatient for my own. These lines tell an enviable story: that of a life filled with merriment. I grinned and crinkled my eyes as much as I could to bring them on, but I soon learned I had to earn them by building a life of laughter and positivity. That continues to be a daily aim.

ENGAGED, EXPRESSIVE, EXTRAORDINARY YOU

There is an abundance of inspirational figures who seem to have ageing nailed. Think about the people whose older years are or were a time of power, joy, and creativity: Maya Angelou, Yayoi Kusama, Stevie Nicks, Miriam Margolyes, Shirley Collins, David Bowie, Patti Smith, David Attenborough, trans writer Jan Morris, Iggy Pop, Iris Apfel, Betty White, Alan Alda—this list goes on and on. You don't have to believe the bad press about getting older if you don't want to.

Concentrating on the stories of people like this can revolutionise how we feel and talk about ageing, steering us into a more positive mindset and reducing the kind of fearful self-talk that becomes self-fulfilling. Words, whether uttered in jest or not, are magic commands—yes, spells. That's why we call it spelling, as many a witch will tell you.

"A woman's work is never done" has, for too many, been the perfect trap and the ultimate distraction, effective at keeping a lot of women out of the way and unfulfilled or feeling guilty for wanting more. There's a maverick inside you. Let her out for some fun. You, and the people around you—your partner, your children, your friends—will all benefit. Another positive side effect to all this is that you will look radiant. That's right: when we cease worrying about "losing our looks" and we live, create, and treat ourselves properly, our cells respond accordingly and we *glow*.

Uprooting Old Attitudes

Many women feel that much of their worth is tied up in their attractiveness. Women are constantly judged and appraised until, *boom*: they get older and suddenly feel invisible. But the treasures of age are many, and they should be celebrated, shared, and expressed. This is something Pagans do very well: cronehood is greeted with joy and reverence. But in the mainstream, a societal suspicion of wise, mature women who don't need rescuing or romancing continues.

We also come across both men and women who are feminists for show: trumpeting how they want marginalised women's voices to be heard in order to appear woke while simultaneously disrespecting women they're threatened by, don't fancy, or don't believe they can be furthered by. All or not at all, please: self-serving agenda feminism is bogus and unhelpful and needs to be called out.

We need to alter how we view ourselves, but we need our men and boys to fundamentally shift their attitudes too, not just gloss over politically incorrect feelings that remain beneath the surface. Those need uprooting: if they aren't uprooted, they will, as we have seen, simply morph into another, less obvious form. We also need more women to be allowed to rise and develop and take positions that put them in charge—and women need to have their sisters' backs, not just on paper or on Instagram, but in reality. It can be a tough and lonely climb up the ladder, but that's no reason to pull it up after you.

Celebrating the Gifts of Change

Something else that needs calling out is the way we talk about our changing bodies. Let's stop buying into the shared idea of women's looks "fading." They're just *changing*. My septuagenarian mother is beautiful. It's different from the beauty of youth, but the essence is the same. As for her magical white hair—she's *earned* that silver. While she was always a beauty in the traditional sense, her spirit is the loveliest thing about her, and it radiates in a way that is magnetic.

Some of the most physically attractive women I know get into a psychological tangle as they hit forty, fifty, sixty, and beyond: we think age brings wisdom and clarity, but if you spend your youth putting too much value on your looks and how others judge them, you're going to miss the gifts we assume just come with old age. Don't take them for granted. Welcome the gifts of the crone. They serve the whole world and are priceless—rough diamonds worn smooth and bright by understanding and compassion, and all the more valuable for it. They are also not guaranteed.

Character doesn't age. Nor does being cool, and there is *nothing* cooler than a super-cool old lady. That's not to say you have to go strutting around in Ray-Bans when you'd really be more comfortable at home knitting and listening to audiobooks. Cool, to me, means finding your perfect self-expression, *whatever that means to you*, and living it without giving two hoots to what anyone else thinks. It means sharing your gifts, having a sense of humour, and allowing your uniqueness to take you right up to your final day on Earth and beyond.

Being Present at Every Age

As we've seen, the "old" taboo has left us all at sea, at least in the West. Growing old is a privilege denied to many, and yet we've come to view it with anxiety, horror, and dread. We rarely focus on the treasures, which are many and powerful. The key to unlocking them is to stay engaged, stay social, and stay creative. Don't stop being you. In fact, be *more* you. Be "glorious Technicolor" you.

Mental and physical decline hastens when we stop reading, stop learning, stop listening to music, stop seeing friends, and stop being interested. Nothing is inevitable, and as we know, there are plenty of examples of vital, engaged elderly people who belie their ages because they are still involved with life in different ways. In fact, they seem younger in themselves than many who are young in years, because of their sheer passion for being alive. I don't mean you have to dress up like Elton John and learn how to mambo—although that sounds pretty great.

Just being mindful of all of the beautiful moments that can make up a day and taking delight in simple things can be enough. Be present. Participate: physically, mentally, and, yes, spiritually, whatever that means to you. Your brain is in charge, so make it work for you.

WELCOME THE GIFTS OF THE CRONE.
THEY SERVE THE WHOLE WORLD
AND ARE PRICELESS ROUGH DIAMONDS
WORN SMOOTH AND BRIGHT
BY UNDERSTANDING AND COMPASSION,
AND ALL THE MORE VALUABLE FOR IT.

UK Artist and Therapist Jane Woollatt

Jane Woollatt's artwork meaningfully addresses the themes of menopause and cronehood, and her work is entwined with an intuitive connection to the Goddess. Here she tells us about working magic into her creative practice and how we can create positive change in the way we think and talk about menopause:

Jane Woollatt: I have worked in the field of psychiatry for over thirty years, and I switch between the two parts of my professional life: each informs the other. Making and being present with art objects is, for me, a connection with the Divine. In the same way that I blend psychological theories with my creative practice, I also weave in sympathetic magic.

I am compelled to move towards subjects that are considered taboo, like suicide, abuse, trauma, and grief. As an artist, I dwell on tough subjects in search of a shape, exploring metaphor, finding ways to hold a hurt or pain and transform or soften it. In my exploration of menopause, I have come to think there should be another phase of the Goddess—the Empress—sitting between mother and crone.

Menopause is associated with ageing and therefore death and a loss of fertility—and therefore, in a crude sense, purpose and status. Society values youth, and so there is negativity surrounding menopause: the information out there is focused on "fixing" it. It does come with a host of changes and challenges: we do need care, compassion, and understanding, but we are not broken and we are not redundant.

We need to be listened to. We need to be protected and our resources valued and preserved for future generations. Life is like a woven spiral. We can touch the generation above and below; we need to make the fabric stronger and stop ripping holes in it. Stronger links make us healthier, stronger, and better protected. We need to talk to each other to break the taboo and not succumb to fear. It may be that [menopause] *isn't* fearful— but if we're told something is to be feared, it will be fearful.

We need positive stories and images, myths and metaphors that inform and encourage. We are transforming, and we hold immense wisdom and strength in our collective minds and bodies.

WE CAN TOUCH THE
GENERATION ABOVE AND BELOW;
WE NEED TO MAKE THE FABRIC
STRONGER AND STOP RIPPING
HOLES IN IT.

THE BEST IS YET TO COME?

If you haven't undergone menopause but are biologically due to, the best way to understand the reality and advantages of this life stage is to talk to women who have undergone it. They contain profound wisdom that too often goes unheard, so ask questions and honour the wise ones and their hard-won lessons.

We often hear about the grief of menopause, but we rarely hear the stories of improved or stabilised physical and mental health. I know women whose lives improved exponentially once they hit menopause because they no longer had to deal with the hormonal challenges of a monthly bleed, which for many can be painful, heavy, and debilitating. The late singer Poly Styrene, from the UK punk group X-Ray Spex, lived with bipolar for years, only to find that the condition, which had dominated not only her life but also that of her family, eased significantly when she reached menopause. The cycle of manic episodes and depressions had been linked to her menstrual cycle. Menopause ushered in the happiest and most balanced time of her life.[50]

Some women don't experience hot flashes. Some do. Some women feel invisible, others liberated. Many times I have seen one of my elders deal with a situation deftly and confidently, and when I express admiration, the response is usually, "Oh, that just comes with age." We become less bothered about what people think, or whether or not we have the respect of people we don't even like. I like the sound of that. One friend of mine told me she felt like a superhero once she'd undergone the change. That's the kind of menopause I want.

It's imperative for us all to hear and share more optimistic stories about getting older as well as understand the potential challenges. We have to talk about this much more, as Jane Woollatt observed, and normalise it—not just for ourselves, but for everyone. This way we stand a better chance of moving through this change in ourselves—and others—with respect, compassion, and understanding, rather than trying to hush it up or treat it like an embarrassing illness.

We must, as always, be deliberate. Don't let a good menopause or older age be a happy accident. *Intend* it as much as you can. Nothing is inevitable, but things *will* develop in a certain way if you don't take control.

✳ WITCH TIP ✳
STOP SAVING IT FOR SPECIAL

The smart outfit, the chic underwear, the expensive perfume, the dreamy shoes, the "good" purse: these lovely things were made to be used and loved, so I'm asking you to cast out the mothballs and enjoy them on an ordinary day. You may find that something extraordinary happens. This kind of behaviour is like a signal.

Never mind "dress for the job you want": dress for the life you want, whether anyone sees you or not. There's also the theory that if you buy things only to hoard and never use them, you end up losing them anyway. I have direct experience of this. I had a bottle of body lotion by Chanel, but I never felt there was an occasion special enough to wear it. One day I changed my mind, unscrewed the lid, and discovered that it had gone rancid, and I had to throw it away. Using it up would *not* have been a waste. Now I wear my favourite scent when I'm going to get groceries.

WANT CHANGE? CHANGE YOUR CHANNELS

By "change your channels," I mean be conscious of the information that you allow in and how it makes you feel. Filter out the things that make you feel down. This is a commitment to yourself, and if you make this commitment, you will have more energy for the things that make you happy in your one beautiful life. Whether you believe in reincarnation or not, we get one go on this planet in this form and guise, so use this opportunity to live this incarnation to the best of your abilities.

Read biographies of inspiring people, and keep a pen and notebook nearby exclusively for the purpose of writing down snippets and quotes that chime with you. You might think you'll remember every *bon mot* that speaks to you, but you won't. Get in the habit of jotting these golden nuggets down, and on a day when you feel uninspired or blue, dig out that notebook and have a read through, or open on a random page to see what presents itself. More often than not, it will be exactly what you need to hear.

Limit your exposure to the news and trashy magazines: we have a distorted view of the world because of how news is reported. If you're empathic, you can start to feel as if you'd rather not be in a world where people behave so abominably. We hear comparatively little about acts of kindness and love and the stories of people who want to make the world a better place—but they are out there and every bit as real. Those are the stories I'm interested in. Yes, we need to keep abreast of what's happening, but at the same time, too many of us get ghoulishly drawn in by negative stories that aren't "for the public interest"; they're just "interesting to the public." I've seen newspapers poison the minds of people I love, and if you are a sensitive, you cannot afford this. Just send a request to the Universe that whatever needs to reach you will, and then get on with your life.

Go on a Gossip Diet

While we are being stringent with our media diet, the same approach must apply to gossip. We humans tend to bond over gossip, but this doesn't mean it's healthy. Don't start it and don't listen to it. Before slagging off a creative project, for example, remember that there was a human behind it who was trying their best according to where they were at that time. If you see something online that isn't your cup of tea, feel free to scroll on past: you don't *have* to ruin someone's day just because you can't resist airing your views. No one changed their opinion just because someone disagreed with them, rightly or wrongly, on Facebook. Save your energy.

This doesn't mean we must lose our critical faculty or our awareness that sometimes things aren't right. I do think it's best not to give any energy or time to people or situations that aren't worth it, rather than getting worked up about them, but sometimes we need to offload to an understanding—and discreet—friend if a person or situation is getting us down. It just becomes problematic when we start gleefully engaging in malicious snipery. It's a bad habit to get into, and an all too easy one. Make up your own mind about people and things, and allow others to do the same.

The exception to this would be if someone is at risk of a negative situation that could otherwise be avoided: if your sibling has fallen in love with someone who you know is a philanderer, or you've spotted that a neighbour has hired the services of a builder who is a known charlatan, you're going to want to say something. Witches believe in free will and autonomy, but we also believe in protecting those we care about and, of course, in the significance of divine timing and serendipity. If you feel you are the right person at the right time to warn a friend about something that might compromise or harm them, use your instincts and act accordingly. The Universe often places sensitives like us in just the right place to step in for the highest good, even if we don't realise it at the time.

I personally don't believe that maxim that "Everyone is trying their best" all the time; we've all known manipulators and chancers or people who are just coasting by with minimum effort. At the same time, while we don't have to love it, we'd do well to remember that there's *always* a reason for every behaviour. Remembering this really helps; it's certainly lighter on the psyche not to get consumed by anger towards other people's behaviours. It's also easier to manifest what you *do* want when you're not shaking your fists at what you don't. The latter takes a lot of energy and is more likely to draw exactly what you hate right into your life.

JUST SEND A REQUEST TO THE UNIVERSE THAT WHATEVER NEEDS TO REACH YOU WILL, AND THEN GET ON WITH YOUR LIFE.

Magical Musing
The Transformative Magic of Standing Up Straight

Here's a spell that will change perceptions instantly—your own and other people's. No hocus-pocus: all you have to do is stand up straight. It's something our elders nagged us about, and with good reason. Not only is good posture better for everything from spine health to improving digestion; it changes people's impression of us and even our perception of ourselves. As we know, perception is reality, and reality is subjective, so let's make it work for us.

Many women and girls have a journey with their posture. As a child, I was very straight-backed, because "Stand up properly" and "Don't slouch" were commands I heard a lot growing up. This was soon to change. Prepuberty, it was all, "Doesn't she have good posture?" but as soon as I hit tweenage-hood, I'd hear, "Stop sticking your boobs out." All I was doing was—you guessed it—standing up straight, shoulders back, exactly as I'd been instructed to a year or so earlier. Soon, I was rounding my shoulders, and a complex was born. Throughout childhood, women are encouraged to smile, stand nicely, be pretty, and people-please. Then puberty hits and all that training is suddenly wrong, because it can attract unfavourable attention. These microaggressions stem from various sources, often well-meaning, sometimes not. Sometimes they emerge because of someone's subliminal irritation at the sight of a blossoming young woman with everything ahead of her. Sometimes they are born of someone's repressed anger at having been exploited during their own innocent years, with this shiny new teenager a mirror to a previous self.

Whatever the origins, complexes set up in childhood take work to unchisel. I still find myself rounding my shoulders—"mustn't be too much" for people—but then I catch sight of a mirror and chastise myself for looking like a sack of potatoes. But when I straighten, lift my face, and hold back my shoulders instead of hunching in a bid to conceal myself, I look better in every way. If people look, fine. I'm wearing clothes, not nipple tassels.

Notice the magical things that happen when you straighten up. People pay attention, they hear you, they see you, and they listen, because they perceive a confident woman at ease with herself, unapologetic and present, graceful and strong, and worthy of respect. Perception is reality. I think, therefore I am. Abracadabra, baby.[51]

CONCLUSION

Embracing the Wise Woman Within

There can be no better ambition than to be a wise woman. Having this as your mission will allow you to live more freely throughout all of your life stages. As we know, wisdom doesn't just come: we must work towards it, seek it, and develop it, every day. For me, life improved when I *really* stepped into being a woman and a witch, in all its forms and meanings: while I was born to be both of these things, I had to grow into them over time. We do this by gifting ourselves control and awareness, self-protection, and a soul friendship, and the greatest magic is that, far from youth closing off as you get older, life in all its magnificence *opens up* to you.

By growing up that inner little girl, you are gaining, not losing. This doesn't mean you have to lose touch with your inner child and that which feels wonder and delight—quite the opposite. The witchful way reminds us to reconnect with the magic that is around us all the time. It's easy to miss it, but it's always there to help us, teach us, and reflect us. Treasure it and treat it with love and the awe that true magic deserves. As the ways of the Wise have shown me, again and again, there is so much enchantment to be found in life. The more you actively seek, the more you'll be inspired to create, and so it goes. Life gets better that way, and not just for you. It's catching, self-propelling, thrilling—and easy: it just takes a shift in perception and some determination.

We are rewarded in so many ways when we employ a little witchful thinking.

RECOMMENDED READING

Want to take your reading further but need some inspiration? Here's a dip into my magical library to give you some ideas.

Heinrich Cornelius Agrippa. *Three Books of Occult Philosophy*. Translated by James Freake. Edited and annotated by Donald Tyson. Saint Paul: Llewellyn Sourcebook Series, 1992.

> This Early Modern grimoire is considered the 101 by many adepts. Exploring the laws of natural, celestial, and ritual magic, Agrippa draws on the Kabbalah, Hermetic philosophy, and Neoplatonism to provide a textbook of philosophy, symbolism, secret knowledge, and advice. This was on the shelf of many a literate wise woman or man from the 1500s onwards, and it remains a resource to this day. That said, it is still a reflection of a patriarchal, polarised, and often cruel time in history that, at best, did not take female practitioners seriously.

Phil Baker. *Austin Osman Spare: The Life and Legend of London's Lost Artist*. London: Strange Attractor Press, 2011.

> Beloved by Aleister Crowley and hailed as a genius in his prime, the artist and visionary Austin Osman Spare (1886–1956) turned his back on commercial success, going under the radar to develop his personal creative and occult practice. This included visionary psychic art and working with sigils, often with rather unexpected results. Baker's biography of A.O.S. is exceptional: an inspiring and evocative portal into Spare's strange and compelling world.

Rae Beth. *Hedge Witch*. London: Robert Hale, 1992.

> This thoughtful and absorbing book consists of a collection of letters written to two apprentice witches. Filled with guidance, rites to mark the sabbats, and suggestions as to how to heal our connection with the natural world, this book has long been a favourite of mine. I often want to lend it to people who haven't yet read Rae Beth's beautiful teachings, but the risk of never getting it back is far too great for me.

Deepak Chopra. *Ageless Body, Timeless Mind: The Quantum Alternative to Growing Old*. New York: Harmony Books, 1993.

> This is a book I turn to again and again. The ideas here bear repeating, and we all too often need reminding of just what's possible. This is not just "positive thinking"; this is quantum physics. *Ageless Body, Timeless Mind* urges us to be aware, moment by moment, of the reality that nothing is inevitable if we consciously work for a different result.

Laurie Cabot with Tom Cowan. *The Power of the Witch*. London: Michael Joseph, 1990.

> Published on my eleventh birthday, this book is a wonderful friend: it shines with warmth. Salem's favourite witch, Laurie Cabot, generously shares wisdom about everything from ancient Goddess-worshipping cultures to practical magic working. All of it is underpinned with powerful positivity and an ethical core.

Scott Cunningham. *Cunningham's Encyclopedia of Magical Herbs*. Saint Paul: Llewellyn, 1985.

> Clear, vibrant, authoritative, and comprehensive—not to mention beautifully written. Like many witches, I refer to

this book a lot, dipping in to find specific herbal correspondences for spells or magical recipes.

Clarissa Pinkola Estés. *Women Who Run with the Wolves*. New York: Ballantine Books, 1992.

While this book initially built a base of devotees by word of mouth, the magic of *Women Who Run with the Wolves* soon spread like a fire, becoming a global bestseller. This book continues to change lives by waking up the "wild woman" within by way of ancient folktales and archetypes, challenging the reader to connect with long-buried instincts in a bid to live more authentically. I try to read it once a year; it's the kind of fortifying wisdom you want to absorb into your bones.

Titania Hardie. *Enchanted: Titania's Book of White Magic*. New York: William Morrow & Company, 1999.

Titania's books are gorgeous inside and out, filled with personally chosen charms and spells to take you through the year, all accompanied by luscious photography. Perfect for the magical aesthete. You'll be tying coloured satin ribbons to everything by the time she's through with you.

Michael Howard. *East Anglian Witches and Wizards*. Richmond Vista, CA: Three Hands Press, 2017.

This account of magic workers in Essex and East Anglia (where I live) is a fascinating historical document that provides us with a window into another time, further clarifying the connections and uneasy crossovers between witchcraft and early Christianity. Michael Howard, editor of *The Cauldron* between 1976 and his death in 2015, wrote over thirty-five books about witchcraft, Paganism, occult parapolitics, and more. Time to get more bookshelves.

Judika Illes. *Magic When You Need It*. San Francisco: Red Wheel/ Weiser, 2009.

Judika's books don't only look gorgeous, they contain deep, essential wisdom that comes from Judika's many years of practice, research, spell collecting, and developing original ideas. I love how generous Judika is with the sharing of the magical knowledge she has so lovingly collated, and she also provides the recipes for condition oils, which is an absolute boon. Be aware: the spells in this book pack a punch.

Lisa Lister. *Code Red: Know Your Flow, Unlock Your Superpowers, and Create a Bloody Amazing Life*. London: Hay House UK Ltd., 2020. First published 2015 by SHE Press UK.

Giving a greater understanding of the connections between the menstrual cycle and magical and creative practices, *Code Red* has been a game changer for many menstruating women. While Lister is not the first to explore menstruation in this way, hers was the first book on the subject that reached my awareness, and I'm forever grateful that it did.

Sam McKechnie and Alexandrine Portelli. *The Magpie & the Wardrobe: A Curiosity of Folklore, Magic & Spells*. London: Pavilion Books, 2015.

This is a coffee-table essential: an exquisitely compiled compendium of traditional beliefs and symbols, charms, recipes, and customs. The attention to detail alone is bewitching as it takes us through the turns of the Wheel of the Year and mingles the Old Ways with newer conventions. No solstice or equinox goes by without me diving in to gaze upon the magical montages that connect with the different sabbats.

Madame Pamita. *The Book of Candle Magic*. Woodbury, MN: Llewellyn, 2020.

> You met Madame Pamita earlier in this book, as she was kind enough to talk to us about candle magic and divination. Well, this delightful handbook of hers takes the study deeper and equips practitioners with skills to set their dreams aglow and good things in motion with the help of a candle and a flame.

Linda Yael Schiller. *Modern Dreamwork: New Tools for Decoding Your Soul's Wisdom*. Woodbury, MN: Llewellyn, 2019.

> Another wise woman who contributed to this book, Linda Yael Schiller provides us with a dream book unlike any other, taking us beyond symbol interpretation and into practical, active approaches through which we can decode the messages our subconscious is trying to give us. Dream on, dreamer.

Betty Shine. *Mind Magic: The Key to the Universe*. London: Corgi Books, 1992.

> British healer Betty Shine was—and continues to be—a powerful healer and lightworker. She wrote a number of books about her mediumistic experiences and harnessing the power of the mind, but this one is my favourite.

Florence Scovel Shinn. *The Complete Writings of Florence Scovel Shinn for Women*. Camarillo, CA: DeVorss & Company, 2003.

> Florence Scovel Shinn was an artist, early-twentieth-century metaphysical writer, and New Thought teacher whose words continue to resonate with all who discover them. Her "treatments" on any problem you can think of are inspiring, and she effortlessly articulates everything from divine universal laws to the vibratory nature of words.

Doreen Valiente. *Natural Magic*. London: Robert Hale, 1975.

> This is real cunning-woman magic: age-old folk charms and practical natural lore, the like of which was practiced and observed by the village wise ones of yore, can be found within these pages. Valiente was a pivotal figure in British witchcraft and a Wiccan high priestess, most famous for working with Gerald Gardner, the founder of Gardnerian Wicca, in the 1950s and beyond. She is often referred to as the mother of modern witchcraft.

Marion Weinstein. *Positive Magic: Occult Self-Help*. Surrey, BC: Phoenix Publishing, 1981.

> I discovered Weinstein's writing as a teenager; her positive ethical witchcraft techniques using Words of Power made sense to me. She is now on the other side of the veil, but you can still view her warm, funny videos on YouTube, which she uploaded in the early years of the platform: Weinstein was always ahead of her time. I keep *Positive Magic* close by and still find new elements revealing themselves to me. Believe it or not, there have been times when I have observed blue light glowing from between the pages as I've read. This is a book of power.

Colin Wilson. *The Occult*. London: Hodder & Stoughton, 1970. Reprint, London: Watkins, 2015.

> Best known as the author of the cult classic *The Outsider*, Wilson surprised many, including himself, when he unveiled this hefty but accessible tome. Wilson had previously dismissed occult matters as mere superstition, but as he said in his introduction, "Writing the book made me aware that the paranormal is as real as quantum physics." Pragmatically and

exhaustively written with wit but also respect, Wilson's *The Occult* is, for me, definitive.

Valerie Ann Worwood. *The Fragrant Pharmacy*. London: Bantam, 1991.

Valerie Ann Worwood. *The Fragrant Heavens*. London: Bantam, 1999.

> I've treasured these books for years, investing in them after first spying their pretty spines on the bathroom shelf of an old friend. Valerie's books about essential oils go beyond any writing on the subject I have ever encountered, sparking a lifelong appreciation of these precious bottles of light. I use these books frequently for reference but also just love to read them from cover to cover, because the writing is transcendent.

W.B. Yeats. *Writings on Irish Folklore, Legend and Myth*. London: Penguin Classics, 1993.

> I urge you to read W.B. Yeats's absorbing collection of writings. Featuring sparkling yarns on fairy mounds, Gaelic love songs, ghosts galore, and magical healing charms, this is very much a happy place for me. Yeats also reveals fascinating tales of Biddy Early, Irish wise woman extraordinaire, healer, diviner, fairy appeaser, and very much a legend herself. Look her up.

BIBLIOGRAPHY

Agrippa, Heinrich Cornelius. *Three Books of Occult Philosophy.* Translated by John French. London: Printed by R.W. for Gregory Moule, 1651; Ann Arbor: Text Creation Partnership, 2011. https://quod.lib.umich.edu/e/eebo/A26565.0001.001/1:13.64 ?rgn=div2;view=fulltext.

Bach Centre. "History of the Bach Flower Remedies." Accessed October 8, 2021. https://www.bachcentre.com/en/remedies/.

Baker, Phil. *Austin Osman Spare: The Life and Legend of London's Lost Artist.* London: Strange Attractor Press, 2011.

Bell, Celeste, and Zoë Howe. *Dayglo: The Poly Styrene Story.* London: Omnibus Press, 2019.

Cabot, Laurie. "Becoming a Witch." Posted by LaurieCabotOfficial. March 28, 2010. Video, 3:14. https://www.youtube.com /watch?v=f2lCLj_KxJg&list=PLBW_F0D4X2IS55Q1L W4uU8xYjK_Rkc06J&index=1.

———, with Tom Cowan. *The Power of the Witch.* London: Michael Joseph, 1990.

Cavendish, Richard. "Tutankhamun's Curse?" *History Today*, March 2014. https://www.historytoday.com/archive/months-past /tutankhamuns-curse.

Centre of Excellence. *Ancient Magic.* Author's Republic, 2017. Audiobook.

Crystalinks. "Tea Leaf Reading: Tasseography." Accessed December 28, 2020. https://www.crystalinks.com/tealeaves.html.

Crystal Vaults. "Aventurine Meanings and Uses." Accessed December 22, 2020. https://www.crystalvaults.com/crystal -encyclopedia/green-aventurine.

———. "Kyanite Meanings and Uses." Accessed December 22, 2020. https://www.crystalvaults.com/crystal-encyclopedia /kyanite.

Diaz, Daniella. "Trump Calls Clinton 'A Nasty Woman.'" *CNN.com*, October 20, 2016. https://www.cnn.com/2016/10/19/politics /donald-trump-hillary-clinton-nasty-woman/index.html.

Duquet, Michèle. "5 Amazing Things You May Not Know About Rose Essential Oil." *Michèle's Blog: For the Love of Our Human Spirit*, April 1, 2014. https://michelesorganics.wordpress .com/2014/04/01/5-amazing-things-you-may-not-know -about-rose-essential-oil/ April 1 2014.

Emoto, Masaru. *The Hidden Messages in Water*. New York: Atria Books, 2011.

Fermenters Kitchen. "Why Fermented Garlic Turns Blue." Accessed January 29, 2021. https://fermenterskitchen.com/fermented -garlic-turn-blue/.

Howard, Michael. *East Anglian Witches and Wizards*. Richmond Vista, CA: Three Hands Press, 2017.

Kelly, Aidan. "About Naming Ostara, Litha, and Mabon." *Patheos*, May 2, 2017. https://www.patheos.com/blogs/aidankelly /2017/05/naming-ostara-litha-mabon/.

Knowles, Lane. "Doctrine of Signatures: Vegetables That Look Like the Parts They Heal." *Huffington Post*, June 6, 2012. https:// www.huffingtonpost.co.uk/laura-knowles/doctrine -of-signatures.

Lane, Jennifer. "Thieves Oil Recipe: DIY Essential Oil Blend for Protection." *DIY Essential Oil Recipes* (blog). *Loving Essential Oils*, August 23, 2020. https://www.lovingessentialoils.com/blogs/diy-recipes/thieves-oil-recipe.

Lister, Lisa. *Code Red: Know Your Flow, Unlock Your Superpowers, and Create a Bloody Amazing Life*. London: Hay House UK Ltd., 2020. First published 2015 by SHE Press UK.

Louv, Jason. "William S. Burroughs' 7 Occult Techniques for Smashing Reality." *Ultraculture*, November 2017. https://ultraculture.org/blog/2017/04/11/william-s-burroughs-occult-technique/.

Luschka. "Four Thieves Vinegar." *Keeper of the Kitchen*, May 13, 2013. https://www.keeperofthekitchen.com/2013/05/13/four-thieves-vinegar/.

Morris, Lucy. "The Stone Age: Victoria Beckham Hides Crystal Pockets in Her Label's Trousers." *Grazia*, July 10, 2018. https://graziadaily.co.uk/fashion/trends/victoria-beckham-crystals/.

Rex, Equanimous. "The Pentagram, Symbol of What Exactly?" *Modern Mythology*, February 22, 2019. https://modernmythology.net/realpentagramhistory-64fdc64866a5.

Schul, Bill, and Ed Pettit. *The Secret Power of Pyramids*. New York: Ballantine Books, 1975.

Shine, Betty. *Mind Magic: The Key to the Universe*. London: Corgi Books, 1992.

Shinn, Florence Scovel. *The Complete Writings of Florence Scovel Shinn for Women*. Camarillo, CA: DeVorss & Company, 2003.

Smith, Mercedes. "Broken a Pot? Copy the Japanese and Fix It with Gold." *BBC Arts*. Accessed November 2, 2020. https://www.bbc.co.uk/programmes/articles/326qTYw26156P9k92v8zr3C/broken-a-pot-copy-the-japanese-and-fix-it-with-gold.

Smith, Michelle. "Gemstone Cleansing—Your Questions Answered—Part 1: Salt Bed." *Gemisphere*, February 27, 2018. https://gemisphere.com/blogs/whats-new/making-sense-of-cleansing.

Steinem, Gloria. *The Truth Will Set You Free, But First It Will Piss You Off!* Crows Nest, NSW: Murdoch Books, 2019.

Weinstein, Marion. *Positive Magic: Occult Self-Help*. Surrey, BC: Phoenix Publishing, 1981.

———. *Earth Magic: A Dianic Book of Shadows*. San Francisco: Red Wheel/Weiser, 2008.

White, Caren. "Baneful Herbs." *Advice from the Herb Lady*. Accessed April 2, 2021. https://advicefromtheherblady.com/plant-profiles/perennials/baneful-herbs/ 2015.

Whitman, Walt. "Song of Myself." Verse 51. https://poets.org/poem/song-myself-51.

Witchipedian, The. "Baneful Herbs." *The Witchipedia*, November 22, 2019. https://witchipedia.com/glossary/baneful-herbs/.

———. "Herbal Lore: Mistletoe." *The Witchipedia*, December 4, 2019. https://witchipedia.com/book-of-shadows/herblore/mistletoe/.

———. "Herbal Lore: Nutmeg," *The Witchipedia*, November 16, 2019. https://witchipedia.com/book-of-shadows/herblore/nutmeg/.

Worwood, Valerie Ann. *The Fragrant Pharmacy*. London: Bantam, 1991.

————. *The Fragrant Heavens*. London: Bantam, 1999.

Yeats, William Butler. *Writings on Irish Folklore, Legend and Myth*. London: Penguin Classics, 1993.

ENDNOTES

PART 1

1. Rae Beth, *Hedge Witch: A Guide to Solitary Witchcraft* (London: Robert Hale, 1992).

2. Marion Weinstein, *Positive Magic: Ancient Metaphysical Techniques for Modern Lives*, rev. ed. (Franklin Lakes, NJ: New Page Books, 2002), 55.

3. Weinstein, *Positive Magic*, 57.

4. Weinstein, *Positive Magic*, 81.

5. Michael Howard, *East Anglian Witches and Wizards* (Richmond Vista, CA: Three Hands Press, 2017), 55.

6. Howard, *East Anglian Witches and Wizards*, 164.

7. Daniella Diaz, "Trump Calls Clinton 'A Nasty Woman,'" *CNN.com*, October 20, 2016, https://www.cnn.com/2016/10/19/politics/donald-trump-hillary-clinton-nasty-woman/index.html.

8. Centre of Excellence, *Ancient Magic*, module 1, Author's Republic, 2017, audiobook.

9. Laurie Cabot, "Becoming a Witch," posted by LaurieCabotOfficial, March 28, 2010, video, 3:14, https://www.youtube.com/watch?v=f2lCLj_KxJg&list=PLBW_F0D4X2IS55Q1LW4uU8xYjK_Rkc06J&index=1.

10. Centre of Excellence, *Ancient Magic*, module 3, Author's Republic, 2017, audiobook.

11. Weinstein, *Positive Magic*.

PART 2

12. Florence Scovel Shinn, *Your Word Is Your Wand* (London: L.N. Fowler & Co., 1968).

13. Laurie Cabot and Tom Cowan, *The Power of the Witch* (London: Michael Joseph, 1990), 89.

14. Equanimous Rex, "The Pentagram, Symbol of What Exactly?," *Modern Mythology*, February 22, 2019, https://modern mythology.net/realpentagramhistory-64fdc64866a5.

15. Madame Pamita, *The Book of Candle Magic* (Woodbury, MN: Llewellyn, 2020).

16. William Shakespeare, *A Midsummer Night's Dream*, act 3, scene 2, line 325. Helena says, "And though she be but little, she is fierce."

17. Aidan Kelly, "About Naming Ostara, Litha, and Mabon," *Patheos*, May 2, 2017, https://www.patheos.com/blogs /aidankelly/2017/05/naming-ostara-litha-mabon/.

18. Howard, *East Anglian Witches and Wizards*, 101.

19. William Shakespeare, *Hamlet*, act 2, scene 2, lines 249–50. Hamlet says, "Why, then, 'tis none to you, for there is nothing either good or bad, but thinking makes it so."

20. Lucy Morris, "The Stone Age: Victoria Beckham Hides Crystal Pockets in Her Label's Trousers," *Grazia*, July 10, 2018, https://graziadaily.co.uk/fashion/trends/victoria -beckham-crystals/.

21. Michelle Smith, "Gemstone Cleansing—Your Questions Answered—Part 1: Salt Bed," *Gemisphere*, February 27, 2018, https://gemisphere.com/blogs/whats-new/making-sense-of -cleansing.

22. "Aventurine Meanings and Uses," Crystal Vaults, accessed December 22, 2020, https://www.crystalvaults.com /crystal-encyclopedia/green-aventurine.

23. "Kyanite Meanings and Uses," Crystal Vaults, accessed December 22, 2020, https://www.crystalvaults.com /crystal-encyclopedia/kyanite.

24. Michèle Duquet, "5 Amazing Things You May Not Know About Rose Essential Oil," *Michèle's Blog: For the Love of Our Human Spirit*, April 1, 2014, https://michelesorganics .wordpress.com/2014/04/01/5-amazing-things-you-may -not-know-about-rose-essential-oil/.

25. Masaru Emoto, *The Hidden Messages in Water* (New York: Atria Books, 2011).

26. Laura Knowles, "Doctrine of Signatures: Vegetables That Look Like the Parts They Heal," *Huffington Post*, June 6, 2012, https://www.huffingtonpost.co.uk/laura-knowles/doctrine -of-signatures-ve_b_1622844.html.

27. "History of the Bach Flower Remedies," The Bach Centre, accessed October 8, 2021, https://www.bachcentre.com/en /remedies/.

28. The Witchipedian, "Baneful Herbs," *The Witchipedia*, November 22, 2019, https://witchipedia.com/glossary/baneful -herbs/.

29. Caren White, "Baneful Herbs," *Advice from the Herb Lady*, accessed April 2, 2021, https://advicefromtheherblady.com /plant-profiles/perennials/baneful-herbs/.

30. The Witchipedian, "Herbal Lore: Mistletoe," *The Witchipedia*, December 4, 2019, https://witchipedia.com/book-of -shadows/herblore/mistletoe/.

31. The Witchipedian, "Baneful Herbs."

32. The Witchipedian, "Herbal Lore: Nutmeg," *The Witchipedia*, November 16, 2019, https://witchipedia.com/book-of -shadows/herblore/nutmeg/.

33. "Why Fermented Garlic Turns Blue," Fermenters Kitchen, accessed January 29, 2021, https://fermenterskitchen.com /fermented-garlic-turn-blue/.

34. Luschka, "Four Thieves Vinegar," *Keeper of the Kitchen*, May 13, 2013, https://www.keeperofthekitchen.com/2013 /05/13/four-thieves-vinegar/.

35. Jennifer Lane, "Thieves Oil Recipe: DIY Essential Oil Blend for Protection," *DIY Essential Oil Recipes* (blog), *Loving Essential Oils*, August 23, 2020, https://www.lovingessentialoils .com/blogs/diy-recipes/thieves-oil-recipe.

PART 3

36. Heinrich Cornelius Agrippa, *Three Books of Occult Philosophy*, trans. John French (London: Printed by R.W. for Gregory Moule, 1651; Ann Arbor: Text Creation Partnership, 2011), chap. 64, p. 144, https://quod.lib.umich.edu/e/eebo/A26565 .0001.001/1:13.64?rgn=div2;view=fulltext.

37. Marion Weinstein, *Positive Magic*, 201.

38. *Paddington 2*, directed by Paul King (London: StudioCanal UK, Heyday Films, 2017).

39. Gloria Steinem, *The Truth Will Set You Free, But First It Will Piss You Off!* (Crows Nest, NSW: Murdoch Books, October 2019).

40. Richard Cavendish, "Tutankhamun's Curse?," *History Today*, March 2014, https://www.historytoday.com/archive /months-past/tutankhamuns-curse.

41. Jason Louv, "William S. Burroughs' 7 Occult Techniques for Smashing Reality," *Ultraculture*, November 2017, https:// ultraculture.org/blog/2017/04/11/william-s-burroughs -occult-technique/.

42. Bill Schul and Ed Pettit, *The Secret Power of Pyramids* (New York: Ballantine Books, 1975), 168.

43. Schul and Pettit, *The Secret Power of Pyramids*, 101.

44. "Tea Leaf Reading: Tasseography," Crystalinks, accessed December 28, 2020, https://www.crystalinks.com/tealeaves .html.

45. Phil Baker, *Austin Osman Spare: The Life and Legend of London's Lost Artist* (London: Strange Attractor Press, 2011).

46. Florence Scovel Shinn, *The Complete Writings of Florence Scovel Shinn for Women* (Camarillo, CA: DeVorss & Company, 2003), 74.

PART 4

47. Mercedes Smith, "Broken a Pot? Copy the Japanese and Fix It with Gold," *BBC Arts*, accessed November 2, 2020, https:// www.bbc.co.uk/programmes/articles/326qTYw26156P 9k92v8zr3C/broken-a-pot-copy-the-japanese-and-fix-it -with-gold.

48. Betty Shine, *Mind Magic: The Key to the Universe* (London: Corgi Books, 1992), 17–19.

49. Walt Whitman, "Song of Myself," verse 51, https://poets.org /poem/song-myself-51.

50. Celeste Bell and Zoë Howe, *Dayglo: The Poly Styrene Story* (London: Omnibus Press, 2019), 165.

51. *Abracadabra* is an ancient magic word that translates from Hebrew as, "What I say becomes real," or, "I create what I speak."

To Write to the Author

If you wish to contact the author or would like more information about this book, please write to the author in care of Llewellyn Worldwide Ltd. and we will forward your request. Both the author and the publisher appreciate hearing from you and learning of your enjoyment of this book and how it has helped you. Llewellyn Worldwide Ltd. cannot guarantee that every letter written to the author can be answered, but all will be forwarded. Please write to:

Zoë Howe
℅ Llewellyn Worldwide
2143 Wooddale Drive
Woodbury, MN 55125-2989

Please enclose a self-addressed stamped envelope for reply,
or $1.00 to cover costs. If outside the U.S.A., enclose
an international postal reply coupon.

Many of Llewellyn's authors have websites with additional information and resources. For more information, please visit our website at http://www.llewellyn.com.